YOUR PERFECT RIGHT

A Guide to Assertive Behavior

Robert E. Alberti, Ph.D.
and
Michael L. Emmons, Ph.D.

with Foreword by
John Vasconcellos
Member of the California State Legislature

Impact Publishers

POST OFFICE BOX 1094
SAN LUIS OBISPO, CALIFORNIA 93406

First Edition, October, 1970
Second Printing, June, 1971
Third Printing, March, 1972
Fourth Printing, June, 1973

Second Edition, January, 1974
Second Printing, July, 1974
Third Printing, February, 1975
Fourth Printing, May, 1975
Fifth Printing, November, 1975
Sixth Printing, June, 1976
Seventh Printing, December, 1976
Eighth Printing, April, 1977
Ninth Printing, September, 1977
Tenth Printing, January, 1978

Third Edition, May, 1978
Second Printing, November, 1978
Third Printing, November, 1979
Fourth Printing, June, 1980
Fifth Printing, October, 1981

Copyright ©1970, 1974, 1978
by Robert E. Alberti and Michael L. Emmons

Library of Congress Cataloging in Publication Data

Alberti, Robert E.
  Your perfect right.

  Bibliography: p.
  1. Assertiveness (Psychology)   I. Emmons, Michael L.,
joint author. II. Title.
BF575.A85A43   1978   158'.1   78-6059
ISBN 0-915166-04-6
ISBN 0-915166-03-8 pbk.

Impact Publishers   BOX 1094, SAN LUIS OBISPO, CA 93406

ACKNOWLEDGEMENTS

Response to *Your Perfect Right* has been continuous and increasing. With thirteen printings and two editions now in circulation, it is time to up-date this work. We reiterate with sincere appreciation that no book is the product of the authors alone. Several persons have made vital contributions to this volume, and we acknowledge with thanks their dedicated efforts:

We thank John Vasconcellos for placing our work in the context of his educational and humanistic concerns and for his thoughtful foreword. Special appreciation is due to Joseph Wolpe, and to the late Michael Serber, both of whom stimulated and encouraged our approach to assertiveness training.

Lachlan P. MacDonald edited the first two editions, and helped in many ways to launch this book, as well as serving for a time as agent and consultant for Impact Publishers.

Charles and Carita Merker, owner-operators of Grandview Printers, Glendale, Arizona, gave generously of their time and talents to help make possible the publication of the first edition of the book.

Deborah Alberti and Kay Emmons have been models of assertiveness, have encouraged, loved, and waited. Without them there would be no book. To them we dedicate this effort.

R.E.A.
M.L.E.

San Luis Obispo, California
January, 1978

CONTENTS

PUBLISHER'S NOTE

This publication is designed to provide accurate and authoritative information in regard to the subject matter covered. It is sold with the understanding that the publisher is not engaged in rendering psychological, medical, or other professional services. If expert assistance or counseling is needed, the services of a competent professional should be sought.

FOREWORD
By
John Vasconcellos
Member of the California Legislature

We are undergoing significant changes in every aspect of our society: religion, family, work, life style, education and government. Many of our social institutions through which persons found security in the past are no longer secure or present in the same way. Education, like society and all its other institutions, is experiencing painful and profound crisis and confusion.

As Chairman of the Joint Committee on California's Master Plan for Higher Education, and of the Joint Committee on Educational Goals and Evaluation, I enjoy a privileged role in shaping the emerging character of education, and consequently of our future society.

I am aware that many persons continue to believe in a thrust towards betterment—call it evolutionary, intellectual, scientific or humanistic. It is vital that human beings, especially those with responsibility to and for others, attempt to make sense of what's happening—for their own fulfillment, and for that of others.

What we are going through now is the deepest and most dramatic of changes: how the human being views the human being, how one envisions oneself as a person, what it means to be human, what consciousness means, what it means to have a body, to express emotions, and to relate authentically.

In traditional Western culture, we have been conditioned to see and experience ourselves in negative ways—with much fear and shame and guilt. Whatever the relationship (parent and child, teacher and student, priest and worshipper, politican and constituent), one was impressed to look outward and upward, to the authority figure, for instruction on how one ought to be.

Today this relationship is radically changing. Many persons are looking inward and envisioning personhood in a positive way. And when I radically change my self concept (or better, self esteem), then all social structures and relationships built upon self-denial, repression and authority come sharply into question. I challenge the assumption that someone else knows better than I do what's best for me. I question those institutions that tell me I need someone else to dictate to me how I ought to be.

In my own experience (raised as a Roman Catholic), the authority figure faced the wall and spoke in a foreign language. My grade school teacher had all the mystery, the grades and the power. We students were supposed to sit still, shut up, and take it in, conform, deny our experience and learn not to trust our own bodies or feelings of existence.

Those ways are no longer adequate for me. So we are trying to give breath to those movements which exalt rather than put down the human, and which encourage persons to question in a positive way what human beings are and can become.

It is likewise with education today. It must be relevant to our radically and rapidly changing society. It must become responsive to the needs and wants of human beings who envision and experience themselves differently.

Traditional educational experiences gave young persons the painful sense that they had to deny their feelings, lock away their questions, and stay quiet for fear of looking stupid. I recall myself going through school: the bright kid who got all the awards, yet always afraid to ask questions for fear of being scorned or ridiculed by the authority figure.

That is no longer adequate. Perhaps the best evidence emerges from what we are hearing throughout California. Every group concerned with education (conservatives and liberals, educators and students and parents, all races, both sexes) is telling us emphatically that readin', writin' and 'rithmetic have been joined by a fourth basic goal of education: self esteem. I believe self esteem is a basic, vital goal of every human relationship and institution.

The goal of self esteem, and the demands of many humans, make it clear that the very questions about humanness and human nature and human potential are the most important questions for schools and education today. I want especially to see our schools become places where students, teachers, administrators, trustees, and parents together explore what it means to be human. And it is possible, as well as necessary, to involve the entire community, even its most traditional members, in a dialogue about self-esteem—and about freedom and responsibility and honesty (authenticity), and loving (caring). Though sadly lost in our current dealings with each other, these remain very basic traditional values.

Unless we do that, we simply aren't going to resolve our major social problems: violence, drugs, racism, sexism and war. Building self esteem, increasing our understanding of ourselves and facilitating appropriate human behavior are becoming ever more vital and inherent responsibilities of our educational system.

This book is important because it speaks directly to those issues. It strikes directly at the roots of low self esteem, whether the behavior traits are non-assertive or aggressive—by elaborating the values and techniques of the alternative—assertive behavior. It discusses how we learn it for ourselves, and how we can facilitate its learning by others (my only reservation is my skepticism about behavior modification, and my commitment to humanistic psychology).

Along with Bob Alberti and Mike Emmons, my conviction is that the human being has tremendous capacity growth in being/becoming authentic, responsible and caring, as well as for relating and growing and learning. Although *Your Perfect Right* is not solely concerned with education, we share the view that schools should be places where human beings are encouraged to be open and express themselves—rather than places where they are conditioned to feel bad about themselves, to take orders and fit in, to pursue studies without questioning, and to perpetuate the old system and its stereotypes.

We are hoping to open California education to the exploration of many alternatives and assumptions. Schools ought to generate the dialogue necessary to create alternative structures, styles and curricula that will enable young human beings to respect themselves and to discover their capacities for living meaningfully.

Education ought to be a process that affirms the right of a child not to be ashamed of him/her self, not to be afraid to declare his/her own needs and wants. It ought rather to enable him/her to recognize his/her body and mind and emotions as legitimate and valuable and equal components of being/becoming fully human. Education ought to affirm and respect the whole child.

Your Perfect Right extends the boundaries of human rights education. Its clear message is for the classroom and for the clinic and hopefully, for a far broader audience. Learning to be assertive is education for living, for being human, for becoming ourselves in much more human ways, and for making society more human too.

But finally, it is a matter of your own personal choice, and your own sense of yourself, and your own willingness to take the kinds of risks that make your own life personal, creative, meaningful and fulfilled.

Sacramento
December 6, 1973

Human Rights and Personal Power

> *Between people, as among nations, respect of each other's rights insures the peace.*
>
> *Benito Juarez*

Have you ever felt helpless, powerless, ineffective? We know and sometimes share the sense of personal powerlessness felt by many individuals in our society today, living in crowded, noisy, polluted, unfriendly places, where individuals count for little or nothing, where giant industries, or public utilities, labor unions, or political establishments are in control. Despite an occasional Ralph Nader or John Gardner, the average citizen continues to feel controlled, exploited, and used by whoever finds in him/her a source of power or profit. The average citizen may feel regarded merely as an expendable resource.

We don't agree. It is our conviction that the individual counts for more.

And that is the value of this book, to help overcome personal powerlessness, to help persons who feel somehow insignificant or frustrated in the total scheme of things. We do not simply blame the human condition upon the modern technological world, but we do recognize that in such a world the need to reaffirm each person's individual value is of the highest priority. We have found, while helping thousands of people to learn to express themselves more effectively, that there are three significant barriers to self-assertiveness:

1

1) Many people do not believe that they have the *right* to be assertive;
2) Many people are highly *anxious/fearful* about being assertive;
3) Many people lack the *social skills* for effective self-expression.

In this book we address these barriers to personal power, and present proven, effective tools to overcome them.

The reader should understand that this is not a proposal for political, economic, or social revolution. We are here concerned with power on a much more personal level—at home, on the job, at school, in stores and restaurants, in club meetings, wherever the sense of personal insignificance or frustration is encountered.

Has anyone ever cut in front of you in a line? Do you have difficulty saying "no" to persuasive salesmen? Are you able to express warm, positive feelings to someone? Can you comfortably begin a conversation with strangers at a party? Have you ever regretted "stepping on" someone else in trying to gain your own objectives?

Many people find these and similar situations uncomfortable or irritating, and often seem at a loss for just the "right" response. *Behavior which enables a person to act in his or her own best interests, to stand up for herself or himself without undue anxiety, to express honest feelings comfortably, or to exercise personal rights without denying the rights of others we call* assertive behavior. (These five dimensions of assertive behavior are examined in detail in Chapter III.) The person who typically acts in a non-assertive manner is likely to think of the appropriate response after the opportunity has passed. The aggressive response is too vigorous, making a deep and negative impression for which one may later be sorry. It is our purpose in this book to assist you in developing a more adequate repertoire of assertive behavior, so that you may choose appropriate and self-fulfilling responses in a variety of situations.

Research has shown that learning to make assertive responses will inhibit or weaken the anxiety previously experienced in specific interpersonal relationships. Developing the ability to stand up for yourself and do things on your own initiative, can reduce appreciably anxiety or tenseness in key situations, and increase your sense of worth as a person. This same sense of worth is often lacking in the person who uses aggressiveness to mask self-doubts and guilt.

We endorse without qualification the concept of the equality of human beings. Each individual has the same fundamental human rights as the other person in an interpersonal relationship, roles and titles notwithstanding. It is our goal to help more people to learn to exercise their perfect rights, without infringing upon the rights of others. We urge you to become thoroughly familiar with The Universal Declaration of Human Rights (Appendix A).

We are greatly concerned about the strong tendency in our society to evaluate human beings on scales which make some persons "better" than others. Consider the following assumptions:

adults are better than children
bosses are better than employees
men are better than women
whites are better than blacks
physicians are better than plumbers
teachers are better than students
government officers are better than voters
generals are better than privates
winners are better than losers

and so on, *ad infinitum.* Our social structures perpetuate these and similar myths, and allow individual human beings in these roles to be treated as if they are of lesser value *as human beings,* rather than in the context of the hierarchy of roles.

If you go through life inhibited, giving in to the wishes of others, holding your own desires inside yourself, or conversely, destroying others in order to have your way, your feeling of personal worth will be low. Even such bodily complaints as headaches, general fatigue, stomach disturbances, rashes, and asthma are often related to a failure to develop assertive behavior. The assertive individual is fully in charge of self in interpersonal relationships, feels confident and capable without cockiness or hostility, is basically spontaneous in the expression of feelings and emotions, and is generally looked up to and admired by others.

Commonly, people mistake agression for assertion, but the assertive individual does not malign others or deny their rights, running roughshod over people. The assertive person is open and flexible, genuinely concerned with the rights of others, yet at the same time able to establish very well his or her own rights.

It has been our sincere desire to avoid anything which may be construed as a gimmick on "how to manipulate others" or anything resembling "gamesmanship." We are only concerned with helping to bring about enduring, positive behavior patterns based upon scientific principles of learning. The concepts of aggressive, assertive, and non-assertive behavior are defined and ilustrated in order to demonstrate how to bring about positive changes in your own behavior. Specific instructions to help you achieve greater assertiveness are provided in clear, non-technical terms. A concluding section discusses issues of concern in the use of assertiveness. Included is a varied collection of illustrations of assertive situations which are useful for anyone who is interested and diligent in a course of self-improvement. Part Two of the book expands upon the theoretical and technical aspects of assertive behavior, and is designed as a guide for professionals who are engaged in facilitating personal growth in their clients.

Why This Book Was Written

As our friend John Vasconcellos noted in his thoughtful foreword to this book, the basic structures of the family, educational and business worlds frequently squelch assertive behavior. Moreover, the teachings of religious organizations have frequently inhibited complete expression in interpersonal situations.

Women, children, and members of ethnic minorities in the United States have characteristically been taught that assertive behavior is the province of the white male adult. Indeed, such attitudes run deep and die hard in our culture.

It has been extremely difficult for the *haves* to acknowledge the human rights of the *have nots.* The gains resulting from the civil rights movement of the 1950's and 1960's were slow, painful, and tragically costly. In retrospect, one wonders too if the changes are more than slight. Lyndon Baines Johnson and Martin Luther King, Jr., agreed that the Civil Rights Acts of 1964 and 1965 were "the best bills we could get" from a Congress powerfully influenced by individuals who had dedicated their lives to the preservation of the *status quo ante.* (Johnson later commented similarly about the 1968 Act).

Most recently, women have encountered similar resistance to their new efforts of self-assertion. Their husbands, their employers, their legislators, their President, have all demonstrated reluctance ranging from foot-dragging to open hostility to political battles. The phenomenal resistance to ratification of the Equal Rights Amendment is a powerful example. Yet women, too, are making overdue gains in recognition of their individual rights. We have noted an increase in assertiveness training for women, including a tremendous number of specialized workshops for women. (Ironically, a group of concerned women informed us that in the "Acknowledgements" for the first edition of this book, we apparently recognized our wives for much non-assertive behavior: "waiting").

The message is clear. Our cultural orientation to the development of appropriately assertive behavior is inadequate. We must begin to value and reward the assertions of each individual, acknowledging the right of self expression without fear or guilt, valuing the right to an opinion, and recognizing the unique contribution of each person.

In the family, the individual who decides to speak up for his or her rights is often promptly censored. Familiar admonitions are: "Don't you dare talk to your mother (father) that way! Children are to be seen, not heard." Never let me hear you say that word again!" Obviously these common parental commands are not conducive to a child's assertion of self!

Teachers especially are guilty of anti-assertive behavior, in basically the same manner as parents. Quiet, well-behaved children who do not question the system are rewarded, whereas those who buck the system in some way are dealt with sternly. It is an acknowledged conclusion among educators that the child's natural spontaneity in learning is conditioned out no later than the fourth or fifth grade.

The residue of parental and educational upbringing affects our functioning in our occupations and daily lives. Every employee is aware that typically one must not do or say anything that will "rock the boat" in an organization. The boss is "above" and others are "below" and feel obliged to go along with what is expected of them even if they consider the expectations completely inappropriate. Employees' early work experiences teach that if you "speak up" you are likely not to obtain a raise or recognition, and you may even lose your job. You quickly learn to be a "company person," to keep things running smoothly, to have few ideas of your own, to be careful how you act lest it "get back to the boss." The lesson is quite clear: be non-assertive in your work!

The teachings of contemporary churches seem to indicate that to be assertive in life is not the "religious" thing to do. Such qualities as humility, self-denial, and self-sacrifice are usually fostered to the exclusion of standing up for oneself. There is a mistaken notion that religious ideals of brotherhood/sisterhood, must, in some esoteric way be incompatible with feeling good about oneself and with being calm and confident in relationships with others. We believe, and show herein, that being assertive in life is in no way incongruent with the teachings of the major religious groups. Your escape from freedom-restricting behavior *allows* you to be of more service to others as well as to yourself. What could be irreligious about that?

Political institutions, while not so likely as the home, school and church to influence early development of assertive behavior, do little to encourage its expression by individual adults. Political decision-making has come only a short distance from the days of "star chambers," and then remains largely inaccessible to the average citizen. Nevertheless it is still true that the "squeaking wheel gets greased," and when individuals do become expressive enough, governments usually respond. It is our hope that more adequately assertive expression will preclude the necessity of aggressiveness among the activist politically alienated.

It is common for a person who has been aggressive in a given situation to feel some guilt as a result of this behavior. It is less widely recognized that the assertive person may also experience such guilt produced by childhood conditioning. The institutions of society have so carefully taught the inhibition of expression of even one's reasonable rights, that one may feel badly for having stood up for oneself.

It is not healthy to suffer guilt feelings for being yourself. Although families, schools, business, churches and governments tend to deny self-assertion, we contend that *each person has the right to be and to express himself or herself, and to feel good [not guilty] about doing so, as long as he or she does not hurt others in the process.*

The anti-assertive influence of these basic societal systems has resulted in a "built-in" set of limits on the self-fulfilling actions of many persons. Many people whose lives were constricted by an inability to be adequately assertive have achieved self-fulfillment by following the assertiveness training program of this book.

Who Will Read This Book

This book is for all who wish to develop a more enhancing personal existence on their own, and for those who will be instrumental in facilitating the personal growth of others.

The book is aimed toward both a general audience, and those who are engaged in, or training for, professional therapeutic or behavior modifying roles. Teachers, coaches, counselors, and personnel workers in schools and colleges find this book useful, as do those whose responsibilities are school-related, but more specialized, such as speech therapists. Professionals in private and agency therapeutic practice— psychiatrists, psychologists, medical doctors, marriage and family counselors, pastors, social workers, rehabilitation and employment counselors—find assertiveness training valuable in their practice. They also offer the book as helpful reading for their clients. For some professionals this book provides a brief review and an organized approach to methods they already employ in varying degrees, and may serve to increase their effectiveness. Personnel and training officers, as well as line managers, in large industrial or government organizations find useful the concepts and techniques described here. Also, this material is valuable for a variety of individuals engaged in community and youth organizations. A more detailed discussion of potential applications of assertive training in these and other settings will be found in Part Two.

This material was written with practical application in mind and is organized to facilitate its usefulness in practice. We urge you to become familiar with the concept of assertiveness, recognize its validity in your own experience, and then apply its principles in your personal life.

In this first part we have intentionally avoided concepts and terminology which might deter the general reader. Part Two of this book is designed to fill the need for a clinically-oriented book on assertiveness training, with documentation of extensive research. The practicioner is referred further to the literature referenced there. You are invited to make the most of what we offer here to help yourself and others. We invite ''feedback'' and reports of both lay and professional work employing assertiveness training, so that we may continually refine and update this work, and for possible publication in *ASSERT*, the bi-monthly ''Newsletter of Assertive Behavior and Personal Development.'' (A sample copy is available at no charge from Impact Publishers, Inc., Post Office Box 1094, San Luis Obispo, California, 93406).

II

Assertive, Non-Assertive, and Aggressive Behavior

> *...There are three possible broad approaches to the conduct of interpersonal relations. The first is to consider one's self only and ride roughshod over others . . . The second . . . is always to put others before one's self . . . The third approach is the golden mean . . . The individual places himself first, but takes others into account.*
>
> —*Joseph Wolpe, M.D.*

Our way of life cultivates conflicting ways of behaving in many interpersonal areas (although there are some important differences within specific ethnic subcultures). A typical example is found in the common attitudes and teachings about human sexuality. Sexual restraint is the societal norm of the American middle class family, school and church. The popular media, however, virtually bombard audiences with a different view of sexuality. On one hand, girls are expected to be sweet and innocently non-assertive, whereas on the other they are rewarded for being sultry, vampish and sensual. Sexual aggressiveness, especially in the male, is highly valued: the "lover" is glorified in print and on the screen, and admired by his peers. Paradoxically, he is cautioned to date "respectable" girls and warned that sexual intercourse is guiltless only after marriage.

Further examples of conflicts between "recommended" and "rewarded" behavior are evident. Even though it is typically understood that one should respect the rights of others, all too often we observe that parents, teachers, and churches contradict these values by their own actions. Tact, diplomacy, politeness, refined manners, modesty, and self-denial are generally praised, yet to ''get ahead'' it is often acceptable to ''step on'' others.

The male child is carefully coached to be strong, brave, and dominant. His aggressiveness is condoned and accepted, as in the pride felt by a father whose son is in trouble for busting the neighborhood bully in the nose. Ironically (and a source of much confusion for the child), the same father will likely encourage his son to ''have respect for his elders,'' ''let others go first,'' ''be polite.''

Although it is seldom openly admitted, the athlete who participates in competitive sports knows when he or she has been aggressive or perhaps ''bent'' the rules a little, that is O.K. because ''it is not important how you play the game, it is important that you win.'' (The physical fitness purist who would argue with this statement is invited to contrast the

FIGURE II-1

Non-Assertive Behavior	Aggressive Behavior	Assertive Behavior
As Actor	*As Actor*	*As Actor*
Self-denying	Self-enhancing at expense of another	Self-enhancing
Inhibited	Expressive	Expressive
Hurt, anxious	Depreciates others	Feels good about self
Allows others to choose	Chooses for others	Chooses for self
Does not achieve desired goal	Achieves desired goal by hurting others	May achieve desired goal
As Receiver	*As Receiver*	*As Receiver*
Guilty or angry	Self-denying	Self-enchancing
Depreciates actor	Hurt, defensive, humiliated	Expressive
Achieves desired goal at actor's expense	Does not achieve desired goal	May achieve desired goal

rewards for winning coaches with those for losing coaches who "build character.") Woody Hayes, much acclaimed football coach at Ohio State University, is quoted as saying, "Show me a good loser, and I'll show you a loser."

We believe that one should be able to *choose for one's self* how to act in a given circumstance. If the "polite restraint" response is too well developed, one may be unable to make the choice to act as he or she would like to. If the aggressive response is overdeveloped, one may be unable to achieve one's own goals without hurting others. This freedom of choice and exercise of self-control is made possible by the development of assertive responses for situations which have previously produced non-assertive or aggressive behavior based on anxiety.

Examples contrasting assertive with non-assertive and aggressive actions will help to clarify these concepts. The pattern which appears in Figure II-1 is also demonstrated in each of the examples presented later in the chapter. The chart displays several feelings and consequences typical for the person (actor) whose behavior is non-assertive, assertive or aggressive. Also shown, for each of these modes of behavior, are the likely consequences for the person toward whom the action is directed (receiver).

It may be seen in Figure II-1 that in the case of a *non-assertive* response in a given situation, the actor is typically denying self, and is inhibited from expressing actual feelings. Often feeling hurt and anxious as a result of this inadequate behavior and allowing others to choose for him or her, this person seldom achieves his or her own desired goals.

The person who carries a desire for self expression to the extreme of *aggressive* behavior accomplishes goals usually at the expense of others. Although frequently self-enhancing and expressive of feelings in the situation, aggressive behavior hurts others in the process by making choices for them, and minimizing their worth as persons.

Aggressive behavior commonly results in a "put down" of the receiver. Rights denied, she or he feels hurt, defensive, and humiliated. His or her goals in the situation, of course, are not achieved. The aggressive person may achieve goals, but may also generate hatred and frustration which may later return as vengeance.

In contrast, appropriately *assertive* behavior in the same situation would be self-enhancing for the actor, an honest expression of feelings, and usually achieve goals. Having chosen for oneself how to act, a good feeling typically (not *always*) accompanies the assertive response (even when one's goals are *not* achieved).

Similarly, when the consequences of these three contrasting behaviors are viewed from the perspective of the "receiver," (i.e., the individual toward whom the behavior is directed) a parallel pattern emerges. Non-assertive behavior often produces feelings ranging from sympathy to outright contempt toward the actor. Also the receiver may feel guilt or anger at having achieved goals at the actor's expense. In contrast, a transaction involving assertion enhances feelings of self-worth and permits full expression of self. In addition, while the actor achieves his or her goals, the goals of the receiver may also be achieved.

In summary, then, it is clear that the actor is hurt by self-denial in non-assertive behavior; the receiver may be hurt in aggressive behavior. In the case of assertion, neither person is hurt, and unless their goal achievement is mutually exclusive, both may succeed.

It is important to note that assertive behavior is *person-and-situation-specific,* not universal. Although we believe the definitions and examples presented in this book to be realistic and appropriate for *most* people and circumstances, individual differences must be considered. Cultural or ethnic background, for example, may create an entirely different set of personal circumstances which change the nature of "appropriateness" in assertive behavior. In the following section, we look in more detail at the differentiation of assertive, non-assertive, and aggressive behavior.

"The CRIB" - A Framework for Classifying Behavior

"I told my father-in-law not to smoke his cigar in my house! Was that assertive or aggressive?"

In AT groups and workshops, we are often asked to classify a particular act as "assertive" or "aggressive." What criteria *do* make the important difference?

A good deal of controversy exists over the relative difinitions of these concepts. We have suggested that assertive and aggressive behavior differ principally in that the latter involves hurting or stepping on others in the course of expressing oneself. Albert Bandura (1973), notes that aggression is defined by both the *behavior* and the *social labels* applied to it. Others have proposed that *intent* must be considered. That is, did you intend to *hurt* your father-in-law (aggressive) or to *inform* him of your wishes (assertive)?

In his extensive research on AT, Richard McFall has followed the assumption that behavior must be measurable according to its *effects*. Thus, if your father gets the assertive message and *responds* accordingly (i. e. by agreeing not to smoke), your behavior may be classified as assertive. If he pouts in a corner, or shouts "Who do you think you are?", your statement may have been aggressive, as described by this criterion. Finally, Donald Cheek (1976) has pointed out that the *social-cultural context* must be taken into account in classifying behavior as assertive or aggressive or non-assertive. A culture, for example, which regards honoring one's elders as one of its ultimate values may view the requests as clearly out of line and aggressive: regardless of the behavior, response, or intent.

It is clear that there are no absolutes in this area, and that some criteria may be in conflict. A particular act may be at once assertive in *behavior* and *intent* (you wanted to and did express your feelings), aggressive in *response* (the other person could not handle your assertion), and non-assertive in the social *context* (your subculture expects a powerful, "put-down" style). It may not be possible to reconcile such mutually exclusive classifications. Nevertheless, it is useful to consider these four criteria [*Context, Response, Intent, Behavior*] when attempting to evaluate a given action.

The "CRIB" chart shown in Figure II-2 may help to clarify this system of looking at non-assertive/assertive/aggressive behavior. Entries in the chart, of course, are representative only, particularly in the area of the response of others. It should be noted that a specific situation may vary considerably from the "usual case" shown here. In any event, the question "Is it assertive or aggressive?" is not one which may be answered simply!

The issues are complex, and each situation must be evaluated individually. Indeed, the labels "non-assertive," "assertive," and "aggressive" themselves carry no magic, but within the framework described here they may be useful in assessing the *appropriateness* of a particular action.

Such a framework may be more complex than your interest in

FIGURE II-2
"THE CRIB"
A FRAMEWORK FOR CLASSIFYING BEHAVIOR
YOUR ACTIONS MAY BE LABELED AS . . .

	NON ASSERTIVE	ASSERTIVE	AGGRESSIVE
When the Society or Culture or context calls for . . .	Strength; "Cool;" Ambition; "Macho;" Drive; Self-Serving; Hardness; Toughness; Lack of regard for others.	Honesty; Forthrightness; Firmness; Courage; Directness; Caring; Respect for others; Equality in relationships.	Self denial; Sacrifice; Quiet; Softness; Submission to others; "Not making waves;" "Staying in your place."
When you feel this response . . .	Emotional pain; failure to gain your goals; loneliness; Physical ailments (headaches, etc.); Low self confidence; Low self-respect.	Good feeling; Accomplishment of your goals; Closeness (in long run—sometimes distance at first); Confidence; Self respect; Affection; "I did all I could."	Guilt; Loneliness; Accomplishment of your goals; Distance from others; Power; Confidence; Low self-respect.
And the response of others is . . .	Scorn; Derision; Lack of respect; Pity; "Winning; Ignoring you; "Turning off."	Good feeling; Friendliness; Affection; Cooperation; Respect; Closeness; Openness. OR SOMETIMES: Fear; Withdrawal OR SOMETIMES: Anger, Dislike.	Fear; Withdrawal; Submission; Avoidance OR Anger; Disrespect; Dislike; Hostility OR Firmness; Assertion; Resistance.
When your intent is primarily . . .	Deny yourself; Avoid risks; Stay out of trouble; Put yourself down; Avoid hurting others; Avoid hurting yourself; Be liked; Hide your anger.	Express yourself; Reach out; Gain your goals; Show respect for others; Be honest and direct; Stand up for your rights; Express friendship or affection; Show your anger.	Express yourself; Dominate; Set others straight"; Win; Do it your way; Gain your goals; Disregard others.
And others interpret that . . .	You are afraid you are a pushover; You don't believe in your ideas; You don't know what you're talking about.	You are confident; You are friendly; You are honest; You know your feelings; You respect yourself & others; You care.	You want to hurt others; You are thoughtless and rude; You are mean; You have no feelings; You are pompous.
When you behave with . . .	Downcast eyes; Soft voice; Hesitation; Helpless gestures; Denying importance of the situation; Slumped posture; Words like "anything you want is okay with me", OR avoiding the situation altogether.	Direct eye contact; conversational voice level; Fluent speech; Erect posture; "I" messages; Honesty; Positive statements; Direct response to the situation.	Glaring; Loud voice; Fluent/fast speech; Confrontation; Threatening gestures; Intimidating posture; Dishonesty; Impersonal messages.
And others Behave by . . .	No eye contact; Not listening; Being pushy; Making unreasonable requests; Taking advantage of you; Disagreeing; Denying your requests; Head shaking; Manipulation.	Making eye contact; Interested conversation; Open posture & gestures; Listening; forthright comments; Agreeing or disagreeing. OR SOMETIMES: giving in; OR SOMETIMES: aggression.	Backing away; Hesitating; Agreeing; Closed posture; Accepting; Giving in; Looking away or down; Head nodding OR counter aggression; hostile remarks; loud voice; glaring; threats; violence OR direct eye contact; firm posture & gestures; forthright comments.

assertiveness. It is not necessary that you be familiar with the detail of this view. It is sufficient to recognize that the answer to ''what is assertive?'' is not simplistic, and that it is necessary to deal uniquely with each person and situation. We are presenting in this book a basic viewpoint and a procedure for increasing your capacity to *choose for yourself!*

General and Situational Non-Assertiveness

> *An appeaser is one who feeds a crocodile—hoping it will eat him last.*
>
> —*Sir Winston Churchill*

Two concepts of non-assertiveness are useful in understanding and developing more adaptive responses to life situations which call for assertiveness. The first concerns those individuals whose behavior is typically adequate and self-enhancing; however, *certain situations* stimulate a great deal of anxiety in them which prevents fully adequate responses to that particular situation. We identify this category as *situational non-assertiveness.*

The second category, *generalized non-assertivenss,* includes those persons whose behavior is typically non-assertive. This individual, often observed as shy, timid, or reserved, is unable to assert rights or act on feelings under *most or nearly all circumstances.* He or she will not do anything to disturb anyone, is constantly giving in to any request (or feeling guilty for turning someone down), has always done what his or her parents wanted, denies having any ideas of his or her own, and is cowed by others. Whereas most persons will at least protest a little when their rights are badly abused, the general non-asserter will say nothing at all. For example, if others are making undue noise and interfering with one's enjoyment of a performance, most of us will, when sufficiently provoked, ask them to respect our desire for quiet, whereas the generally non-assertive person will suffer in silence, perhaps even levelling self accusations of being non-accepting or non-loving at having the slightest thought that the other person is wrong!

It is not unusual for the general non-asserter to go out of the way to let others take advantage. Some will ask permission to do what most regard as commonly accepted. One woman felt it necessary to ask her husband if she could kiss him or sit on his lap! A man named Fred let someone borrow his car, supposedly for the day. When, three days later, the person returned the car with little gas and no explanation whatsoever as to what had happened, Fred said nothing, although his head was in a "fog" and his stomach in turmoil!

The generally non-assertive person, therefore, is one with very low self-esteem and for whom very uncomfortable anxiety is generated by nearly *all* social situations. Feelings of inadequacy, lack of acknowledgement of self-worth, and physical discomfort brought on by generalized anxiety may call for in-depth treatment. The extreme inhibition and lack of emotional responsiveness of this non-assertive person may require a depth of attitude and behavior development which is possible only in a relationship with a trained therapist. Thus, although a comprehensive set of assertive-training situations is included in this book's program for assertiveness development, no attempt is made here to deal fully with the therapeutic conditions necessary to help the *generally* non-assertive person. It is suggested that individuals identified as generally non-assertive seek help from a qualified counselor or therapist.

Ellen was a particularly notable example of such a person. Although beautiful and very bright, she permitted herself to see her own value only in terms of service to her husband and her baby son. She picked up her husband's dirty socks without a complaint, and responded with compliance to his every wish. Moreover, she was extremely anxious in social situations and in rooms without windows. Her difficulties called for therapeutic interventions of several types, including assertiveness training. Although Ellen's husband was at first reluctant, then upset, he was finally very pleased with the more independent, self-expressive person Ellen gradually became!

The situational non-asserter may readily recognize the problem and, without too much preparation or prompting, successfully initiate assertion. He or she also has a tendency to recognize ways to be assertive with others spontaneously, without being specifically instructed to do so. An example is Carol, a 27-year old female college student who told of how others took advantage of her a good deal of the time. Her current difficulty was with a classmate who had borrowed her notes and now had kept them for over a month. Carol needed them back in order to prepare for student teaching and once had even asserted herself to some extent by asking for their return, but the other girl did not return them. The concepts of assertiveness were explained to Carol, the difficulty she had asserting herself properly was pointed out to her, and she role-played calling the girl again, this time being firm and insistent. Within the next several days she did call the girl, spoke firmly about needing her notes, and soon got them back. In addition, she spoke up to one of her roommates about some matter that upset her. She even complained about an unjust parking ticket and won! In the past, this woman would have let these things slide or pass; however, she learned her lesson quickly. She has continued to assert herself with a much improved self-image as a result.

In the case of *situational* non-assertiveness, we may assume we are dealing with a relatively healthy person who wishes to develop new ways of handling situations which are now uncomfortable, self-denying, and non-adaptive. If nothing were done about these situations, he or she would still be able to function in a relatively healthy manner, but by asserting in certain key situations, his or her life will run more smoothly and be much more fulfilled. A teacher, counselor, or friend may observe this person's inability to act in his or her own best interest. Or the individual may seek help in overcoming anxiety in a given situation. Should this describe you, don't hesitate to first try the methods described in this book, then to get professional aid if you need it.

General and Situational Aggressiveness

> *I am the inferior of any man whose rights I trample underfoot.*
>
> —*Horace Greeley*

In the preceding section, we described the behavior of the person whose anxiety inhibited appropriately assertive responses. Another person may respond to such anxiety by becoming aggressive, "putting yourself up" by "putting others down."

It is not uncommon for assertive behavior to be confused with aggressive behavior. However, observe that assertion does not involve hurting another person. Often the aggressive individual *wishes* to stand up for self without hurting others but has not *learned* responses which are appropriately assertive. It is easy to misunderstand aggressive acts and to hold low esteem for aggressive people. Some recent popular books have attempted to help improve understanding of aggressiveness, however, much remains to be done with this topic. Unfortunately, as will be discussed later in Chapter VIII, some popularized, oversimplified and inaccurate explanations, such as those which characterize aggressiveness as "instinctive," are misleading and of little value in understanding this mode of behavior. Hopefully, an acknowledgement of aggression as an inadequate response to anxiety and a recognition of the ease with which one may learn more adaptive assertive responses will reduce the out-of-proportion concern many have about individual aggression.

The concepts of "general" and "situational" may be applied to aggressive behavior in a similar fashion to our discussion of non-assertiveness. The *generally aggressive* individual is characterized by behavior toward others which is *typically* aggressive in every type of situation. On the surface, this person may appear to have a high level of self-confidence, to be in command of every situation, to be strong and able to cope with life on his own terms. If male, he may live according to his view of the American cultural ideal: the image of the aggressive, masculine figure who dominates his environment and demonstrates his "manhood" by bravado. The more intellectually oriented may typically dominate conversations, belittle the opinions of others, and leave no doubt that he or she is "the final word" on nearly any topic. One who is generally aggressive appears to have friction in the majority of contacts with people. He or she is likely to be extremely sensitive to criticism and to feel rejected a good portion of the time. General aggressiveness is characterized by the ease with which one is triggered into aggressive outbursts. In extreme cases, there may be such high volatility that the slightest threat to security causes an adverse reaction. The male is often very autocratic in his family relationships, with a submissive wife and cowering children, none of whom dare cross him in any way. He may resort to physical punishment with the children and may be physically abusive with his wife. Often a loner type who is considered sullen and moody, he or she may have great difficulty holding a job.

This generally aggressive person, whose behavior is so offensive to others, finds few friends and little esteem from acquaintances. Needing affection and acceptance as much as anyone, she or he does not know how to be assertive (and thus gain acceptance) or how to ask for affection. Attempts at reaching out to others for human contact usually end in frustration because of abusive behavior.

Again, as in the case of the generally non-assertive person, the generally aggressive individual is, we believe, anxious in nearly all social situations. Unwilling or unable to respond to an emotional event honestly, deceiving others and often self, persons who exhibit this behavior pattern may benefit from a professional therapeutic relationship.

The *situationally aggressive* person responds with aggression only under certain conditions. This individual will usually recognize the condition and voluntarily seek assistance for the specific problem, or respond readily to another's suggestion that he or she could easily learn a more adaptive response than aggression. Examples of situational aggressiveness will perhaps place the idea in clearer perspective. Two college students were referred by the same instructor on separate occasions. Jim, a male sophomore, was described as having a "chip on his shoulder." Adele, a female senior, was sent for "being too pushy" with an instructor and with her classmates. The young man was a disruptive influence in the classroom; he would ask questions in an aggressive manner which intimidated the teacher and in class discussions would barge in with his opinions, showing no respect for the opinions of others. Jim's opinionated attitude was offending but made worse by his contempt for others who did not accept his "obvious" conclusions. He literally disrupted the entire classroom climate by rejecting the validity of any viewpoint other than his own. To say the least, Jim alienated everyone in this classroom situation even though many of his points were well thought out and logical.

Adele only became aggressive after an extended period of non-assertivenes. As she felt others taking advantage of her more and more, she finally could stand it no longer and would have an aggressive outburst. After such display of anger, Adele would appear to function well again until the build up occurred again, producing another outburst. Each of these individuals was "correct," but ruined the effectiveness of their ideas by inappropriate actions. Both found their academic lives improved by learning how to handle situations assertively.

Another example of situational aggressiveness is that of Pat, 37, who was being counseled with her husband after working individually with a therapist for some time. Pat was extremely angry with her husband for his preoccupation with activities outside the home, but avoided direct confrontation. Instead, her responses to him were "super-sweet," including a direct statement that she "didn't mind" his involvements elsewhere. Nevertheless, Pat did express her bitter resentment by such actions as taking the car when she knew he needed it, cutting him down verbally in front of others, and leaving the children with him when he was particularly busy at home. Such subtly aggressive acts were all a substitute for the honest confrontation Pat would not assert herself to achieve.

Case Examples

The following situational examples will help to clarify the concepts of non-assertive, aggressive, and assertive behavior. As you read them, you may wish to pause to reflect on your own response before reading the alternative responses we have presented. These examples are oversimplified, of course, in order to demonstrate the ideas most clearly.

"Dining Out"

Mr. and Mrs. A are at dinner in a moderately expensive restaurant. Mr. A has ordered a rare steak, but when the steak is served, Mr. A finds it to be very well done, contrary to his order. His behavior is:

Non-assertive: Mr. A grumbles to his wife about the "burned" meat, and observes that he won't patronize this restaurant in the future. He says nothing to the waitress, responding "Fine!" to her inquiry "Is everything all right!" His dinner and evening are highly unsatisfactory, and he feels guilty for having taken no action. Mr. A's estimate of himself, and Mrs. A's estimate of him are both deflated by the experience.

Aggressive: Mr. A angrily summons the waitress to his table. He berates her loudly and unfairly for not complying with his order. His actions ridicule the waitress and embarrass Mrs. A. He demands and receives another steak, this one more to his liking. He feels in control of the situation, but Mrs. A's embarrassment creates friction between them, and spoils their evening. The waitress is humiliated and angry and loses her poise for the rest of the evening.

Assertive: Mr. A motions the waitress to his table. Noting that he had ordered a rare steak, he shows her the well done meat, asking politely but firmly that it be returned to the kitchen and replaced with the rare-cooked steak he originally requested. The waitress apologizes for the error, and shortly returns with a rare steak. The A's enjoy dinner, tip accordingly, and Mr. A feels satisfaction with himself. The waitress is pleased with a satisfied customer and an adequate tip.

"Something Borrowed"

Helen is a college sophomore, bright, attractive, a good student liked by teachers and peers. She lives in a residence hall with two roommates, in a suite arrangement with six other girls. All of the girls date quite regularly. One evening, as Helen's roommates are dressing for their dates (Helen plans a quiet evening working on a term paper), Mary says that she is going out with a "really special" young man, and she hopes to make a good impression. She asks Helen if she may borrow and wear a new and quite expensive necklace Helen has just received from her brother, who is overseas in military service. Helen and her brother are very close and the necklace means a great deal to her. Her response is:

Non-assertive: She swallows her anxiety about loss or damage to the necklace, her feeling that its special meaning makes it too personal to lend, and says "Sure!" She denies herself, reinforces Mary for making an unreasonable request, and worries all evening (which makes little contribution to the term paper).

Aggressive: Helen shows her outrage by her friend's request, tells her "absolutely not," and proceeds to upbraid her severely for even daring to ask "such a stupid question." She humiliates Mary and generally makes a fool of herself. Later she feels uncomfortable and guilty, interfering with her work on the paper. Mary's hurt feelings show on her date, and she has a miserable time, puzzling and dismaying the young man. Thereafter the relationship between Helen and Mary becomes very strained.

Assertive: She explains the significance of the necklace to her roommate, and politely but firmly observes that the request is an unreasonable one since this piece of jewely is particularly personal. She later feels good for having asserted herself, and Mary, recognizing the validity of Helen's response, makes a big hit with the young man by being more honestly herself.

"Have a Joint"

Pam is a friendly, outgoing college junior who has been dating an attractive young man for whom she cares a great deal. One evening he invites her to attend a small get-together with two other couples, both of whom are married. As all become acquainted at the party, Pam is enjoying herself. After an hour or so, one of the married men brings out several cigarettes which he identifies as marijuana and suggests that they all smoke. Everyone eagerly joins in except Pam, who does not wish to experiment with marijuana. She is in conflict because the boy she admires is smoking marijuana and as he offers her a cigarette she decides to be:

Non-assertive: She accepts the marijuana and pretends to have smoked it before. She carefully watches the others to see how they smoke. Inside, she dreads the possibility they may ask her to smoke more. Others are speaking of getting "stoned" and Pam is worried about what her friend is thinking about her. She has denied herself, been dishonest with her boy-friend, and feels remorseful for giving in to something she did not wish to do.

Aggressive: Pam is visibly upset when offered the marijuana and blasts the young man for bringing her to a party of this "low type." She states that she wants to be taken home right away rather than stay with such people. When the others at the party says that she does not have to smoke if she doesn't wish to, she is not appeased and she continues to be quite indignant. Her friend is humiliated, embarrassed before his friends, and disappointed in her. Although he remains cordial toward Pam as he takes her home, he does not offer an invitation for a further date.

Assertive: Pam does not accept the cigarette, replying simply, "No, thank you. I don't care for one." She goes on to explain that she hasn't smoked pot before and doesn't wish to. She expresses her preference that the others not smoke, but acknowledges their right to make their own choices.

"The Heavyweight"

Mr. and Mrs. B, who have been married nine years, have been having marital problems recently because he insists that she is overweight and needs to reduce. He brings the subject up continually, pointing out that she is no longer the girl he married (who was 25 lbs. lighter), that such overweight is bad for her health, that she is a bad example for the children, and so on.

In addition, he teases her about being "chunky," looks longingly at thin girls, commenting how attractive they look, and makes reference to her figure in front of their friends. Mr. B has been reacting this way for the past three months and Mrs. B is highly upset. She has been attempting to lose weight for those three months but with little success. Following Mr. B's most recent rash of criticism, Mrs. B is:

Non-assertive: She apologizes for her overweight, makes feeble excuses or simply doesn't reply to some of Mr. B's comments. Internally, she feels both hostile toward her husband for his nagging, and guilty about being overweight. Her feelings of anxiety make it even more difficult for her to lose weight and the battle continues.

Aggressive: Mrs. B goes into a long tirade about how her husband isn't any great bargain anymore either! She brings up the fact that at night he falls asleep on the couch half the time, is a lousy sex partner and doesn't pay sufficient attention. None of these comments are pertinent to the issue at hand, but Mrs. B continues. She complains that he humiliates her in front of the children and their close friends and acts like a "lecherous old man" by the way he eyes the sexy girls. In her anger she succeeds only in wounding Mr. B and driving a wedge between them by "defending" herself with a counter-attack on him.

Assertive: Approaching her husband when they are alone and will not be interrupted, Mrs. B indicates that she feels that Mr. B is correct about her need to lose weight, but she does not care for the way he keeps after her about the problem or the manner in which he does so. She points out that she is doing her best and is having a difficult time losing the weight and maintaining the loss. He acknowledges the ineffectiveness of his harping, and they work out together a plan in which he will systematically reinforce her for her efforts to lose weight.

"The Neighbor Kid"

Mr. and Mrs. E have a boy two years old and a baby girl two months old. Over the last several nights their neighbor's son, who is 17, has been sitting in his own driveway in his car with his stereo tape player blaring loudly. He begins just about the time the E's two young children retire in their bedroom on the side of the house where the boy plays the music. The loud music awakens the children each night and it has been impossible for the E's to get the children to bed until the music stops. Mr. and Mrs. E are both disturbed and decide to be:

Non-assertive: Mr. and Mrs. E move the children into their own bedroom on the other side of the house, wait until the music stops around 1 a.m., then transfer the children back to their own rooms. Then they go to bed much past their own usual bedtime. They continue to quietly curse the teenager and soon become alienated from their neighbors.

Aggressive: Mr. and Mrs. E call the police and protest that "one of those wild teenagers" next door is creating a disturbance. They demand that the police "do their duty" and stop the noise at once. The police do talk with the boy and his parents, who become very upset and angry as a result of their embarrassment about the police visit. They denounce the E's tactics in reporting to the police without speaking to them first, and resolve to avoid further association with them.

Assertive: Both Mr. and Mrs. E go over to the boy's house and indicate to him that his stereo is keeping the children awake at night. They ask what arrangement they could work out concerning the music so that it would not disturb their children's sleep. The boy is reluctantly agreeable to setting a lower volume during the late hours, but appreciates the E's cooperative attitude. Both parties feel good about the outcome.

"The Loser"

Russell is a twenty-two-year-old college drop out who works in a plastics factory. He lives alone in a small one-room walk-up apartment. Russell has had no dates for the past fourteen months. He left college after a series of depressing events—academic failures, a "Dear John" letter, and some painful harassment by other students in his residence hall. He has been in jail overnight for drunkeness on two recent occasions. Yesterday he received a letter from his mother, inquiring about his well being, but primarily devoted to a discussion of his brother's recent successes. Today his supervisor berated him harshly and somewhat unjustly for a mistake which was actually the supervisor's own responsibility. In addition, a secretary in the plant turned down his invitation to dinner.When he arrived at his apartment that evening, feeling particularly depressed and overwrought, his landlord met him at the door with a tirade about "drunken bums" and a demand (one week early) that this month's rent be paid on time. Russell's response is:

Non-assertive: He takes on himself the burden of the landlord's attack, feeling added guilt and even greater depression. A sense of helplessness overcomes him. He wonders how his brother can be so successful while he considers himself so worthless. The secretary's rejection and the boss's criticism strengthen his conviction that he is "no damn good." Deciding the world would be a better place without him, he finds the small revolver he has been hiding in his room, and begins loading it for the purpose of committing suicide.

Aggressive: The landlord has added the final straw to Russell's burden. He becomes extremely angry and pushes the landlord out of the way into his room. Once alone, he resolves to "get" the people who have been making his life so miserable recently, the supervisor, the secretary, the landlord, and possibly others as well. He finds his revolver and begins loading it, with the intent of going out after dark to shoot the people who have hurt him.

Assertive: Russell responds firmly to the landlord, noting that he has paid his rent regularly, and that it is not due for another week. He reminds the landlord of a broken rail on the stairway and the plumbing repairs whch were to have been accomplished weeks earlier. The following morning, after giving his life situation a great deal of thought, Russell calls the local mental health clinic to ask for help. At work he approaches the supervisor calmly and explains the circumstances surrounding the mistake. Though somewhat defensive, the supervisor acknowledges her error and apoligizes for her aggressive behavior.

Recognizing Your Own Non-Assertive and Aggressive Behavior

The examples given in this chapter help to point out what we mean by "assertiveness".

The most effective method of determining the adequacy of your own assertiveness is simply to honestly listen to yourself describe your relationships with others who are important to you. Make a careful examination of your interactions with (depending upon age and life style) parents, peers, co-workers, classmates, spouse, children, bosses, employees, teachers, salesmen, neighbors, relatives. Who is dominant in these specific relationships? Are you easily taken advantage of in dealings with others? Do you express your feelings and ideas openly in most circumstances? Do you take advantage of and/or hurt others frequently?

Your honest responses to such questions provide hints which may lead you to explore in greater depth your assertive, non-assertive or aggressive behavior. We think you will find such self-examination rewarding, and a very important step on your journey toward increased interpersonal effectiveness.

Chapter IV offers a systematic procedure for determining your own strengths and shortcomings in assertiveness, and will help you to plan your own course of acton. But first, let's take a closer look at this elusive concept from another perspective . . .

III

What is Assertive Behavior?

> *A man who trims himself to suit everybody will soon whittle himself away.*
>
> —*Charles M. Schwab*

You have already discovered that assertiveness is not a simple characteristic. At the least, it must be viewed as person-and-situation-specific.

Some have suggested that there is no generalized characteristic of ''assertiveness'' and that the concept is so complex and has such diverse meaning as to be undefinable! Despite these complexities, we know from the experience of thousands of persons that training in assertiveness can be valuable, if training procedures are carefully matched to trainee needs.

In this chapter, we will examine several approaches to the concept of ''assertiveness.'' Our brief definition in Chapter I offers a starting point:

Behavior which enables a person to act in his or her own best interests, to stand up for herself or himself without undue anxiety, to express honest feelings comfortably, or to exercise personal rights without denying the rights of others, we call assertive behavior.

27

Let's examine the elements of that complex sentence in greater detail:

To act in one's own best interests refers to the capacity to make life decisions (career, relationships, life style, time schedule), to take initiative (start conversations, organize activities), to trust one's own judgement, to set goals and work to achieve them, to ask help from others, to comfortably participate socially.

To stand up for oneself includes such behaviors as saying "no," setting limits on one's time and energy, responding to criticism or put downs or anger, expressing or supporting or defending one's opinion.

To express honest feelings comfortably means the ability to disagree, to show anger, to show affection or friendship, to admit fear or anxiety, to express agreement or support, to be spontaneous, all without painful anxiety.

To exercise personal rights relates to one's competency (as a citizen, as a consumer, as a member of an organization or school or work group, as a participant in public events) to express opinions, to work for change, to respond to violations of one's own rights or those of others.

To not deny the rights of others is to accomplish the above personal expressions without unfair criticism of others, without hurtful behavior toward others, without namecalling, without intimidation, without manipulation, without conrolling others.

Thus assertive behavior is a positive self-affirmation which also values the other persons in your life.

"I Couldn't Think Of What To Say!"

Many people view assertiveness as a *verbal* behavior, believing that they must have just the right words to handle a situation effectively. It is our experience that the *manner* in which you express an assertive message is a good deal more important than the exact *words* you use. Although popular with many assertiveness trainers, it has never been our style to offer scripts of "what to say when . . ." We are primarily concerned with encouraging honesty and directness, and much of that message is communicated *non-verbally*.

People in our groups and workshops have enjoyed watching us role-play a scene which makes this point clear: Bob is a dissatisfied customer who wishes to return a defective copy of *Everything You*

Always Wanted to Know About Assertiveness, But Were Too Timid Too Ask to the bookstore; Mike is the clerk. Using essentially the same words, "I bought this book here last week, and discovered that 20 pages are missing. I'd like a good copy or my money back," Bob approaches Mike in three different ways:

(1) Bob walks slowly and hesitatingly to the counter. His eyes are downcast at the floor, he speaks just above a whisper, his face looks as though it belongs on the cover of the book. He has a tight grip on the book, and a "tail-between-the-legs" posture;

(2) Bob swaggers toward the counter, glares at Mike, addresses him in a voice heard all over the store. Bob's posture and almost-fistlike gesture are an obvious attempt to intimidate the clerk;

(3) Bob walks up to the counter facing Mike. He stands relaxed and erect, smiles, and looks directly at Mike with a friendly expression. In a conversational volume and tone of voice, he states the message, gesturing to point out the flaw.

The three styles are over-exaggerated, of course, but the point is clear. The non-assertive, self-defeating style says to Mike that this customer is a pushover, and the slightest resistance will cause him to give up and go away. The second approach may achieve the goal of refund or exhange, but the aggressive Bob will leave with Mike's hostility directed at his back! With the assertive approach, Bob gets what he came for, and Mike feels good about having helped solve a problem for an appreciative customer.

The Components of Assertive Behavior

Increasingly systematic observations of assertive behavior have led behavioral scientists to conclude that there are several important components which contribute to an assertive act. Our thinking in this area was significantly influenced by the late Michael Serber, M.D. (1972). Let us examine the key components of assertive behavior in detail:

Eye Contact: One of the most obvious aspects of behavior when addressing another person is where you look. If you look directly at the person as you speak, it helps to communicate your sincerity an to increase the directness of your message. If you look down or away much of the time, you present a lack of confidence, or a quality of deference to the other person. If you stare too intently, the other person may feel an uncomfortable "invasion."

We do not advocate that you "maximize" eye contact. Continuous looking at someone can make the other person uncomfortable, is inappropriate and unnecessary, and may appear to be a "game." Moreover, eye contact is a cultural variable; many cultural groups limit the amount of eye contact which is acceptable, particularly between age groups or members of the opposite sex. Nevertheless, the importance of eye contact is obvious, and a relaxed and steady gaze at the other, looking away occasionally as it is comfortable, helps to make conversation more personal, to show interest in and respect for the other person, and to enhance the directness of your messages.

As is true with other behaviors, eye contact may be improved by conscious effort, in small steps. Be aware of your eyes as you talk with others, and attempt to gradually optimize your eye attention in conversation.

Body Posture: As you watch other people talking with each other, carefully observe how each is standing or sitting. You may be as amazed as we have been by the number of persons who talk with another while their bodies are turned away from that person! Often while sitting side by side (eg. on an airplane, bus, or train, or on a couch, in a classroom, or at dinner) one may turn only the head toward the other while talking. A significant increase in personalizing the conversation occurs from a slight turn of the torso - say 30 to 45 degrees - toward the other person.

Relative "power" in an encounter may be emphasized by standing or sitting. A particularly evident power imbalance may be seen in the relationship between a tall adult and a small child; the adult who is thoughtful enough to bend to the child's height will find an observable difference in the quality of communication (and usually a much more responsive child!).

In a situation in which you are called upon to stand up for yourself, it may be useful to do just that - stand up. An active and erect posture, facing the other person directly, lends additional assertiveness to your message. A slumped, passive stance gives the other person an immediate advantage, as does any tendency on your part to lean back or move away.

Distance/Physical Contact: An interesting aspect of cross-cultural research into non-verbal communication is that of distance vs. closeness between persons in conversation. As a rough guide, it may be said that, among European peoples, the farther North one goes, the farther apart are found individuals engaged in conversation. In the United States, as in Europe, closeness seems to increase with average annual temperature, but there are important exceptions, notably among ethnic subcultures which value closeness and contact differently.

Closeness is, of course, not universally a function of temperature. Cultural and social customs are products of very complex historical factors. It is fascinating, for example, to contrast the almost obligatory polite distance present in the que for London bus, with the pushing, shoving body contact which is part of the cloak room scramble at a winter play in Moscow!

In any case, distance from the other person does have a considerable effect upon communication. Standing or sitting very closely, or touching, suggests a quality of intimacy in a relationship, unless the people happen to be in a crowd or very cramped quarters. "Coming too close" may offend the other person, make him/her defensive, or open the door to greater intimacy. It is often worthwhile to check out verbally how the other person feels about your closeness or distance (depending, of course, upon your investment in the relationship!).

Gestures: Accentuating your message with appropriate gestures can add emphasis, openness, and warmth. Bob Alberti "traces" his use of gestures in conversation to his Italian heritage. While enthusiastic gesturing is indeed a somewhat culturally-related behavior, a relaxed use of gestures can add depth or power to your messages. Uninhibited movement can also suggest openness, self-confidence (unless the gesturing is erratic and nervous), and spontaneity on the part of the speaker.

Facial Expression: Ever see someone trying to express anger while smiling or laughing? It just doesn't come across. Effective assertions require an expression that agrees with the message. An angry message should be delivered with a straight, non-smiling countenance. A friendly communication should not be delivered with a dark frown. Let your face say the same thing your words are saying!

If you will look at yourself in the mirror, you can learn a great deal about what your face says on your behalf. First, relax all the muscles of your face as much as you can. Let go of your expression, relax the muscles around your mouth, let your jaw go loose, let your cheeks soften, along with the wrinkles of your forehead and around your eyes. Pay careful attention to the relaxed, soft feelings. Now smile, bringing your mouth up as widely as you can. Feel the tightness in your cheeks, around your eyes, all the way up to your ears. Hold that smile, look at the expression in the mirror, and concentrate on the feelings of tightness. Now relax your face completely again. Notice the difference between the relaxed feelings and those of the tight smile, and the difference between the expressions you see in the mirror.

With this greater awareness of the feelings in your face, and of how you look when you smile and when you are relaxed, you can begin to more consciously control your facial expression to be congruent with what you are thinking, feeling, or saying. And you may develop a more natural, less plastic smile for those times when you really want your happiness to show!

Voice Tone, Inflection, Volume: The way we use our voices is a vital element in our communications. The same words spoken through the teeth in anger offer an entirely different message than when they are shouted with joy or whispered in fear.

A level, well modulated conversational statement is convincing without intimidating. A whispered monotone will seldom convince another person that you mean business, while a shouted epithet will bring defenses into the path of communication.

Voice is one of the easiest of the components of behavior on which to gain accurate feedback these days. Most everyone has easy access to a small cassette recorder which can be used to "try out" different styles of your voice. You may wish to experiment with a conversational tone, an angry shouted blast, a supportive, caring message, a persuasive argument.

Consider at least three dimensions of your voice: *tone* (is it raspy, whiny, seductively soft, angry?); *inflection* (do you emphasize certain syllables, as in a question, or speak in a monotone, or with a "sing-song" effect?); *volume* (do you try to gain attention with a whisper, or to overpower others with loudness, or is it very difficult for you to shout even when you want to?).

If you can control and use your voice effectively, you have acquired a powerful tool in your self-expression.

Fluency: Mike Serber employed an exercise he called "sell me something" in which he asked the client to talk for thirty seconds persuasively about an object, such as a watch. For many people, it is very difficult to put together a string of words lasting thirty seconds. A smooth flow of speech is a valuable asset in getting your point across in any type of conversation. It is not necessary to talk rapidly for a long period, but if your speech is interrupted for long periods of hesitation, your listeners may get bored, and will probably recognize you are very unsure of yourself. Clear and slow comments are more easily understood and more powerful than rapid speech which is erratic and filled with long pauses and stammering. Once again, the tape recorder is a valuable tool. If you can use the machine to practice by talking on a familiar subject for thirty seconds. Then listen to yourself, noticing pauses of three seconds or more and space fillers such as "uhhh . . ." and "you know . . ." Repeat the same exercise, more slowly if necessary, trying to eliminate any significant pauses. Gradually increase the difficulty of the task by dealing with less familiar topics, trying to be persuasive, pretending to respond in an argument, working with a friend to keep a genuine dialogue going.

Timing: In general, we advocate spontaneity of expression as a goal. Hesitation may diminish the effectiveness of your assertion, but "he/she who hesitates . . ." is *not* lost! Nevertheless, spontaneous assertion will help keep your life clear, and will help you to focus accurately on the feelings you have at the time.

Nevertheless, at times it may be important to *choose an occasion* to discuss a strong feeling. It is not a good idea to confront someone in front of a group, for example, because extra defenses are sure to be present under those conditions. Remember too, that it is *never too late* to be assertive! Even though the "ideal" moment has passed, you will find it worthwhile to go to the person at a later time and express your feelings. Indeed it is so important that we express feelings constructively that psychologists have developed special techniques to help inidividuals to work through strong feelings toward those (eg. parents) who may have died before the feelings could be expressed. More on ''too late'' assertions in Chapter VII.

Listening: This component is perhaps the most difficult both to describe and to change, yet it may well be the most important of all. Assertive listening involves an active commitment to the other person. It requires your full attention, yet calls for no overt act on your part (although eye contact and certain gestures—such as nodding—can be appropriate elements of listening). It demonstrates your respect for the other person. It requires that you avoid expressing *yourself* for a time, yet is *not* a non-assertive act. Effective listening may involve the act of giving feedback to the other person, so that it is clear that you understand what was said. Listening is not simply the physical response of hearing sounds—indeed, deaf persons may be excellent ''listeners.'' Rather, assertive listening involves *tuning in* to the other person, *attending* to his/her message, and actively attempting to *understand* it before responding.

Attending (or listening) is a new dimension of assertive behavior as this is written. We are not yet sure of its full implications for the concept of assertiveness. We do know, however, that if we are to be faithful to our commitment that assertiveness includes respect for the rights and feelings of others, our conception must be expanded to include assertive *receiving*—sensitivity to others—as well as assertive *sending!*

As with the other components of assertive behavior, listening may be trained and developed. It is hard work, takes patience, and requires other people willing to ''send'' to you. If you truly work at it, you might enjoy yourself so much that you neglect other components! Don't get *that* good at listening, but strengthen your capacity. It will make all of your assertions more effective!

Content: We save this obvious dimension of assertiveness for last to emphasize that, although *what* you say is clearly important, it is often *less* important than most of us generally believe. We encourage a fundamental honesty in interpersonal communication, and spontaneity of expression. In our view, that means saying forcefully, "I'm damn mad about what you just did!" rather than "You're an S.O.B.!" People who have for years hesitated because they "didn't know *what* to say" have found the practice of saying *something*, to express their feelings *at the time*, to be a valuable step toward greater spontaneous assertiveness.

We encourage you to express your own feelings—and to *accept responsibility for them.* Note the difference in the above example between "I'm mad" and "You're an S.O.B." It is not necessary to put the other person down (aggressive) in order to express *your* feeling (assertive).

Your imagination can carry you to a wide variety of situations which demonstrate the importance of the *manner* in which you *express* your assertions. The time you may be spending *thinking about* "just the right words" will be better spent *making* those assertions! The ultimate goal is expressing *yourself,* honestly and spontaneously, in a manner "right" for you.

A recent contribution to the definition of assertive content is described in a paper by Cooley and Hollandsworth (1977). They have proposed a "components" model for assertive statements, which has seven elements grouped in three categories. They note that *saying "no" or taking a stand* includes stating your position, explaining your reason, and expressing understanding. *Asking favors or asserting rights* may be expressed by stating the problem, making a request, and getting clarification. Finally, *expressing feelings* is accomplished by a statement of your emotions in a situation.

Assertiveness does not depend upon you being highly verbal, but if you have difficulty finding the "right words" the Cooley and Hollandsworth model may help you to construct your messages.

We have resisted advocating particular formulas or scripts for assertive expression, preferring to encourage you to use your own language, and to recognize that the *style* of your delivery is more important than the words anyway. We recognize that words are not unimportant, and that many people do stumble over vocabulary. Often, however, we are impressed with how clearly clients may tell *us* how they feel about a particular situation, and then ask "What shall I say to the person?'' Our answer is quite direct: ''Tell that person what you just told me!''

One further word about content is in order. Donald Cheek has pointed out the need to adapt assertiveness to the cultural setting in which you find yourself. Particularly for minorities who may find themselves in ''survival'' situations, he suggests that *what* you say must take into consideration *to whom* you are saying it! Language which would be interpreted as assertive within one's own subculture, for example, could easily be interpreted as aggressive by ''outsiders.'' While we are reluctant to advocate that you change yourself to adapt to whatever the situation seems to call for, we do recognize that all of us deal with individuals differently, depending upon our respective roles and the percieved ''power'' of others over us. Nevertheless, we hope you can behave consistently in a wide variety of circumstances, and the *honest expression of yourself* can be your principal criterion, rather than being whoever you think others want you to be.

In our experience, it is not usually the content that hangs people up. It is the anxiety, or the lack of confidence, or the belief that ''I have no right . . .'' In the next two chapters, we will help you to assess your own assertive strenghts and weaknesses, and to overcome obstacles to more effective expression of yourself.

In Summary: Ten Key Points About Assertive Behavior

By now, you may be feeling somewhat overwhelmed with all of this material which attempts to ''define'' *assertive.* Perhaps we can synthesize a working definition which includes what *we* believe to be the most important elements. To us, then, *assertive behavior* is:

1) self-expressive;
2) honest;
3) direct;
4) self-enhancing;
5) not hurtful to others;
6) partially composed of the *content* of the message (feelings, rights, facts, opinions, requests, limits);
7) partially composed of the *non-verbal style* of the message (eye contact, voice, posture, facial expression, gestures, distance, timing, fluency, listening);

8) appropriate for the person and the situation, rather than universal;
9) socially responsible;
10) a combination of learned skills, not an inborn trait.

Now you have a better idea of what it means to be "assertive," and you are probably ready to begin taking steps toward increasing your own assertiveness. We know you can succeed, and the procedures spelled out in the balance of this book will help.

Bon voyage!

Evaluating Your Assertiveness

"Never play another person's game. Play your own."

—*Andrew Salter*

If you are looking for a simple solution to life's problems, you are reading the wrong book. We do not believe there to be a ''right'' way to handle all life situations. There is no magic formula, script, or potion which will bring order out of the chaos for you. The search for simplistic answers is futile, and we can't help much if that's what you're after.

We can, however, help you to ''play your own game.'' If you want to become able to make choices for yourself, to be assertive when you choose to be, the balance of this book will be of value to you.

No one is assertive all the time. Each of us sometimes acts non-assertively, sometimes assertively, sometimes aggressively. Our goal is to help you to maximize your assertive skills, and your capacity to *choose for yourself how you will act in a given situation.*

Let's continue your journey toward greater assertiveness and freedom of choice by finding out about where you are *now.* What do you know about your own assertiveness?

Figure IV-1, the *Assertiveness Inventory*, provides a list of questions which should be useful in increasing your awareness of your own behavior in situations which call for assertiveness. The Inventory is not a standardized psychological test. There are no ''right'' answers. There is no formal scoring procedure. The only ''score'' is your own evaluation of how you measure up to what you would *like* to be able to do. Be honest with yourself. After you complete the Inventory, we'll discuss further how you can use the results to help plan your own program of growth. Take a few minutes right now to respond to the Assertiveness Inventory.

Figure IV-1
ASSERTIVENESS INVENTORY

The following questions will be helpful in assessing your assertiveness. Be honest in your responses. All you have to do is draw a circle around the number that describes you best. For some questions the assertive end of the scale is at 0, for others at 4. Key: 0 means **no** or **never**; 1 means **somewhat** or **sometimes**; 2 means **average**; 3 means **usually** or **a good deal**; and 4 means **practically always** or **entirely**.

1. When a person is highly unfair, do you call it to attention? 0   1   **(2)**   3   4
2. Do you find it difficult to make decisions? 0   1   2   3   **(4)**
3. Are you openly critical of others ideas, opinions, behavior? 0   1   **(2)**   3   4
4. Do you speak out in protest when someone takes your place in line? 0   1   2   **(3)**   4
5. Do you often avoid people or situations for fear of embarassment? 0   1   2   **(3)**   4
6. Do you usually have confidence in your own judgment? 0   1   2   **(3)**   4
7. Do you insist that your spouse or roommate take on a fair share of household chores? 0   1   **(2)**   3   4
8. Are you prone to "fly off the handle?" 0   1   2   **(3)**   4
9. When a salesman makes an effort, do you find it hard to say "No" even though the merchandise is not really what you want? 0   **(1)**   2   3   4
10. When a latecomer is waited on before you are, do you call attention to the situation? 0   1   **(2)**   3   4
11. Are you reluctant to speak up in a discussion or debate? 0   **(1)**   2   3   4
12. If a person has borrowed money (or a book, garment, thing of value) and is overdue in returning it, do you mention it? 0   1   2   **(3)**   4
13. Do you continue to pursue an argument after the other person has had enough? 0   **(1)**   2   3   4
14. Do you generally express what you feel? 0   1   2   **(3)**   4
15. Are you disturbed if someone watches you at work? 0   **(1)**   2   3   4
16. If someone keeps kicking or bumping your chair in a movie or a lecture, do you ask the person to stop? 0   1   **(2)**   3   4
17. Do you find it difficult to keep eye contact when talking to another person? 0   **(1)**   2   3   4
18. In a good restaurant, when your meal is improperly prepared or served, do you ask the waiter/waitress to correct the situation? 0   1   2   **(3)**   4

19. When you discover merchandise is faulty, do you return it for an adjustment? . . . . 0 1 2 3 ④

20. Do you show your anger by name-calling or obscenities? . . . . 0 1 ② 3 4

21. Do you try to be a wallflower or a piece of the furniture in social situations? . . . . 0 ① 2 3 4

22. Do you insist that your property manager (mechanic, repairman, etc.) make repairs, adjustments or replacements which are his/her responsibility? . . . . 0 1 2 ③ 4

23. Do you often step in and make decisions for others? . . . . 0 ① 2 3 4

24. Are you able openly to express love and affection? . . . . 0 1 2 ③ 4

25. Are you able to ask your friends for small favors or help? . . . . 0 1 2 ③ 4

26. Do you think you always have the right answer? . . . . 0 1 2 ③ 4

27. When you differ with a person you respect, are you able to speak up for your own viewpoint? . . . . 0 1 2 ③ 4

28. Are you able to refuse unreasonable requests made by friends? . . . . 0 1 2 ③ 4

29. Do you have difficulty complimenting or praising others? . . . . 0 ① 2 3 4

30. If you are disturbed by someone smoking near you, can you say so? . . . . 0 1 ② 3 4

31. Do you shout or use bullying tactics to get others to do as you wish? . . . . 0 1 ② 3 4

32. Do you finish other people's sentences for them? . . . . 0 ① 2 3 4

33. Do you get into physical fights with others, especially with strangers? . . . . ⓪ 1 2 3 4

34. At family meals, do you control the conversation? . . . . 0 ① 2 3 4

35. When you meet a stranger, are you the first to introduce yourself and begin a conversation? . . . . 0 1 2 ③ 4

Because the concept "assertiveness" is so complex, it is not possible to answer the simple question "How assertive are you?" Now that you have assessed your own behavior on the items of the Assertiveness Inventory, we suggest that you do a systematic examination of yourself in terms of four separate dimensions: *situations, attitudes, behaviors,* and *obstacles.*

In order to perform a thorough and systematic assessment of yourself, and to provide a valuable tool for your continued personal growth, we urge you to obtain a special notebook in which to record your progress. It has been our experience, and that of many other therapists, that regularly keeping such a log or journal is of major benefit to a program of personal growth.

A sample page of your log might look like this:

```
ASSERTIVENESS LOG FOR _____ 19 _____

Situations

Attitudes

Behaviors

Obstacles

Progress / Problems / Comments
```

Used in this way, your log becomes a very important tool for your growth program, helping you in self-assessment, recording progress, and as a "motivator" to continue working on your personal development.

Here are some ideas which may help you to be thorough in your self-assessment:

Situation assessment may be conducted by referring to the Assertiveness Inventory, determining those situations and persons which you can handle effectively and those which are troublesome. Write down the results in the log. Pay particular attention to any *patterns* which may appear. Are you, for example, more adequate with strangers than with intimates (or perhaps vice versa)? Can you readily stand up for your rights, but fall down on expressing affection? Do such factors as age, sex, or roles of the other person make a difference?

Attitude assessment has plagued psychologists for decades. It is very difficult to accurately measure *any* attitudes, and particularly difficult to be "objective" about one's own. Nevertheless, we encourage you to approach this task (in a much-less-than-scientific manner!) by simply writing down in your log how you feel about *your right* to behave assertively. Look at the various situations and people noted in each of the five categories of the definition of assertive behavior (preceding chapter), and in the situations described in the Assertiveness Inventory. What we're getting at here is simply to determine how you feel about whether it's even *okay*, for example, to respond to criticism.

Behavior assessment is not so difficult, but may take longer. In the last chapter, we described in detail several "components" of behavior which are key to any assertive act. If you monitor your own behavior carefully for a time (a week or more is a good idea), and record your observations regularly in your log, you will have a good idea of your own effectiveness with eye contact, body posture, and the other components noted there. It will probably help if you make it a point to watch some other people whom you consider effectively assertive, and to note in your log some of their behavioral qualities as well.

Obstacle assessment may be the easiest area for you to complete. We know that most people *want* to act assertively. However, for many, there are barriers which seem to make assertion more difficult. Common obstacles: *anxiety* (fear of the possible consequences: maybe the other person won't like me, or will hit me, or will think I'm crazy, or maybe I'll make a fool of myself, or maybe I will fail to get what I want); *lack of skills* (I don't know how to meet girls, what do I do to express a political opinion?, I never learned how to show affection); *other people in your life* (parents, friends, lovers, roommates, and others have an interest in making it difficult for you to change, even if they *believe* they want you to be more assertive). Record in your log those obstacles which you feel are making assertiveness more difficult for you.

If you will take the time and effort to proceed carefully and thoroughly with your self-assessment, you will find that the results will pinpoint quite specifically what you will need to do to increase your assertiveness. At every point, of course, you have the choice of whether to carry this personal growth project further. And *choice* is the most key element in your assertiveness anyway!

After you have kept your log or journal for a week, examine carefully the four entries: situations, attitudes, behaviors, obstacles. Look for patterns. Assess your particular strengths as well as your weaknesses. (If you have complex and severe shortcomings in the four dimensions you have evaluated, it is possible that you will need professional assistance in reaching your goal. Particularly for those individuals with very high levels of anxiety about being assertive, we suggest contact with a qualified counselor, psychologist, psychiatrist or other therapist. Your local community mental health center and/or college/university counseling center can assist you in finding someone to help. Also,

Appendix B identifies standards which will help you to evaluate a professional therapist).

The first week's entries in your journal should give you a pretty good picture of how you are doing now, and provide a basis for setting goals for yourself.

Your results, for example, might indicate that you have difficulty with people in authority, that you do not believe you have a right to speak up to them, that you cannot maintain eye contact well, and that you are very anxious around such people. Each of these items is something you can work on individually and overcome through the process of assertiveness training described in this book.

As you proceed, use your log to keep a careful record of how you're doing. It will provide a series of ''bench marks'' so you can watch yourself grow. It will help motivate you to work at your progress. It will allow you to be more systematic about your work on assertiveness.

V

Overcoming Obstacles:
A Foundation for Assertive Behavior

*If a person continues to see only giants, it means
he is still looking at the world through the eyes of
a child.*

—*Anais Nin*

"OK," you say, "maybe I am not as assertive as I'd like to be. You can't teach an old dog new tricks. That's just the way I am. I can't change it."

We don't agree. Thousands of persons have found that becoming more assertive is a *learning* process, and that it *was* possible for them to change. Sometimes it takes longer for an "old dog." But, the rewards are great, and the process not really that difficult. How do I know that I realy want to change in the first place? Are there potential dangers involved in assertion? What about the significant other persons in my life; won't they object if I suddenly become more expressive? This chapter will help you lay the ground work for your self-directed development of assertive behavior.

Why Should I Change?

"Yes, I'm non-assertive; so what?" Well, consider for example, how well do you recognize consequences of such behavior? Take a look at the results of your Assertiveness Inventory in Chapter IV. Have you observed how you come across to others? Do people often take advantage of you? Do you avoid certain social situations because you feel too anxious? Have you lost out on a job or date because you couldn't bring yourself to talk to someone? Has it ever cost you money because you "just couldn't" take a faulty item back to a store? Do you own some things you don't want because you "couldn't say no?" Have you been criticized by your spouse or others for indecisiveness?

Any of these consequences of non-assertiveness is bound to produce personal anguish, disappointment, perhaps self-recrimination. If you have experienced this kind of pain, you already have felt the motivation to change. You are ready to get on with it, and we are convinced that the procedures presented here will be of great value to you. Learning to express "your perfect right" is not a cure-all, but it is a big step toward freeing yourself of the burdens of self-denying behavior.

It is often more difficult for those with aggressive styles to admit the need for help since they are accustomed to controlling the environment to suit personal needs. If aggressiveness is your style, you may wish to consider that your present relationships may become worse unless you seek change. Unhealthy relationships tend to deteriorate, and may leave you feeling worse than you do now. Generally we have found that the person who behaves aggressively may seek to change as a result of the suggestion of others. Sometimes, she or he is moved by frustration with the inadequacy of aggressive responses.

Do you always take the lead in social relationships? Do you find you continually have to call first in making contact with friends? Do others seldom engage you in discussion willingly? Are you invariably the "winner" in arguments? Do you often berate clerks and waitresses for inadequate service? Are you the "ruler" of your subordinates on the job? Of your family at home? Do you find people trying to "get back" at you? Alienation of those close to you is a high price to pay for having things go your own way. Assertiveness can often achieve the same ends, with fewer casualties in your relationships.

One example, which interestingly demonstrates both non-assertive and aggressive responses to anxiety, is the case of young Caren, who was having fits of anger, expressed toward the man she planned to marry. Her anxiety was caused by his lack of consideration; he would pick her up quite late for dates, not inform her until the last minute about engagements he wanted her to attend with him, and other similar discourtesies. Caren would not assert her right to demand due courtesy, until her anger had built up to an irrational level, then she would explode at him. Once she was aware that the situation would likely only grow worse after marriage, what it would be like to be married for years with such a relationship existing, and the potentiality of her marriage ending in divorce, Caren agreed to assertiveness training. Unfortunately, many women go through their entire marriage "under the thumb" of their husbands because they feel it is "their place" in the marriage relationship.

Your Perfect Rights

When suggesting assertion to individuals, we emphasize the fact that no one has a right to take advantage of another simply on a human-being-to-human being level. For instance, an employer has no right to take advantage of an employee's rights to courtesy and respect as a human being. A doctor does not have the right to be discourteous or unfair in dealing with a patient or nurse. A lawyer should not feel she or he can "talk down" to a laborer. Each person has a perfect right to express opinions even though he or she may "only have a grade school education" or be "from the wrong side of the tracks" or be "just a secretary" in a large office. All persons are indeed created equal on a human-to-human plane and deserve the privilege of expressing their inborn rights. There is so much more to be gained from life by being free and able to stand up for oneself, and from honoring the same right for others! By being assertive one is actually learning to give and take more equally with others, and to be of more service to self and others.

Another facet which motivates many to become assertive is the likelihood that physical ailments will be reduced as assertion progresses. Complaints such as headaches, asthma, gastric disorders, and general fatigue often times clear up. The reduction in anxiety and guilt, which is experienced by non-assertive and aggressive persons who learn to be assertive, often results in the elimination of such physical symptoms.

This is a good time to realize that you are not alone, that thousands of others have faced similar challenges and situations and have changed for the better.

The hope and courage necessary to initiate training may be bolstered by studying case descriptions to learn how others successfully overcame similar difficulties. We suggest Andrew Salter's (1949) book

Conditioned Reflex Therapy, particularly Chapter 6 on the "inhibitory personality" and several of his case examples. The aggressive person, on the other hand, is encouraged to read Bach and Wyden's *The Intimate Enemy* (particularly Chapters 6, 9 and 13).

You may be able to "see yourself" in one of these descriptions of others and as a result desire to overcome this problem. You probably "see yourself" in examples we have given earlier, or those which appear later in this book.

One implication of assertion recurs time and again with non-assertive individuals: self-denying behavior subtly reinforces another's bad or unwanted behavior. Two examples help to make this point clear.

Diane, a married woman of 35, had a husband who desired sexual intercourse every evening. At times she would clearly be tired from the day's activities as a housewife and mother of three, and not wish intercourse. However, when Diane would refuse him, her husband would begin to pout and feel hurt, carrying on until she would finally "feel sorry" for him and give in. This sequence was a consistent pattern in their marriage and the more Diane would not give in, the more he would pout until she did so. Of course, by eventually giving in she promptly reinforced all of his pouting, not to mention the reinforcement value of his sexual gratification! Diane was thus *teaching* her husband that he could have what he wanted if he would pout.

Another example is a college student, Wendy, age 20, who, although surviving quite well on her own, was living off-campus in a cheap habitat with another girl and boy. By living together they cut expenses and saved a good deal of money. Wendy and her roommates had a reputation for being "anti-administration." Word of her behavior and living conditions got back to her parents, who then confronted her with a long tirade about the younger generation, respect for authority, her mother's health, being disgraceful, and so on. This happened on several occasions and each time Wendy would eventually get upset and either ask what she could do to help ease things or simply give in to some of their demands. Here again, by her action of getting upset and giving in. Wendy simply reinforced her parents' unwanted behavior; that is, *she taught them* how to have these tirades against her.

Although it may be more difficult for the generally aggressive individual to admit the negative consequences of aggressive actions, he or she usually recognizes the reaction of others to denial of their rights. The aggressor reacts internally with acknowledgement and pain when confronted with the alienation this behavior brings about. If you are seeking help, you may admit to yourself your concern and guilt for the hurt you cause others, and acknowledge that you simply do not know how to gain your goals non-aggressively. At this point you are an excellent candidate for assertiveness training.

One individual of this type was ''reached'' in a therapy group setting. After considerable time had been spent listening to Jerry's loud dominance over the group, several members took him to task. Although he was a large rugged man, Jerry soon responded to this *caring but confronting* response by the others and began to cry. He confessed that he had developed this facade of bravado to protect himself from the closeness which he feared. He really felt himself to be quite an inadequate person, and had used the ''strong man'' mask to keep others at a distance. The group responded to Jerry's need for others to care for him and later helped him to shape adequately assertive responses to replace his previously gruff, bellicose behavior.

Members of our assertive behavior groups have commented upon how much *attitudes* can change as a result of taking part in the group. The group provides support for acting assertively, expressing oneself and standing up for rights. For some group members the group's support and encouragement of assertiveness is as important as the opportunity for *practice* which the group affords. Throughout life many of them have experienced people in authority (parents, teachers, even peers) saying, ''You have no right . . .'' Now, a group of people, including some psychologists are saying, ''You have a *perfect right* . . .'' Thus a key part of our message to you is that it's *good*, it's *right*, it's *okay* to assert yourself!

''But I'm Really Afraid!''

The process of assertiveness training was originally developed as a treatment for anxiety (see Salter, 1949 and Wolpe, 1969). Early work in the field was done by psychotherapists who recognized that learning and practicing assertive responses was an affective way to overcome fears in social situations.

Many readers of *Your Perfect Right*—perhaps you, too—find anxiety to be the most significant obstacle to greater assertiveness. "Sure," you say, "I know *how* to express myself! I just get really uptight about doing it. The risks seem too great. I want people to like me . . ." Moreover, you may not even be aware of the source of such fears. Often they result from childhood experiences; well-meaning parents may have taught you that "children are to be seen and not heard" for example.

Although learning to be assertive will help to reduce such fears, when the level of anxiety is very high, it may be necessary to deal more directly with the anxiety itself. Once again it is AT pioneer Dr. Joseph Wolpe (1969) who has developed an immeasurably valuable procedure: *systematic desensitization.* Like AT, systematic desensitization is based on learning principles; you *learned* to be anxious about expressing yourself, and you can *unlearn* it! *No one* was *born* fearful! The process of desensitization simply involves repeated association of an anxiety-producing situation (imagining yourself "talking back" to your boss, for example) with a feeling of deep relaxation throughout your body. Gradually, you learn to "automatically" associate relaxation, instead of anxiety, as a response to that scene. The intricacies of the procedure are somewhat more complex, but that is the essence of desensitization. It has been proven effective for a wide range of fears, including phobic reactions to heights, public speaking, animals, flying, test taking, and social contact.

Although it is possible to desensitize yourself, we suggest, as we have mentioned previously, that you seek out a competent therapist to assist you if your anxiety about being assertive is high enough to require this special procedure.

A simple way to help determine your anxiety level about assertiveness is called the "SUDS scale." SUDS is an acronym for Subjective Units of Disturbance; simply rating your own physical feelings of anxiety on a scale from 0—100. Because anxiety, *by definition,* has physical components, you can become aware of your own degree of discomfort in a situation by "tuning in" to your body's indicators: heart rate (pulse), breathing rate, coldness in hands and feet, perspiration (particularly in hands), muscle tension (there are others, but we usually cannot easily be aware of them; biofeedback training is allowing many people to learn when they are relaxed or anxious by monitoring physical indicators).

Try this: get yourself as relaxed as you can right now—lie flat on the couch or floor or relax in your chair, breathe deeply, relax all the muscles in your body, imagine a very relaxing scene (lying on the beach, floating on a cloud, etc.). Allow yourself to relax in this way for *at least* five minutes, paying attention to your heartbeat, breathing, hand temperature and dryness, muscle relaxation. Those relaxed feelings can be given a SUDS scale value of 0, to represent near-total relaxation. If you did not do the relaxation exercise, but are reading this alone, relatively quietly and comfortably, you may consider yourself somewhere around 10 on the SUDS scale.

At the opposite end of the scale, visualize the most frightening scene you can imagine. With your eyes closed, picture yourself narrowly escaping an accident, or being near the center of an earthquake or flood. Pay attention to the same bodily signals: heart rate/pulse; breathing; hand temperature/moisture; muscle relaxation. These fearful feelings can be given a SUDS scale value of 100—almost *totally* anxious. Now you have a roughly calibrated comfort/discomfort scale which you can use to help yourself evaluate just how anxious you are in any given situation. Each 10 points on the scale represents a "just noticeable difference" up or down from the units above and below it. Thus 70 is slightly more anxious than 60, and by the same amount more comfortable than 80. (The SUDS scale is too subjective to be able to define much more closely than 10 units.)

Most of us function normally in the range of 20-50 SUDS. A few life situations will raise our anxiety above 50 for short periods, and on rare occasions (rare for most of us anyway!), we will relax below 20.

Now, here's where the SUDS scale becomes really useful:

1) Make a rough estimate of your usual SUDS level;

2) Estimate your SUDS level in each of the situations listed in the Assertiveness Inventory (Chapter IV). If you place your *usual* (most of the time) SUDS level much above 50, or if your responses to the second SUDS estimate places your SUDS level over 70 or so in more than a few assertive situations, we suggest you work (with help if you need it) to overcome this high anxiety *before* (or at least concurrently with) your attempt to develop your assertive skills further.

This discussion of anxiety about assertiveness is not meant to discourage you. On the contrary, most readers will find themselves able to handle their mild discomfort about self-expression without major difficulty. There are some of us, however, who *do* need some extra help in overcoming obstacles. If you do, *don't be embarrassed or hesitant about asking for it*, just as you would seek competent medical help for a physical problem. Then, when you've cleared up the anxiety obstacle, turn back to the procedures outlined here for developing your assertiveness.

"Sometimes It Doesn't Work!"

There will be some failures with your assertions. These procedures will not turn you into a 100 percent success in all your relationships! There are no instant or magic answers to life's problems. Assertiveness does not always work (for us either!). Sometimes your goals will be incompatible with the other person's. When two people head for the same parking space, someone has to give! At times, others may be unreasonable or unyielding, and your best assertions (or *ours!*) will be to no avail.

Also, because you're human, you'll blow it sometimes, as we all do. Allow yourself to make mistakes! You'll be uncomfortable, disappointed, down, discouraged. Allow yourself to be human, then pick yourself up and try again. You'll find that every home run king was also a strikeout king! If you are going to hit the ball, you've got to keep swinging the bat!

If you feel your assertions are failing a bit too often, take a close look at what's going on. Are you setting your goals too high? Take small steps to insure success! Are you overdoing it and becoming aggressive? Monitor your behavior carefully—refer to Chapter IV and check yourself. (Some aggression is to be expected at first. The pendulum will balance in a short time.)

We all want our assertions to work, and to achieve our goals. Nevertheless, the greatest value of self-assertion is the good feeling that comes from having expressed yourself. To know that you have a *perfect right* to self-expression, to feel free to say what you're feeling, and to *do* it are the best benefits of all.

Usually you'll find assertiveness *will* make things happen. But whether it works or not, remember how good it felt to speak up for yourself! You did what you could, even if the outcome wasn't what you hoped for. If you *have* genuinely tried, and done all you can, that's all you can ask of yourself!

A Few Words of Caution Before You Begin

Once you are well motivated and ready to begin asserting yourself, you must *first* make certain that you understand thoroughly the basic principles of assertion. Realizing differences between assertive and aggressive behavior is important to your understanding and success. *Second,* you must decide whether you are ready to begin trying self-assertive behavior on your own. Usually *situationally non-assertive* or *situationally aggressive* persons are able to begin assertion quite successfully.

With the *generally non-assertive* and *generally aggressive,* however, or those who are highly anxious, more caution is involved and we recommend slow and careful practice and work with another person, preferably a trained therapist, as a facilitator. This recommendation is particularly strong for those who feel *very* anxious about beginning.

Third, your initial attempts at being assertive should be chosen for their high potential of success, so as to provide reinforcement. This point, of course, is important with all beginning asserters, but especially the *generally non-assertive* and *generally aggressive.* The more successfully you assert yourself at first, the more likely you are to be successful from then on.

Initially, begin with small assertions that are likely to be rewarding, and from there proceed to more difficult assertions. You may wish to explore each step with a friend or trained facilitator until you are capable of being fully in control of most situations. You should proceed with care when taking it upon your own initiative to attempt a difficult assertion without special preparation. And be especially careful not to instigate an assertion where you are likely to fail miserably, thus inhibiting further attempts at assertiveness.

If you do suffer a setback, which very well may happen, take time carefully to analyze the situation and regain your confidence, getting help from a facilitator if necessary. Especially in the early stages of assertion, it is not unusual to make mistakes either of inadequate technique or of overzealousness to the point of aggression. Either miscue could cause negative returns, particularly if the other individual becomes hostile and highly aggressive. Don't let such an occurrence stop you. Consider your goal again, and remember that although successful assertiveness requires practice, the rewards are great.

Fourth, give some thought to your relationship with those who are closest to you. Typically, patterns of non-assertive or aggressive behavior have been operational in an individual for a long period of time. Both non-assertive and aggressive patterns of interaction will be well established with those significantly close such as family, spouses, and friends. A change in these relationships is very likely to be quite upsetting to those others involved.

Parents are often targets of assertive behavior, especially during the late teens and early twenties, when children are striving for independence. Of course, some people defer to their parents' wishes and commands as long as they are living (because it is the "right thing" to do to respect one's elders, primarily parents, who sacrificed so much for you). Many parents believe this same line of thinking and therefore are likely to be quite disconcerted when their child "rebels" assertively. On the other hand, parents who have patterned their lives in response to an aggressive child could be equally unsettled to find the child's behavior changing to assertive, even though they have often wished for such a day. Consequently, it may be valuable to ask someone to intervene and talk to the parents to prepare them for what is to come. This intervention can often prevent their reactions from becoming exacerbated, and avoid causing deeply strained relations between parents and child.

Marriage relationships which have been functioning for years based upon the non-assertive or aggressive actions of one partner are similarly prone to be turned "topsy-turvy" when assertion commences. If the spouse is not properly prepared, and possibly willing to change to some degree, a marital break-ip is a definite possibility. Cooperation from the spouse through one or more conferences with a facilitator can help a great deal in "cushioning" the change in behavior. Hopefully assertive training for one spouse will also strengthen the marital relationship. Nevertheless there is a potential for damage to an intimate relationship from a significant behavior change by one partner, and caution must be observed in proceeding with these likely consequences in mind. A conference with parents and/or spouse is definitely recommended.

We hope you have successfully overcome the obstacles to your own greater assertiveness! If you are ready to go on, and have carefully considered the cautions noted here, you will find a step-by-step process detailed in the next chapter.

VI

One Step at a Time:
The Development of Assertive Behavior

He that respects himself is safe from others; he
wears a coat of mail that none can pierce.
                                        —*Henry Wadsworth Longfellow*

Perhaps you have heard it said that "when two engineers (lawyers, housekeepers, plumbers, nurses) are talking together and a psychologist walks up and joins the conversation, there are now two engineers and a psychologist, but when two psychologists are talking and an engineer (substitute your own favorite) walks up and joins them, there are now three psychologists!" Everyone believes she/he is a psychologist in some sense. Indeed, we all have some practical, first-hand knowledge of human behavior, beginning with ourselves.

Changing Behavior and Attitudes

Unfortunately there are shortcomings in popular views of how people behave. One popular view which has been found by psychologists to be inaccurate is the notion that attitudes must be changed before one can change the way she or he acts. In our experience with hundreds of clients in clinical assertiveness training, and in the feedback from some of the thousands of readers of this book, as well as from countless reports from our colleagues in psychological practice and research, it is now clear that *behavior can be changed first,* and it is easier and more effective to do so in most cases.

As you begin the process of becoming more assertive, we won't ask you to wake up some morning and say, "Today I am a new, assertive person!" You will find here instead a guide to systematic, step-by-step changes in behavior. The key to developing assertiveness is *practice of new behavior patterns.* This chapter is devoted to leading you through the steps involved in such practice, and showing how you can put the newly assertive behavior to work in your relationships with others.

We have observed a cycle of non-assertive or aggressive behavior which tends to perpetuate itself, until a decisive intervention occurs. A person who has acted non-assertively or aggressively in relationships for a long period of time usually has a poor self-image. His or her behavior toward others—whether self-denying or abusive—is responded to with scorn, disdain, avoidance. Observing the response, this person says, "See, I knew I was no damn good." Confirmed in this low self-evaluation, the inadequate behavior patterns are continued. Thus the cycle is repeated: inadequate behavior; negative feedback; attitude of self-depreciation; inadequate behavior.

The most readily observable component of this pattern is the *behavior* itself. We can easily see overt behavior in contrast with attitudes and feelings which may be hidden behind a practiced facade. In addition, *behavior* is the component most amendable to change. Our efforts to help you improve your interpersonal functioning and increase your valuing of yourself as a person focus on changing your *behavior* patterns.

The cycle can be reversed, becoming a positive sequence: more adequately assertive (self-enhancing) behavior gains more positive responses from others; this positive feedback leads to an enhanced evaluation of self-worth. ("Wow, people are treating me like a worthwhile person!"); and improved feelings about oneself result in further assertiveness.

Harold had for years been convinced that he was truly worthless. He was totally dependent upon his wife for emotional support, and despite a rather handsome appearance and ability to express himself well, had literally no friends. Imagine his utter despair when his wife left him! Fortunately, Harold was already in therapy at the time, and was willing to try to make contact with other people. When his first attempts at assertiveness with eligible young women were successful beyond his wildest hopes, the reinforcing value of such responses to his assertions was very high! Harold's entire outlook toward himself changed rapidly, and he became much more assertive in a variety of situations.

Not everyone, to be sure, will experience such an immediate "payoff" for his/her assertions, and not all assertions are fully successful. Success often requires a great deal of patience, and a gradual process of handling more and more difficult situations. Nevertheless this example emphasizes a general rule we have found in facilitating assertive behavior: *assertiveness tends to be self-rewarding*. It feels good to have others begin to respond more attentively, to achieve one's goals in relationships, to find situations going one's way more often. *And you can make these changes happen!*

Remember to begin with assertions where you are somewhat certain of success before proceeding to more difficult ones requiring greater confidence and skill. It is often quite helpful and reassuring to obtain support and guidance from another person, perhaps a friend, teacher, or professional therapist.

Keep in mind that changed behavior leads to changed attitudes about oneself and one's impact upon people and situations. The balance of this chapter presents the steps involved in bringing about that changed behavior. Read *all* the material here carefully *before* you begin. Then return to this point and begin to follow the steps in your own life. You'll like the difference in you!

The Step-by-Step Process

Step 1: Observe your own behavior. Are you asserting yourself adequately? Are you satisfied with your effectiveness in interpersonal relationships? Look over the discussion in Chapter IV again, and assess how *you* feel about yourself and your behavior.

Step 2: Keep track of your assertiveness. Keep a log or diary for a week. Record each day those situations in which you found yourself responding assertively, those in which you "blew it," and those you avoided altogether so that you would not have to face the need to act assertively. Be honest with yourself, and systematic, following the guidelines for self-assessment described in Chapter IV.

Step 3: Set realistic goals for yourself. Your self-assessment will help you to select specific targets for your growth in assertiveness. Pick out situations, or people, toward which you want to become more effective. Be sure to start with a small, low-risk step, to maximize your chances of success.

Step 4: Concentrate on a particular situation. Spend a few moments with your eyes closed, imagining how you handle a specific incident (being short-changed at the supermarket, having a friend "talk your ear off" on the telephone when you had too much to do, letting the boss make you "feel like 2¢" over a small mistake). Imagine vividly the actual details, including your specific feelings at the time and afterward.

Step 5: Review your responses. Write down your behavior in Step 4 in terms of the components of assertiveness noted in Chapter III (eye contact, body posture, gestures, facial expression, voice, message content, etc.) Look carefully at the components of your behavior in the recalled incident. Note your strengths. Be aware of those components which represent non-assertive or aggressive behavior. If a major element of your response involves anxiety, refer to the discussion in Chapter V, "But I'm Really Afraid!" Do not attempt to force yourself into very painful situations. On the other hand, do not avoid new growth if it is only moderately uncomfortable!

Step 6: Observe an effective model. At this point it would be very helpful to watch someone who handles the same situation very well. Watch for the components discussed in Chapter III, particularly the style—the words are less important. If the model is a friend, discuss his/her approach, and its consequences.

Step 7: Consider alternative responses. What are other possible ways the incident could be handled? Could you deal with it more to your own advantage? Less offensively? Refer to Figure II-1, and differentiate between non-assertive, aggressive, and assertive responses.

Step 8: Imagine yourself handling the situation. Close your eyes and visualize yourself dealing effectively with the situation. You may act similarly to the "model" in Step 6, or in a very different way. Be assertive, but be as much you "natural self" as you can. Repeat this step as often as necessary until you can imagine a comfortable style for yourself which succeeds in handling the situation well.

Step 9: Get help if you need it. As we have noted several times before, the process of becoming more assertive may require you to stretch yourself considerably. If you feel unable on your own to deal with the situations you have visualized, seek help from a qualified professional (see Appendix B).

Step 10: Try it out. Having examined your own behavior, considered alternatives, and observed a model of more adaptive action, you are now prepared to begin trying out for yourself new ways of dealing with the problem situation. A repeat of Steps 6, 7 and 8 may be appropriate until you are ready to proceed. It is important to select an alternative, more effective way of behaving in the problem situation. You may wish to follow your model and enact the same approach taken by him or her in Step 6. Such a choice is appropriate, but should reflect an awareness that you are a unique person, and you may not find the model's approach one which you could feel good about adopting for yourself. After selecting a more effective alternative behavior, you now should role-play the situation with a friend, teacher, or therapist, attempting to act in accord with the new response pattern you have selected. As in Steps 2, 4, and 5, make careful observation of your behavior, using available mechanical recording aids whenever possible.

Step 11: Get feedback. This step essentially repeats Step 5 with emphasis on the positive aspects of your behavior. Note particularly the strengths of your performance, and work positively to develop weaker areas.

Step 12: Behavior shaping. Steps 8, 10, and 11 should be repeated as often as necessary to "shape" your behavior—by this process of successive approximations of your goal—to a point wherein you feel comfortable dealing in a self-enhancing manner with the previously threatening situation.

Step 13: The real test. You are now ready to test your new response pattern in the actual situation. Up to this point your preparation has taken place in a relatively secure environment. Nevertheless, careful training and repeated practice have prepared you to react almost "automatically" to the situation. You should thus be encouraged to proceed with an *in vivo* trial. If you are unwilling to do so, further rehearsals or help may be needed. (Repeat steps 8-12). Again, remember that *doing,* honestly, spontaneously, is the most important step of all.

Step 14: Further training. You are encouraged to repeat such procedures as may be appropriate in the development of the behavior pattern you desire. You may wish to undertake a similar program relative to other specific situations in which you wish to develop a more adaptive repertoire of responses. Chapter X includes some examples which may be helpful in planning your own program for change.

Step 15: Social reinforcement. As a final step in establishing an independent behavior pattern, it is very important that you understand the need for on-going self-reinforcement. In order to maintain your newly-developed assertive behavior, you should achieve a system of reinforcements in your own social environment. For example, you now know the good feeling which accompanies a successful assertion and you can rest assured that this good response will continue. Admiration received from others will be another continuing positive response to your growth. You may wish to develop a check list of specific such reinforcements which are unique to your own environment. One good idea: start saying positive statements to yourself, rather than self defeating put downs! More on this in Chapter VII.

Although we emphasize the importance of this systematic learning process, it should be understood that what is recommended is not a lock-step forced pattern without consideration for the needs and objectives of each individual. You are encouraged to provide a learning environment which will help *you* to grow in assertiveness. No one system is "right" for everyone. We encourage you to be systematic, but to follow a program which will meet your own unique individual needs. There is, of course, no substitute for the *active practice* of assertive behavior in your own life, when *you* choose to, as a means of developing greater assertiveness and enjoying its accompanying rewards.

Because a number of approaches to assertiveness training have proved valuable, we are providing in the following section a brief commentary on each of several important contributions to AT practice. Most of these are available in book form, so you should have a minimum of difficulty in locating any which are of interest to you.

Other Approaches to Assertiveness Training

Andrew Salter, truly the pioneer in developing a therapeutic approach to increasing personal effectiveness, describes *excitation* (a behavioral style he later agrees is like assertion) as "a matter of emotional freedom." In his classic book *Conditioned Reflex Therapy* (1949), Salter says excitatory responses must be honest, direct, outward, energetic, unaffected, and free of anxiety. Salter teaches six major elements of excitatory (assertive) behavior: *feeling talk, facial talk, contradiction and attack, deliberate use of "I," agreement with praise,* and *improvisation* (spontaneity). That's a pretty good description of what we are calling *assertiveness!*

Another key figure in the development of assertiveness training is psychiatrist Joseph Wolpe. Wolpe's definition (1969, 1973), is broad and direct: "*Assertive behavior is defined as the proper expression of any emotion other than anxiety towards another person.*" His approach to training, from which we have drawn heavily, emphasizes desensitization and behavior rehearsal.

As assertiveness training has grown in popularity, trainers and researchers have looked at the concept of assertiveness in greater detail, much as we are doing in this chapter. Patricia Jakubowski was the first to present a systematic approach to AT for women (1973). Later, in her book with Arthur Lange, *Responsible Assertive Behavior* (1976), several types of assertive behavior are proposed: *Basic assertion* (standing up for personal rights); *Empathic assertion* (communicating understanding and empathy); *Escalating assertion* (gradually increasing firmness); *Confrontive assertion* (pointing out mistakes, giving directions); *I-language assertion* (expressing negative feelings phrased in "how I feel" language).

The Assertive Woman (1975), by Stanlee Phelps and Nancy Austin, is the first AT book specifically devoted to the concerns of women. Phelps and Austin have integrated AT procedures with consciousness raising, and include helpful material on such topics as manipulation, putdowns, humor, sexuality, children, and social change. The book includes many exercises and self-assessment surveys.

A different book with a similar title, *The New Assertive Woman* (1975), by Lynn Bloom, Karen Coburn, and Joan Pearlman, presents material related to women's rights, irrational beliefs, and games women play in avoiding self-assertion. AT procedures similar to *Your Perfect Right* are included.

Don't Say Yes When You Want to Say No (1975), by Herbert Fensterheim and Jean Baer is a presentation of AT within the context of behavior therapy, and includes assignments and exercises, as well as material on weight control, sex therapy, and relaxation training.

In her own book, *How to Be an Assertive [not Aggressive] Woman* (1976), Jean Baer draws much from the Fensterheim/Baer volume, applying it to women. She describes many "blocks" to assertiveness, and discusses the differences between "therapy" and "education".

I Can If I Want To (1975), by Arnold Lazarus and Allen Fay, although not an AT book *per se,* is a brief series of self-affirmation exercises based on AT and humanistic-behavioral principles. Lazarus was a pioneer in developing the AT model in the 1960's with Joseph Wolpe, although their views have diverged markedly in recent years, with Lazarus adopting a style he calls "broad spectrum behavior therapy."

Among other major contributors to the AT field whose works we consider worthy of your attention are John and Merna Galassi (1976), Eileen Gambrill and Cheryl Richey (1976), Iris Fodor and Janet Wolfe (1975), Robert Liberman and associates (1976), and Spencer Rathus (1975, 1977). We consider the work of all of the professionals mentioned thus far to be positive and constructive. Others whose work is primarily directed toward AT professionals are discussed in Chapter XII.

It is our opinion that such styles as those in the books of Manuel Smith (1975) and Robert Ringer (1976), although often popularly identified with AT, are more oriented toward *manipulating* others in pursuit of one's goals (and are thereby aggressive rather than assertive as we define it). Thus we cannot support the approaches advocated in their work.

There is a considerable range and variety of approaches to assertiveness training. Although highly structured techniques and "scripts" can be useful in learning assertiveness, our preference is to offer the general set of steps presented in this chapter. We do not wish to tell you what to say, or even to give a "formula" for what to say, in a given situation. Rather, we encourage your individuality, and hope that you will develop your own assertive style, following guidelines of *honesty, directness, respect for the rights of others,* and *your own*

--

freedom of choice in your self-assertion. Examine other approaches, and select a method which will be of maximum value to *you!*

A Gentle Shove

Now that you know what is involved in the process of developing assertive behavior, don't allow yourself to remain a passive observer. If you are interested enough to read this far, you are either thinking seriously about improving your own assertiveness or considering how you can help others to become more assertive. In either case, *do something about it!* You cannot change solely by sitting there reading this book. If we don't move you to action in your own life, we have served only as a diversion and we are disappointed. If, on the other hand, you go out now and handle *one* interpersonal situation more in your own best interests, we are pleased to have had a part in your growth.

Try it!

VII

The "Soft" Assertions:
Caring for Self, Friends, and Family

> *Is not the expression of affection toward other
> people also assertion?*
> —*Michael Serber, M.D.*

"Stand up for yourself" is the slogan often cited as synonymous with
the development of assertive behavior. Indeed, the first edition of *Your
Perfect Right* was devoted almost exclusively to fostering that type of
behavior. In a critical review of that first edition, published in *Behavior
Therapy*, a professional journal, the late psychiatrist Michael Serber
noted our oversight. A colleague who had substantial influence on our
work, Serber wrote in that early review (1971):

> *Certainly, behavioral skills necessary to stand up to the multi-
> ple personal, social, and business situations confronting the
> majority of people are imperative to master. But what of other
> just as necessary skills, such as being able to give and take
> tenderness and affection? Is not the expression of affection
> toward other people also assertion? There are many behavior
> modifiers who are completely "turned off" to sensitivity-
> training groups. The majority of such groups, if they try to
> fashion that it is difficult to imagine anything concrete being
> learned. Nevertheless, the content of sensitivity training, the
> ability to express warmth and affection, to be able to give and*

*take feelings, including anger, badly needs the special atten-
tion behavior modifiers can bring to it. Sensitivity training can
become a unique area in which humanistic goals and behavioral techniques can yield both meaningful and concrete new
behaviors.*

We have found that *positive, caring feelings* or *constructive anger* are
often more difficult to express for non-assertive and aggressive persons
that "standing up" behavior. In addition, to express one's feelings after
the moment has passed often calls for an extra measure of assertiveness.

Caring Begins at Home

Particularly for adults, expressions of warmth are often inhibited.
Embarrassment, fear of rejection or ridicule, the "superiority of reason
over emotion" are all excuses given to explain the inhibition of
spontaneous expressions of warmth, caring and love.

Freedom of such expression has not been encouraged in our culture.
As we discussed in Chapter I, "polite restraint" is in the accepted order
of things. Nevertheless, the new life styles and youth subcultures,
which have been most obvious among potent forces for change,
encourage greater spontaneity. We heartily endorse greater openness in
the communication of genuine positive feeling toward other persons.

It is encouraging to note the freedom in expression of caring, joy, and
warm feelings among young people, blacks, and Latinos. Each of these
groups is becoming more influential in shaping our social order. Perhaps
future generations will find such emotional freedom more natural!

Sadly, for some people even "thank you" is difficult. An
acquaintance of ours, president of a multi-million dollar giant
organization, is noted for rarely expressing appreciation to the people on
his staff. A job well done is seldom openly rewarded, recognized, or
even acknowledged. Because the chief executive is apparently afraid to
act in warm and positive ways (Perhaps because he might appear
"soft?" Or because others might come to *expect* rewards?), the morale
of staff members in that organization is not very high.

To be a caring person, and to openly express that, seems to be a
"high-risk" style in our society. How sad for all of us that we make it so
difficult for warmth to be expressed openly! A California public official

has been scorned and ridiculed for signing letters to other public officers with the closing "Love . . ."

Psychologist Erich Fromm has differentiated five types of love in his excellent book *The Art of Loving*: fraternal, maternal, erotic, love of God, and self-love. We hope you can view love in this broader context, and allow yourself to love *you* and *others* more openly.

"The hardest step for most people I know," commented high school counselor Gail McPhail at an AT group meeting, "is to *be assertive with yourself*: to convince yourself to go ahead and express your feelings in a situaion. Now that we know *how* to be assertive, can we spend some time on those self-barriers to assertion?" The group did spend some time working on those self-barriers to assertion, and we learned something of the importance of "being assertive with yourself."

If your thoughts are filled with self denying "rules" and "attitudes," your behavior will in all likelihood be similar. You may think in "negative self statements" ("I am not important," "My opinions don't count," "No one will be interested in what I have to say," "I'll probably make a fool of myself if I say anything," "I'm really not sure," "I have no right to say that,"). If so, chances are very good you will act accordingly - that is, you'll keep quiet and let others control the situation!

Try, for a short period of time, to allow yourself to say the *positive* form of those statements: "I am important," "My opinions count," "Some one will be interested in what I have to say," "I have a right to say that." You needn't *act* on any of these at this point, just "get the feel" of saying positive things to yourself.

After you have practiced the positive thoughts for a while, you may wish to begin - still in your own thoughts - to consider the ways you would be acting in those situations if you followed through on the thoughts. Perhaps, for example, you were thinking "Someone will be interested in what I have to say," in regard to joining in on a group discussion. If you were to imagine *acting* on that thought, you might see yourself asking a question of one of the more outspoken participants. Or maybe you could just start out by saying "I agree." Think about ways you could *act* like a person who *thinks* positively! Then go back to Chapter VI, and follow the Step-by-Step process toward more assertive *action!*

Figure VII-1
A BEHAVIORAL MODEL FOR PERSONAL GROWTH

Dr. Carl Rogers, in his 1961 book **On Becoming A Person,** has identified three characteristics of personal growth. These lend themselves to use as models in the process of developing personal growth. The checklist has been developed by Dr. Alberti, based upon Rogerian phrases:

"An Increasing Openness to Experience"
How recently have you
- participated in a new sport or game?
- changed your views on an important (political, personal, professional) issue?
- tried a new hobby or craft?
- taken a course in a new field?
- studied a new language or culture?
- spent fifteen minutes or more paying attention to your body feelings, senses (relaxation, tension, sensuality)?
- listened for fifteen minutes or more to a religious, political, professional, or personal viewpoint with which you disagreed?
- tasted a new food, smelled a new odor, listened to a new sound?
- allowed yourself to cry? or to say "I care about you"? or to laugh until you cried? or to scream at the top of your lung capacity? or to admit you were afraid?
- watched the sun (or moon) rise or set? or a bird soar on the wind's currents? or a flower open to the sun?
- traveled to a place you had never been before?
- made a new friend? or cultivated an old friendship?
- spent an hour or more really communicating (actively listening and responding honestly) with a person of a different cultural or racial background?
- taken a "fantasy trip"—allowing your imagination to run freely for ten minutes to an hour or more?

"Increasingly Existential Living"
How recently have you
- done something you felt like doing at that moment, without regard for the consequences?
- stopped to "listen" to what was going on inside you?
- spontaneously expressed a feeling—anger, joy, fear, sadness, caring— without "thinking about it"?
- done what you wanted to, instead of what you thought you "should" do?
- allowed yourself to spend time or money on an immediate "payoff" rather than saving for tomorrow?
- bought something you wanted "on impulse"?
- done something no one (including you) expected you to do?

"An Increasing Trust in One's Organism"
How recently have you
- done what felt right to you, against the advice of others?
- allowed yourself to experiment creatively with new approaches to old problems?
- expressed an unpopular opinion assertively in the face of majority opposition?
- used your own intellectual reasoning ability to work out a solution to a difficult problem?
- made a decision and acted upon it right away?
- acknowledged by your actions that you can direct your own life?
- cared enough about yourself to get a physical exam (within a year)?
- told others of your religious faith, or philosophy of life?
- assumed a position of leadership in your profession, or an organization, or your community?
- asserted your feelings when you were treated unfairly?
- risked sharing your personal feelings with another person?
- designed and/or built something on your own?
- admitted you were wrong?

Let's take a look at your good feelings toward yourself. Can you give expression to the feeling of elation which accompanies the achievement of a highly-valued personal goal? Do you allow yourself the pleasure of feeling satisfied with a job well done? Of making someone else happy? Of congratulating yourself?

Look over Figure VII-1, "A Behavioral Model for Personal Growth." How are you treating yourself? Can you honestly answer those questions and say you are behaving in a caring, loving way toward yourself? Like Gail, we are increasingly convinced that a key element of assertive behavior is *being assertive with yourself!* Caring enough for yourself to *believe* you can, then *doing it.* In the therapeutic setting, we overcome a lack of self-love by *authorizing* the assertive behavior. The result of the "authorized" action is an enhanced concept of self-worth, which is the beginning of a positive turn in the attitude-behavior-feedback-attitude cycle. Encouragement from a professional therapist enables a person to begin acting more assertively. *You* can achieve the same results on your own or with a minimum of help by following the procedures we have described.

Reaching Out

Expressing your warm feelings for another person is a highly assertive act. And, as with other assertions we have noted, the act itself—that is, *doing it*—is more important by far than the words you use or your own style of communication. This is even more true for expressions of caring. Nothing represents a more personal, individual expression that that which says, "You mean a great deal to me at this moment."

Consider some ways of communicating that message:

A warm, firm, and extended handshake (ever notice the duration and feeling of a "brotherhood" hand clasp—e.g., Black Power, fraternity members?)

A hug, the squeeze of an arm, an arm around the shoulders, an affectionate pat on the back, the squeeze of a hand held affectionately.

"Thank you."

"You're great!"

"I really understand what you mean."

"I like what you did."

A warm smile.

Extended eye contact.
"I'm here."
A gift of love (made by the giver, or uniquely special to the recipient).
"I believe you."
"I trust you." (better yet an *act* of trust)
"I love you."
"I believe in you."
"I'm glad to see you."
"I've been thinking of you."
"You've been on my mind."

Probably none of these messages is a new thought to you. Yet you may find it difficult to allow yourself to say or do them. It is too easy to be hung up on embarrassment, or to assume: She knows how I feel," or "He doesn't care to hear that." But *who* doesn't care to hear that? All of us need to know we are cared about and admired and needed. If those around us are *too* subtle in their expressions of positive regard, we can too easily begin to doubt, and perhaps look elsewhere for what the Transactional Analysis people call our "strokes"—positive feedback from others.

In very *intimate relationships,* between lovers for example, it is often assumed that each partner "knows" the feelings of the other. Such assumptions often lead to the marriage counselor's office, with complaints such as "I never know how he feels," "She never tells me she loves me," "We just don't communicate any more." Frequently it is necessary only to re-establish a communication pattern in which each partner is expressing *openly* his/her feelings—particularly those of caring. The expression of caring is seldom a panacea for all the ills of an ailing marriage, but can "shore up the foundation" by helping each partner to remember what was good about the relationship in the first place!

Psychologists Herbert A. Otto and George R. Bach have developed extensive systems for improving spontaneous expression of caring in intimate relationships. Readers particularly interested in this area are referred to their works, noted in the Bibliography.

Not long ago, we asked a group of university students to tell what makes each of them feel especially good. Some of their favorite experiences are in the following list (Notice how many involve someone else caring!):

Acceptance of an invitation	Independence
Achievement	Jobs completed
Affection	Keeping my plants alive
Appreciation	Laughter
Approval	Making new friends
Assurance	My boyfriend's/girlfriend's actions
Compliments from the opposite sex	of love toward me
	Personal satisfaction with myself
Encouragement	Positive comment
Expressed interest of others	Praise
Friendliness	Receiving a compliment
Getting an A on an exam	Recognition
Giving a compliment	Recognition when speaking
Good grades	Request to repeat a job previously
Greeting someone else	done
Having a friend	Satisfaction
Having someone say "hello"	Security
Helping Others	Singing
Implementation of ideas	Spoken affirmation
	Touch

We all need to *hear* positive feedback from others. Therapists encounter many, many clients who are unhappy precisely *because* they are not getting such "strokes" in their lives.

Compliments are a frequent source of discomfort for non-assertive and aggressive persons. To praise someone as a person or something someone has done may be a difficult thing for you. Again, we encourage *practice* of that which causes you some anxiety. Go out of your way to praise others—not dishonestly or insincerely, but whenever a genuine opportunity presents itself. Don't concern yourself with waiting for the "right words" either. Your thoughtfulness—the honest expression of what you are feeling—will convey itself with almost any vehicle *if you act!* Try simply, "I like what you did" or "Great!" or a big smile.

Accepting compliments—to hear someone else direct a very supportive statement to you, or about you to a third person, is perhaps an even more challenging task, particularly difficult if you are not feeling good about yourself. Nevertheless, it is an assertive act—a mutually enhancing response—to accept praise from another person.

Consider first that you really have no right to deny that person his/her perception of you. If you say "Oh, you just caught me on a good day!" or "It wasn't anything special" or "it was an accident that it turned out well," you have in effect, told the complimentor that he or she has poor judgment. It is as if you said to that person, "You're wrong!" Try to allow everyone the right to feelings, and if they are positive toward you, do others—and yourself—the service of accepting.

We are not suggesting that you go about praising yourself, or accepting credit for achievements which are not your own. We do urge, however, that when another person sincerely wishes to convey a positive comment about you, that you allow the expression of that feeling without rejection or qualification. Try saying at the least, "It's hard for me to accept that, but thank you," or better yet is simply "That feels good." or "I like to hear that."

Imagine the following scenes:

While you are wandering alone at a large gathering, a stranger walks up to you and starts a conversation, and you no longer feel anxious and lost.

Three days after you arrive in a new neighborhood, the couple next door come to welcome you, with a pot of coffee and a freshly baked-cake.

During your visit in another country, you are looking in vain for a street sign. A native appears, and asks "May I help you find something?"

Thoughtful acts like these are not only "strokes" for the receiver, they produce warm feelings for the person who reached out assertively. People often hesitate to initiate contact in these ways, for fear of rejection - a common reason for avoiding assertions! Such initiative involves concern for the other person, and some courage of your own. Yet, realistically, who could reject such a kindness?

Often actions like these are easier than you might suppose. As you enter a classroom, meeting, bus, airplane, think how easy it would be to simply approach a vacant seat and ask the person in the next seat "Is anyone sitting here?" Not only have you found a place to sit - assuming the seat *is* available - *you have begun a conversation!* Having thus opened contact, you may easily proceed to find out more about the other person ("Where are you headed?" "Have you heard this lecturer before?" "My name is Mary Doe/John Doe.").

Don't wait for others to take the initiative. Take the risk of reaching out! It's a key means to caring about yourself and about others, and an important step toward greater assertiveness (and more fun!)

"It's Too Late Now!"

We often hear from clients who are in assertive therapy, or as questions raised in our assertiveness training groups, about situations which have occurred in the past. These persons, who feel they can do nothing about the problem "at this late date" are frustrated by the consequences of their earlier lack of assertion, but feel helpless to change the situation now.

An example of such a case involved the relationship of Charlene K., a business executive and her secretary, George. The busy executive found herself regularly completing letters and reports late in the day, and asking George to have them typed and duplicated for meetings the following morning. The secretary had, the first time, assumed that the request—which required that he remain after hours to complete the work—was due to unique circumstances at that time. He willingly agreed to help out. Later, he found the "special request" had become an expectation, and occurred two or three times a week. Although he enjoyed the work, his personal life was being interfered with, and he began to think of quitting the job. Fortunately, he sought help in an assertiveness training group where he somewhat tentatively brought the situation up for discussion. George found the therapist and group members very supportive. He selected a relatively assertive woman in the group and "rehearsed" with her a scene in which he confronted Charlene with his feelings. He did poorly at first, apologizing and allowing the "boss" to convince him that such "loyalty to the company" was necessary to the job. With feedback and support from the group, however, he improved his ability to express his feelings effectively and not be cowed by the executive's response. The next day, George confronted Charlene at the office, made his point, and arranged a more reasonable schedule for such projects. In the two months that followed she made "special requests" only twice, and only when the circumstances clearly *were* unusual. Both were pleased with the result.

The point of this discussion is that it is seldom "too late" for an appropriate assertion—even if a situation has grown worse over some time. Approaching the person involved—yes, even a family member, spouse, lover, boss, employee—with an honest "I've been concerned about———for some time" or "I've been wanting to talk with you about———" can lead to a most productive effort at resolution of an uncomfortable issue. And, as no small side benefit, it can open communication of feelings in the future.

Keep in mind, as we have noted before, the importance of stating your feelings in such a way as to accept responsibility for them: "I'm concerned . . ." *not* "You've got me upset . . ."; "I'm mad . . ." *not* "You made me mad . . ."

Another important reason to "go back" and take care of old business with others is that "unfinished business" continues to gnaw away at you. Resentment from experiences which created anger, or hurt won't just "go away." Such feelings result in a widening gap between people, and the resulting mistrust, and potential grudge is hurtful to both persons.

Even if the old issues cannot be amicably resolved, doing all you can to *attempt* reconciliation is a very healthy and worthwhile step for you. We recognize that opening up old wounds can be painful. And there are certain risks - the outcomes *could* be worse than before. Despite these risks, we have seen so many people gain great rewards from resolving old conflicts that we do not hesitate to encourage you to do all *you* can to work out any such problems in your own life.

One more point: As we have cautioned before, do not attempt to *begin* your journey toward new assertiveness with highly risky relationships. This is a rather advanced step, and should come after you have mastered the basics.

Assertive Women, Men & Children Too!

A tremendous source of interest in AT has been the women's movement, and not solely from the "liberationist" perspective. Women of all social viewpoints, ethnic and socio-economic backgrounds, educational and professional involvements, homemakers, hard hats, and high ranking executives are asking for help in their efforts to become more adequately assertive.

At the same time, a smaller but equally committed number of men were acknowledging a great gap in their own preparation for interpersonal relationships. They had found themselves limited to only two options in behavior: the powerful dominating aggressor or the "97 pound weakling" with sand in his face. Neither was particularly satisfying.

The mid-1970's have seen public recognition in our society of the inadequacy of a social "ideal" which identifies women as characteristically "passive, sweet, submissive, accepting, warm, loving, nurturing, empathetic" and the counterpart male (as if by "nature") as "strong, active, decisive, dominant, cool, rational." We have, at long last, begun to value the *assertive* woman and the assertive man.

Assertive Women

In their excellent book *The Assertive Woman* (which is good reading for men too, incidentally), Stanlee Phelps and Nancy Austin present the behavioral styles of four "women we all know." Their characterizations of "Doris Doormat," "Agatha Aggressive," "Iris Indirect," and "April Assertive" are self explanatory by the names alone. Yet, in describing the patterns of each, Phelps and Austin help us to gain a clearer picture of the social mores which have *devalued* assertiveness in women. Agatha gets her way, though she hasn't many friends. Iris, the sly one, also gains most of what she wants, and sometimes her "victims" never even know it. Doris, although denied her own wishes much of the time, is highly praised by men and by the power structure as "a good woman." April's honesty and forthrightness have often led her into trouble (at least until recently), at home, at school, on the job, and even with other women.

Beginning to evolve, however, is a new social more: women are persons, have rights, deserve equal recognition/status/pay, are not inherently "weaker," do not (except when they freely so choose) "belong in the home." Thus the *assertive* woman has become - albeit slowly and not without considerable effort - a person valued by society, by men, by other women. She is capable of choosing her own lifestyle, free of the dictates of tradition, government, husband, children, social groups, bosses. She may *elect* to be a homemaker and not fear intimidation by her "liberated" sisters. She may elect to pursue a male-dominated profession and enjoy confidence in her rights and her abilities.

In her sexual relationships, she can be comfortable taking initiative, asking for what *she* wants (and thereby freeing her partner from the "automatic" role of making the first move). She can also say "no" with firmness, and make it stick.

As a consumer, she makes the marketplace respond to her needs, by refusing to accept shoddy merchandise or service, or marketing techniques, which often assume "she doesn't know any better."

In short, the assertive *woman* is an assertive *person*, who exhibits the qualities we espouse throughout this book, and likes herself better for it!

Assertive Men

Imagine the following scene: John's day has been exhausting: he has washed windows, mopped floors, completed three loads of wash and continuously picked up and cleaned up after the children. He is now working hurriedly in the kitchen preparing dinner. The children are running in and out of the house banging the door, screaming, and throwing toys.

In the midst of this chaos, Mary arrives home from an equally trying day at her office. She offers a cursory "I'm home!" as she passes the kitchen on her way to the family room. Dropping her briefcase and kicking off her shoes, she flops in her favorite chair in front of the television set, calling out, "John, bring me a beer! I've had a helluva day!"

This scene is humorous partly because it seems highly unusual. After all, shouldn't *John* be the breadwinner, working at an office rather than at home? Isn't it a man's *place* to go out and conquer the world on behalf of his family? To demonstrate his *man*hood, his *macho*, his strength and courage?

Unfortunately, we have for too long accepted as proper the stereotype of the male as "mighty hunter," who must protect and provide for his family. Indeed, from earliest childhood the "accepted" male roles have encouraged assertive and often aggressive behavior in pursuit of this "ideal." Competitiveness, achievement, striving to be "the best" are integral components of male child-rearing and formal schooling, to a considerably greater extent than for their sisters.

Yet there are encouraging signs. An increasing number of men, through the late 1960's and early 1970's, have begun to reject that aggressive, climbing, "success" stereotype, in favor of a more balanced role and lifestyle. Psychological concepts of "masculinity" have changed to acknowledge the caring, nurturing side of men as well. And perhaps most significantly, men have recognized that they can accomplish their own life goals in *assertive*—not aggressive—ways. Professional advancement in all but the most stubbornly competitive (and often dehumanizing) fields is available for the competent, confident, *assertive* man.

Similarly, the assertive man is held in greater esteem in personal relationships. Family and friends are closer and have greater respect for the man who is comfortable enough with himself that he needn't put others down in order to put himself up. The honesty of assertiveness is an incalculable asset in close personal relationships, and assertive men are coming to value such closeness much more than the fleeting rewards of a competitive economic system.

Gail Sheehy's enormously successful book *Passages* (1976) records the recognition, by men who have lived the aggressive style in their 20's and 30's, that those achievements mean little in their later years: The values of personal intimacy, family closeness, and trusted friendships - all fostered by assertiveness, openness, honesty - are the lasting and *important* ones. The assertive man is finding himself too!

Parents and Children in the Assertive Family

How long has it been since you were on a see-saw ("teeter-totter")? Remember how you could affect the ride of the person on the other end by shifting your weight forward or back? If you moved forward quickly, your friend would likely drop with a solid bump! By leaning way back, you could keep the other suspended in mid-air for a time.

Families and other interpersonal systems have a balance system not unlike that of the see-saw. A change in one member of the family will generally "upset" the balance of the total system, affecting everyone. Often families are strong "resistors" of change because of the delicate balance, even though it may be a painful or even destructive system.

Becoming more assertive is clearly a change which may upset the family balance. A formerly passive mother, for example, may severely strain family relationships as she begins to express a new assertiveness. Children who were able to easily manipulate her must find new and more direct avenues to achieve their goals. Her perhaps "pampered" husband may soon be ironing his own shirts and sharing in household chores. Such changes present a difficult adjustment for everyone, and offer a considerable obstacle to the woman (for example) who wishes to become more assertive. Similar problem potential exists for the newly assertive father, of course. For the children, a whole new set of difficulties are introduced into the path of their growing assertiveness.

It has been said that "the last frontier of human rights is that of the rights of chidren." Despite the history of apparent dedication to individual rights in the United States, and even despite the recent gains in rights for minorities, women, and others who have been denied and oppressed, we have made few changes in our basic notions that children are indeed second class citizens. The veneration of "youth" in popular media, dress styles, music, literature has not carried over into a comparable respect for the rights of those who *are* young.

Without debating the relative concerns of innocence and inexperience *vs.* age and wisdom, let us simply suggest that *assertive* children, like assertive adults, are likely to be healthier and happier, more honest, less manipulative, to feel better about themselves, and to be headed toward more self-actualized adulthood. We favor a conscious effort in families, schools, churches, and public agencies to foster assertiveness in young people - and to create conditions which will facilitate their "natural" spontaneity of expression and will value the honesty and openness which typically characterizes the young before fearful parents and schools destroy it.

Let us be clear - we do not advocate totally "permissive" child-rearing. The "real world" places limits upon us all, and children need to learn that early if they are to develop adequate life s-u-r-v-i-v-a-l skills. However, we do consider it vital that families, schools, and other child rearing social systems view children as human beings worthy of respect, honor their basic human rights, and teach them 1) that honest self expression is a valued behavior and 2) the skills to act accordingly.

Most of the principles and procedures advocated elsewhere in this book are applicable to the development of assertiveness in children, so we will not present here any specialized material. Interested readers may wish to consult the approach presented directly to younger children by Pat Palmer (1977).

It is worth mentioning here that parents - and we don't mean just those who may be physically or emotionally *abusing* their children - often have difficulty discriminating between assertion and aggression when disciplining or otherwise dealing firmly with their youngsters. We believe that the same general rules we have discussed earlier for defining assertiveness apply in the case of parent-child relationships (you may wish to refer to Chapters 2 and 3). Although each situation is unique in terms of its context, response, intent and behavior, the key to defining assertiveness in family interactions is the notion of *mutual respect*. Notwithstanding the unique nature of the parent-child relationship, both persons are individual human beings, deserving of all the respect and valuing due any other person, child or adult.

A few words about teen age and adult "children" are in order. Independence from our parents may be the single most important life issue we all face, certainly it is the core around which "growing up" revolves. Some rebelliousness is normal and healthy for teenagers, and facilitates their developing independence. Parental dominance and teenage inhibition may slow down that process, and delay the necessary steps toward independent adulthood. Unresolved ties with parents sometimes restrict independence in the lives of adults of all ages. In our experience, an assertive approach by the "child" can clear the air, make the situation clear to the parent, and allow needed expression of feelings on both sides.

Such a confrontation is almost inevitably painful, and it is a considerable risk for both parent and child to open up old wounds. Despite this considerable obstacle, we believe continued silence exacts much too high a price. Adults who avoid dealing with their parents or adult children as they would any other adult (with whom they feel a special closeness) can suffer unmeasured guilt, self-denial, inhibition, repressed anger, and often depression. Our colleagues in New York City, Drs. Janet Wolfe and Iris Fodor, have done excellent work with the relationship of adult mothers and daughters (1977), and their model of assertiveness in the mother-daughter relationship is useful for anyone who is dealing with this issue.

Summing up this discussion of assertiveness in the family, it may be useful to itemize our viewpoint:

1) Assertive behavior enhances both individuals and relationships;

2) Honest, open and non-hurtful assertive communication is desirable and highly valuable in families;

3) Children as well as adults should learn to be assertive within the family and beyond it;

4) The principles and procedures for defining and learning assertiveness which are described in this book are applicable to adults and to children (i.e. modelling, rehearsal, feedback, practice, reinforcement, mutual respect, and individual rights).

Changing family systems is more difficult, more time and energy consuming, and potentially more risky (families can and do break up) than is changing individual behavior. We encourage you to carefully evaluate, to proceed slowly, to involve everyone openly, to avoid coercion, to tolerate failure, to remember that nobody, and no approach is perfect! Notwithstanding these cautions, we also encourage you to work toward the development of an "assertive family." It can be a tremendously exciting and growth enhancing environment in which to live!

VIII

Anger is Not Aggression!

> *If people would dare to speak to one another
> unreservedly, there would be a good deal less
> sorrow in the world a hundred years hence.*
> —*Samuel Butler*

The common confusion of angry feelings with aggressive behavior creates a tremendous barrier to expression of the natural, healthy, universal and useful human emotion we call anger.

Non-assertive people often say, "I never get angry." We don't believe it! Everyone *gets* angry. Some people have so controlled themselves as to not openly *show* anger. Typically, such a controlled individual suffers from migraine headaches, asthma, ulcers, or skin problems.

We are convinced, along with psychologist George Bach and many others, that expression of anger is a healthy thing, and that it can be done constructively. Dr. Bach's book *The Intimate Enemy* deals in detail with constructive expression of anger in an intimate relationship. Persons who develop spontaneous assertiveness can release anger effectively in non-destructive ways, and thus preclude the necessity for aggressive actions.

An important step in non-destructive expression of anger is to *accept responsibility for your own feelings*. It is *you* who feel the anger, and that doesn't make the other person "stupid," "an S.O.B.," or the cause of your feeling.

A physical expression of a strong feeling can be a useful means for "venting" hostility. Banging the table, stomping the floor, crying, striking at the air, hitting a pillow can all be good devices for releasing strong feeling without aggression toward another person. However, they are *not* adequate alone as will be discussed in "The Myth of Instinctive Aggression" later in this chapter.

Preventing the build-up of hostility over time by exercising spontaneous expression when you feel it is the healthiest way we know to deal with anger. Some of the verbal expressions others have found useful include:

"I am very angry"   "I am extremely upset"
"I am becoming very mad"   "Stop bothering me"
"I strongly disagree with you"   "I think that's unfair"
"I get damn mad when you say/   "Don't do that to me"
  do that"
"I am very disturbed/   "You have no right to say/
  distressed by this whole thing"   do that"
"It bothers me"   "I really don't like that"

All too often we have observed persons who express anger, frustration, or disappointment with another by cowardly, indirect, and unnecessarily hurtful methods. Moreover, if the desired goal is to change the behavior of the intended target, these approaches are rarely successful. A "classic" example is the case of the newlyweds, Martha and John. In the first few weeks of their marriage, Martha had discovered at least a dozen of John's habits which she found objectionable. Unfortunately for both, she was unable—or unwilling—to find the courage to confront John openly with her concerns. Martha instead chose the "safe" way to express her dislike of John's behavior; she confided in her mother. Worse yet, not content with almost daily telephone conversations with mother about John's shortcomings, she also used family get-togethers as an occasion to berate John before the rest of the family.

This "see-how-bad-he-is" style, relating to a third person (or persons) one's dislikes of another, may have disastrous effects upon a relationship. John feels hurt, embarrassed, and hostile about Martha's attacks upon him. He wishes she had chosen the privacy of their own relationship to tell him of her annoyances. Instead of being motivated to change his habits, he responds to her aggressive approach with bitterness and a resolve to strike back by intensifying the very behaviors she would have him change.

Had Martha chosen courageously to assert herself directly by telling John of her feelings, she would have created a good foundation for a cooperative effort in modifying John's behavior.

Another example will help clarify our attitudes concerning the expression of anger:

Adam took his car to a large repair shop for a several-hour repair job. The maintenance was done on a first-come, first-served basis. He arrived at 8 a.m., but told the manager he would pick the car up around 4:30 p.m. When he arrived, the following verbal interchange took place:

Adam: "Hi, my name is Adam Z., and I'm here to pick up my car."

Manager: (looking through his worksheets) "I'm sorry, sir, we haven't gotten to your car yet."

A: "Damn! That really makes me mad! This is first-come, first-served and I was here at 8 a.m. What happened?"

M: "It was our mistake, we put it in the back and got busy and overlooked it."

A: "Well, hell that doesn't do me any good. It is an inconvenience for me to get my car in and leave it all day."

M: "I know that and I apologize. I promise to get it done first thing in the morning if you want to bring it back."

At this point the customer could decide what his options are and choose accordingly. Adam could try to get the manager to have someone fix his car by working overtime; he could decide to take his car elsewhere; he could return the next day for the repair work; he could demand a loan car.

Notice the anger expressed without being aggressive toward the manager. He was rightfully mad and told the manager so without downgrading him as a person. He might have responded aggressively:

"You can take that repair job and shove it," and stormed out, or said, "You damn S.O.B.'s never do anything right around here. I demand that you fix my car right now!"

Either of these statements would likely inflame the manager and not accomplish much. The important thing is to express your anger feelings without hurting someone (physically or mentally) in the process.

Honest, spontaneous, "gut-level" assertive expression will help to prevent inappropriate and destructive anger. First, it will often achieve your goals at the outset. Even when assertion doesn't gain what you're after, however, it still prevents the anger you might direct toward yourself if you had done nothing.

Despite its advocacy by some popular psychological theorists, the current fad of *venting* aggression (by hitting other people with foam bats or by shouting obsenities), is *not* psychologically healthy. Anger may be expressed in assertive ways. By "releasing" angry feelings through aggressive acts (however "benign" they may *appear*), one simply learns to handle anger aggressively. The following discussion of "The Myth of Instinctive Aggression" will help to clarify our thoughts on this controversy.

The Myth of "Instinctive Aggression"

"Look at the history of humankind," you say, "wars, violence, inhumanity, street fights, child abuse, senseless killings. I *must* believe that we are *naturally* aggressive beings!" And after all, our social systems tend to give a great deal of reinforcement for "aggression" even in its less violent forms: the "aggressive" salesperson; the "highly competitive" athlete; the "hard nosed" manager; the "strong willed" politician, all tend to be esteemed.

Popular views of the "aggression-is-natural" viewpoint include those of such heavyweights as psychoanalyst Sigmund Freud, ethologist Konrad Lorenz, and psychotherapist George Bach. They offer persuasive arguments:

> *Freud:* "The tendency to aggression is an innate, independent, instinctual disposition in man." (*Civilization and Its Discontents,* Chapter 6)

Lorenz: "We find that aggression . . . is really an essential part of the life-preserving organization of instincts." (*On Aggression,* page 44)

Bach: "The healthy fusion of aggression with developmental process is crucial to the child's eventual mastery of the environment and his struggle for survival in a difficult, competitive culture." (*Creative Aggression,* page 45).

Can we dismiss our disagreement with these views as merely an honest difference of opinion? No. We submit that the most enlightened evidence supports a view of aggression as a *potential, but not universal* form of behavior. It would be foolish to deny the existence of human aggression, but good cross cultural studies show that it is not a universal form of human expression.

It is worth special mention here, that *aggression* is not the same thing as *anger!* Anger is a perfectly natural, healthy human emotion which may be expressed in a number of ways, including aggressively, non-assertively, assertively, or not at all. Anger is a *feeling,* an emotion we all feel at times. Aggression is a *behavioral style* of expression.

We have come a long way since 1970 when in the first edition of *Your Perfect Right,* we cited Lorenz' *On Aggression* as a helpful resource in understanding aggressive behavior. Our own understanding of the research literature, and the general level of knowledge of aggression and assertion, have increased tremendously.

Simplistic "instinctive" theories of aggression are no longer viable, if indeed they ever were. Ethologists like Lorenz, aided by popular writers such as Robert Ardrey (1966) presented a view of instinctive human aggressive behavior which, like the animal cousins we were said to emulate, appeared whenever we were called upon to defend honor, life, or territory. Lorenz further advocated the regular release of our aggressive energy, lest it "build up" and come out spontaneously in uncontrolled, potentially destructive ways.

Paralleling the work of Lorenz, an entire school of psychotherapy grew up around the notion of "letting it out," integrating Freudian concepts of the innate need to express energy with Gestalt notions of the oneness of mind and body and existential philosophy of living each moment "in the here-and-now." Therapists Fritz Perls, George

Bach and a host of their followers got clients up off the couch, shouting at each other in groups, flailing each other with foam bats and epithets, confronting feelings honestly, and expressing aggression "creatively."

There is no doubt some value in such "venting" of strong feelings. However, the overwhelming evidence from more recent careful experimental studies is that *aggression begets aggression*. Thus if you learn - as a young child under your parents tutelage, or as an adult taught by a therapist - to express strong feelings aggressively (hurtfully), you will adopt an aggressive style.

Psychologist Leonard Berkowitz (1965, 1969), for example, has reported experimental studies which confirm our contention that there are non-violent methods of emotional release which contain the benefits but not the harmful effects of direct aggression. He suggests that a direct aggressive attack provokes additional aggression, both in the attacker and in the subject.

In one study, for instance, women who were insulted were permitted two styles of response. Group one was allowed to describe their angry feelings to the insulter (e.g., "That really makes me mad"). Group two women were given freedom to strike back and attack the insulter. After the experiment, women in the "feeling description" group (one) maintained less hostile feelings toward their insulter than did the women in group two, who were permitted to attack directly.

Berkowitz concludes, from the results of many such studies, that although persons may "feel better" after venting hostility aggressively, such reinforcement of destructive acts leads to further hurtful behavior. We agree heartily.

Assertive responses, on the other hand, can both effectively express your strong feelings *and* give the other person a chance to respond non-defensively - and perhaps even to change that behavior toward you which angered you in the first place!

As research and more sophisticated analyses of human behavior have evolved, it is the position of social learning theory which most adequately explains the nature of aggressive - and other - behavior. Albert Bandura, leading theorist of the social learning viewpoint states it succinctly (1973):

The social learning theory of human aggression adopts the position that man is endowed with neurophysiological mechanisms that enable him to behave aggressively, but the activation of these mechanisms depends upon appropriate stimulation and is subject to cortical control. Therefore, the specific forms that aggressive behavior takes, the frequency with which it is expressed, the situations in which it is displayed, and the specific targets selected for attack are largely determined by social experience. (pp. 29-30)

Thus, in a refinement of the "instinct" notion, contemporary theorists of the social learning and socio-biology schools agree that humans have the genetic *potential* which makes aggression *possible* - but not automatic or universal. *Social and cultural learning* determines how a person will respond under particular circumstances, and governs one's personal standards for the appropriateness of particular actions.

"Assertive Aggression"

Although examples of physical aggression proliferate in the news media, its more common cousin, mental aggression, is much more of a problem in most of our lives. Physical aggression itself is seldom pure, because there is most often "a story" behind the violence. Mental aggression is usually the catalyst that triggers the physical outburst. The overt forms of mental aggression can be quite varied and unique, depending upon the inventiveness of the person engaging in the act. A threatening gesture, a firey look, a caustic remark, an inflammed body stance, sly innuendos; the parade of instigations and retaliations goes on.

The question is - are there any forms of non-physical aggression which are justifiable? If an in-law writes you a nasty letter, do you have a right to be aggressive in return? If your boss calls you a foul name because you botched up a job, can you "give it right back?" If your spouse maligns you, is it ever acceptable to engage in the battle with full force? If you assert yourself with a line jumper and get told to "go to hell!", are you then free to lamblast the offender? If you have been repeatedly assertive about a situation and there are still no changes forthcoming, do you then have a right to be aggressive?

When someone has done something which you feel is aggressive in nature, a first step should be to assertively ask for clarification. In other words, don't assume aggression was intended without checking it out. The next step is to assertively deal with the act of aggression rather than to take flight or to stay and fight. This is a true "turning the other cheek" response. It is a misconception to believe that the best thing to do is to leave the situation, because such an action at this point does not resolve anything. Neither does a fighting-back response. Many people mistakenly feel justified in retaliating against the aggressive person, feeling that someone who can dish out this type of response is not easily hurt, can take it, is hard-shelled. Our clinical experience has been that the person who comes across aggressively, even chronically so, is often as personally insecure as those who behave non-assertively. We feel that it is good to treat them with care as most of us do with the overtly cowering non-assertive type: in an assertive, not aggressive, manner, even if you feel anger.

The third and fourth steps are interchangeable depending upon your feelings. Regular assertive responses allow one to be slow to anger, but if those feelings arise, they should be expressed assertively, not aggressively. Do not be afraid to use assertive anger if you have feelings of anger. One need not become aggressively angry in order for the other person to feel the intensity of one's upset. Along with being able to express anger, do not hesitate to moralize with the individual about his or her behavior toward you. Statements such as "I feel what you are saying is really unfair," and "It seems to me you are being dishonest," may help the individual to settle down. Most will begin to de-escalate when met with an initial assertive return, but if the individual "stays with" the aggression, assertive anger and moralizing may help bring the situation to an adequate resolution.

This leads us to the inevitable question: *Is it ever acceptable to be aggressive?* What if the individual doesn't respond to any of the above steps? What recourse do you have if the individual continually rebuffs your assertive attempts to ameliorate the conflict? The choice boils down to either leaving the encounter or to becoming aggressive in return. Your choice must necessarily focus on the "cruciality" of the issue at stake. We advocate leaving the situation whenever the issues are not matters of moral or ethical importance, but only "ego" importance. However, if the issue is a morally important one, the answer is "yes," we consider it acceptable to be mentally aggressive at times.

Even if one if forced to be aggressive, it should not be with an attitude of relish, but with an attitude of regret. If you find that there are times you "need" to be aggressive, be careful that you don't find yourself enjoying the chance to "pay the bastard back." In this respect, we might even conclude that there are two types of aggression, aggressive aggression and assertive aggression, which is aggression born of righteous indignation rather than hate.

Put-Downs and Indirect Aggression

One of the most frequent questions we hear from workshop participants is how to handle a put-down. Perhaps the stimulus for this request is the fact that there are a multitude of reasons others find to put us down: for the way we dress, for our cultural background, for our speech, for our mannerisms, for our work performance. There is a large area from which to select to criticize another's behavior. To add to the dilemma, most people also engage in self-put-downs. In this section, we discuss four basic types of put-down behavior: (1) the direct verbal put-down, (2) the indirect verbal put-down, (3) the non-verbal put-down, and (4) the self put-down.

The Direct Put-Down: Verbal Aggression: This type of behavior is obvious: another person is verbally blasting you for something. Let us say that you are coming out of an elevator, and accidentally brush someone as you pass by. The person responds immediately in a hostile manner: "Damn it! Why don't you watch where you're going! You fool, you could have hurt me!" The tirade may continue, but the person's intent is quite "up front", isn't it? How should you respond to such a caustic reaction, triggered by an innocent gesture on your part?

We suggest that your first action be to allow the person to vent the angry feelings until he or she slows down. When the outburst has subsided you could say, "I apologize for brushing against you. I didn't do so intentionally. You're obviously upset, but I do not like your calling me names or yelling at me. I can get your point without that." Observe that we did not say that you should retaliate aggressively in return. Research tells us that aggression begets aggression, but we are asking you to "turn the other cheek" by remaining *assertive* in the face of an aggressive response.

In summary, the four steps we have found valuable when confronted with a direct verbal put-down are: (1) admit it when you are wrong, even in the face of insult, (2) acknowledge the person's feelings, (3) assert yourself about the way he or she is reacting, (4) give a short statement to bring the encounter to an end.

Indirect Verbal Put-Downs: What should you say to a boss who states, "You did an excellent job on that project you turned in yesterday. All the grammatic errors gave it a folksy qualitiy." Or what it your spouse says, "I love the way you look when you wear that outfit; old clothes become you." Do you do a double-take? Are you confused? What is the real meaning in statements of this kind?

Such indirect verbal put-downs are called *indirect aggression*. In their book, *The Assertive Woman* by Stanlee Phelps and Nancy Austin, they speak of indirect aggressive behavior in the following way: ". . . in order to achieve her goal she may use trickery, seduction, or manipulation." They note further that the reactions this behavior causes in others are confusion, frustration, and feelings of being manipulated. Because indirect aggressive behavior comes out as a concealed attack, Phelps and Austin label the person who behaves in this manner a "mad dog in a lamb's suit."

We suggest that the best way to handle an indirect verbal put-down is to first ask for more information. In either of the situations given above, one might reply with "What are you saying?" or "What do you mean?" Such a response tends to help clarify the other person's true intent. (You may have misunderstood!)

Your second response will depend upon the answer of the other person. Part of your goal in the interaction, however, is to teach the person a new way of behaving toward you. If the boss indicates on the second exchange that, "Oh, I think you did a good job," you might still want to say, "Well, thank you, but I was a little confused. If you are really concerned about my errors in grammar, I hope you can say so directly. I couldn't really tell if you thought the project was good or bad." The message you are trying to teach the boss is that you prefer that he or she be straightforward with you because you are then less confused.

In marriage relationships it is nice to have good-natured teasing, but too often, underlying hostilities come out under the guise of such behavior. Your spouse may have been kidding you all along, but there are more straightforward and less destructive ways to kid or tease people.

Non-Verbal Put-Downs: "Sticks and stones may break my bones, but words will never hurt me" is a taunt children throughout the ages have used to rebuff name-callers. Unfortunately, no reply has yet been invented for our "adversaries" who put us down *without* words. What is the best way to respond to an obscene gesture or a dirty look? How should pouting and silly grins or smirks be dealt with when the person uses no words to help you verify his or her intention precisely? The non-verbal put-down is much harder to deal with because the person responding in this manner, first, is not using words and, second, may not always be consciously aware of the put-down. Moreover, you cannot be certain you accurately "read" the non-verbal message.

If another person responds toward you with an obviously aggressive non-verbal put-down, we feel that it is best to attempt to get the person to use words instead of gestures. You might say, in an assertive manner, "Could you translate that look (gesture) into words for me? I have trouble knowing what you're feeling unless you tell me directly." Be prepared for a verbal put-down at this point and respond accordingly, as per the suggestions given above.

The non-assertive non-verbal put-down is the least direct of all. When someone aggressively shakes a fist in your face it is usually difficult to misinterpret the meaning. If you are making a request of someone and he or she begins to stare off into space or grins inappropriately, the intent is not so obvious. There is a good chance that the person who responds with an indirect non-verbal put-down is doing so automatically, or out of habit. We all have mannerisms which take the place of words. Although our purpose is not to have people eliminate all non-verbal messages, we feel that it is good to accompany them with words if there is a chance they might be misinterpreted.

Imagine that you are about to pay for a purchase when the cashier looks at you, grimaces, and sighs in an anguished manner. You may wish to "write this off" as nothing personal, or merely assume the cashier is having a bad day. If you are bothered by the incident, however, we feel it is good to deal with the situation. Ask the person to explain further: "I didn't understand your expression." or "I'm not sure what you mean by that." or "Did I do something wrong?" This serves to place the non-verbal response out in the open, to clear the air. If you have done something that bothers the person, you deserve to know. Your next respose will depend on what transpires, but we feel it is good at some point to explain to the person that it is difficult to interpret, such non-verbal messages.

The Self-Put-Down: We feel that people should be advocates for themselves! Too much time is spent verbally and non-verbally (inward thoughts) putting ourselves down. The human machine works best when uncluttered by negative material. We should all be fair judges or critics of our own behavior, but most of us go beyond the call of duty! Many engage in self-put-down behaviors which *serve no constructive purpose.* We suggest that you start catching yourself when you engage in self-put-down behavior and replace those messages with good, self-confident ones. As we suggested in Chapter VII, be assertive with yourself and think and say self-fulfilling thoughts instead of self-deprecating ones!

Constructive Conflict Resolution

There are some useful guidelines for conflict resolution which have emerged out of the work of behavioral scientists working with marriage relationships and with organizational behavior. Most of these principles are parallel to the methods of assertiveness training presented throughout this book.

Conflict is more easily resolved when both parties:

1) avoid a "win-lose" position. The attitude that "I am going to win, and you are going to lose" will more likely result in *both* losing. By remaining flexible, both can win - at least in part.

2) gain the same information about the situation. Because perceptions so often differ, it is good to make *everything* explicit!

3) have goals which are *basically* compatible. If we both want to preserve the relationship more than to win, we have a better chance!

4) act honestly and directly toward one another.

5) accept responsibility for their own feelings ("I am angry!" NOT "You made me mad!")
6) are willing to face the problem openly, rather to avoid or hide from it.
7) agree upon some means of negotiation or exchange. I probably would agree to give on some points, if you would give on some! (and vice versa).

When conflict involves strong angry feelings, many people fear bringing those feelings into the open. Many of us have been told since early childhood that anger is bad. Recognizing the value of anger, as discussed elsewhere in this chapter, and allowing that natural feeling to be expressed non-destructively, will go a long way toward creating the conditions necessary for constructive conflict resolution.

Buried Anger

Others have noted how central anger is to feeling expression and mental health in general. Psychotherapist Andrew Salter observes that "Whenever I'm feeling depressed, it's because I've forgotten to be nasty to somebody!" Our acquaintance with the delightfully spontaneous Mr. Salter (who is responsible for the fundamental concepts of assertiveness training) suggests that he uses the word "nasty" for effect; it may also be read "direct", "firm," or "openly angry."

Anger is one of the most difficult emotions for many people to express. Our assertive behavior groups often lose members when "assertive expression of anger" becomes the topic. Many are simply *afraid* of their anger. Having "buried" it for years, they are terrified of the potential consequences should they suddenly "let it out." It is as if some evil and forbidding monster will escape from its cage.

In our experience, the gradual freeing of anger expression can be frightening for some people. Moreover, they have not learned constructive, assertive approaches to expressing their anger. Finally, they assume that any anger brought into the open will be hurtful to the other person. "I'd sooner suffer in silence than to hurt anyone," is the common, unfortunate, plea.

Unfortunate, because so much agony in human relationships results from anger which is denied expression. Both persons suffer. There is a good deal of evidence to suggest that buried anger comes out as resentment, envy, migraines, ulcers or skin problems. (No clear proof, however, and the actual mechanisms are not yet known.) The other person doesn't hear of the unexpressed anger, continues to behave in ways which are upsetting, and wonders why the relationship is deteriorating.

So What Can I Do About My Anger?

There *are* constructive ways to handle anger expression. As we noted earlier, psychologist George Bach has described a few useful approaches to dealing with anger in his earlier work *The Intimate Enemy* (1968). A great deal of research by psychologist David Rimm (1977) and his colleagues has demonstrated that chronic "bad tempers" can be modified through AT procedures, and inappropriate anger expression (abusive language, breaking objects), can be significantly reduced.

Our view of a healthy approach to dealing with anger is this:

(1) Recognize and allow yourself to believe that anger is a natural, healthy, non-evil human feeling. Everyone feels it, we just don't all *express* it. You needn't fear your anger.

(2) Remember that *you* are responsible for your own feelings. You got angry at what happened; the other person didn't "make" you angry.

(3) Remember that anger and aggression *are not the same thing!* Anger can be expressed assertively.

(4) Get to know yourself, so you recognize those events and behaviors which trigger your anger. As some say, "find your own buttons, so you'll know when they're pushed!"

(5) Learn to relax. If you have developed the skill of relaxing yourself, learn to apply this response when your anger is triggered.

(6) Develop assertive methods for expressing your anger, following the principles described in this book: be spontaneous; don't wait and let it build up resentment; state it directly; avoid sarcasm and innuendo; use honest, expressive lan-

guage; avoid name-calling, put-downs, and physical attacks.

(7) Keep your life clear! Deal with issues when they arise, when you feel the feelings - not after hours/days/weeks of "stewing" about it.

(8) As a last resort, refer to the discussion of "Assertive Aggression."

Go ahead! Get angry! But develop a positive, assertive style for expressing it. You, and those around you, will appreciate it.

IX

Beyond Assertiveness

God, give us the serenity to accept what cannot be changed, the courage to change what should be changed, and the wisdom to distinguish the one from the other.

—Reinhold Niebuhr

Our theme throughout this book has been the value of assertive behavior to the individual seeking self-direction, particularly in interpersonal relationships. The perceptive reader will have recognized some of the potential shortcomings and hazards inherent in personal assertiveness. Sensitivity is required in taking into account some of these limitations and potentially negative consequences of asserting yourself.

Although assertive behavior will be its own reward for most, the consequences on occasion may deflate its value. Consider, for example, the young boy who assertively refuses the big bully's request to ride his new bike, and as a result finds himself nursing a black eye! His assertion was perfectly legitimate, but the *other person* was unwilling to accept the denial of *his* desire. Therefore, without suggesting that assertiveness be avoided if it appears hazardous, we do encourage persons to consider the probable *consequences* of their assertive acts. Under certain circumstances, the personal value of an assertion will be outweighed by the value of avoiding the probable response to that assertion.

It may be useful to review a number of possible situations in which the potential value of assertiveness is weighed against the likely consequences. It is our conviction that each person should be able to *choose* how to act. If you *can* act assertively under given conditions, but *choose* not to, we have accomplished our goal. If instead you are *unable* to act assertively (i.e. cannot *choose* how to behave, but are cowed in non-assertiveness or triggered into aggression), you will be governed by others, and your mental health will suffer. *Our most important criterion for your well being is that YOU are making the choice!*

Assertiveness in an Holistic Perspective

There is no one cure for all that ails one psychologically. Proponents of various systems of therapy generally overemphasize their particular brand of help to the exclusion of other valuable approaches. In addition, psychologists often do not look beyond mental realms of treatment into physical and spiritual means of help. Assertiveness training is an extremely valuable tool for gaining self-confidence and self-control in life, but it is by no means a cure-all. AT works best when used along with other psychological, physical, and spiritual approaches. We espouse an holistic-eclectic treatment system, integrating a variety of psychological methods with physical and spiritual considerations.

Humans are mental-physical-spiritual beings, and we need to look at ourselves as such. Moreover, although there is an inseparable interrelationship among the mental, physical, and spiritual, it is vital to assess and treat ourselves as a unit.

An analysis of one's psychological functioning should be accompanied by assessment of physical and spiritual areas as well. Medical history, current medical condition, dietary and physical exercise patterns, spiritual strengths and weaknesses, all are important considerations in a thorough assessment of one's well being. Do not assume that a lack of assertiveness, for example, will be adequately dealt with by an AT program. The problem could be largely dietary! Examine all the possibilities, and engage medical and/or spiritual as well as psychological professionals if you need their help.

The Swing of the Pendulum

A question that often arises from the audience when we conduct an AT workshop:

"I have this friend who went through assertion training and now is unbearable! This person, who used to be peaceful and quiet is complaining about everything! He (or she) has really gone overboard. Isn't assertion training dangerous at times because it creates monsters?"

If one has considered him or herself the underdog throughout life, and then learns to be assertive, there is the distinct possibility that he or she will swing beyond assertion into verbal aggressiveness. This type of behavior could be described as, "Now I've got my chance, and I'll set a few people straight!" Feelings held down or covered up for so many years often come out with a "bang" when the person discovers assertiveness training.

The converse of this situation may also be true: The person who has been prone to aggressive behavior, such as manipulating, will often times go overboard when first learning assertion, becoming "super sweet" to people. It can be flabbergasting to suddenly be treated as a queen or king by someone who was formerly derisive and calculating!

Both of these dramatic shifts in behavior are normal reactions and to be expected under the circumstances. The pendulum was "stuck". Now released, the person seeks to experience the full range of behavior. We have never experienced anyone to have been genuinely harmful in this swing, but the notable change will be upsetting to those personally involved. We suggest that you be patient in these instances because our observation has been that the pendulum returns to settle in the middle range after a relatively brief period of experimentation. The middle way of assertion is eventually accepted as the best alternative.

Potential Adverse Reactions

In our experience with facilitating assertiveness in others we have found that negative results occur in a minimal number of instances. Certain people do, however, react in a disagreeable manner when they face assertion from another. Therefore, even if the assertion is handled properly, neither being non-assertive or aggressive to any degree, one may at times still be faced with uncomfortable situations such as the following:

1. Backbiting—After you have asserted yourself, the other person involved may be somewhat disgruntled, but not openly. For example, if you see someone jumping in line ahead of you and you assert yourself, the person may grumble passing you to go to the end of the line. You may hear such things as "Who do you think you are, anyway?", "Big deal!", "Big man!", and so forth. To our way of thinking, the best solution is simply to ignore the childish behavior. If you do retort in some manner, you are likely only to complicate the situation by reinforcing the fact that the words "got to you."

2. Aggression—In this case the other party may become outwardly hostile toward you. Yelling or screaming could be involved, or physical reactions like bumping, shoving, or hitting. Again, the best approach is to avoid escalating the condition. You may choose to express regret that he or she is upset by your actions, but you must remain steadfast in your assertion. This is especially true if you will have further contacts. If you back down on your assertion, you will simply reinforce this negative reaction. As a result, the next time you assert yourself with this person, the probability will be high that you will receive another aggressive reaction.

3. Temper Tantrums—In certain situations you may assert yourself with someone who has had his or her own way for a long period of time. She or he may then react to your assertion by looking hurt, claiming precarious health, saying you don't like him or her, crying, feeling sorry for him or herself or otherwise attempting to control you or make you feel guilty.

4. Psychosomatic Reactions—Actual physical illness may occur in some individuals if you thwart a long-established habit. Abdominal pains, headaches, and feeling faint are just a few of the symptoms possible. To reiterate, however, one should choose to be firm in the assertion, recognizing that the other person will adjust to the new situation in a short time. You should also be consistent in your assertion whenever the same situaion recurs with this individual. If you are inconsistent in asserting your rights, the other person involved will become confused. He or she may eventually just ignore your assertions.

5. Overapologizing—On rare occasions after you have asserted yourself the other party involved will be overly apologetic or overly humble to you. You should point out that such behavior is unnecessary.

If, in later encounters he or she seems to be afraid of you or overly deferent toward you, you should not take advantage. We feel that you could help to develop assertiveness in such a person, utilizing the methods we have described.

6. **Revenge**—If you have a continuing relationship with the person to whom you have asserted yourself, there is the chance that that person may seek revenge. At first it might be difficult to understand what is being attempted, but as time goes on the taunts will become quite evident. Once you are certain that someone is trying to make your life miserable, you should squelch the actions immediately. A recommended method is to directly confront the situation. Usually this is enough to get vengeful tactics to cease.

Choosing Not to Assert Yourself

Choice is the key word in the assertion process. As long as you know in your own mind (from previous successful assertive encounters) that you *can* assert yourself, you may in a given instance decide not to do so. Following are some circumstances where one may *choose* non-assertiveness:

1. **Overly Sensitive Individuals**—On occasion, from your own observations, you may conclude that a certain person is unable to accept even the slightest assertion. When this is apparent, it is much better to resign yourself to this fact rather than chance an assertion. Although there are over-sensitive types who use their apparent weakness to manipulate others, we are all aware that there are also certain individuals who are so easily threatened that the slightest disagreement causes them to explode, either inwardly (thus hurting themselves) or outwardly (thus hurting others). You could avoid contact with such a person as much as possible, but if you must be around someone of this type there are alternative responses. One is to accept the person and cause no friction, if such is feasible. If not, and if someone does cause your life to be miserable, you may wish to use (as a *last* resort!) Potter's technique of "Lifemanship," which allows you to become free of another's control by using manipulation of a vulnerabilty of the other person (see Wolpe, 1969).

2. **Redundancy**— Once in a while the person who has taken advantage of your rights will notice, before you get a chance to assert

yourself, and will then remedy the situation in an appropriate way. Obviously, you should not wait for an extended period of time wishing that the other person will notice. Also, you should not hesitate to be assertive if he or she fails to make the amends which you feel should reasonably be made. If, on the other hand, the other person recognizes what has happened, it is not appropriate on your part to *then* pipe up and assert yourself.

3. **Being Understanding**—Now and then you may choose not to be assertive because you notice that the person is having difficulty; there can be extenuating circumstances. At a restaurant one evening, having ordered our meals a certain way, we noticed that the new cook was having great difficulty with everything. Therefore when our meals arrived, not exactly as we had ordered, we chose not to be assertive, rather than "hassle" him further. Another example is when someone you know is having an "off" day and is in a rare bad mood. In these cases you may *choose* to overlook things that may be going wrong between you, or postpone a confrontation to a more productive time. (Caution: It is easy to use "not wanting to hurt the other's feelings" as a rationalization for non-assertiveness when assertion would be more appropriate. If you find yourself doing this more than occasionally, we suggest that you carefully examine your real motives.)

When You Are Wrong

Especially in your early assertions, you may assert yourself when you have incorrectly interpreted a situation. Also, you may assert yourself with poor technique and offend the other person. If either of these situations does occur, you should be very willing to say that you have been wrong. There is no need to get carried away in making amends, of course, but you should be open enough to indicate that you know when you have been mistaken. Additionally, you should not be apprehensive about future assertions with that person if you again feel that a situation calls for it.

Some Random Thoughts on Assertive Behavior

We have undertaken this book with continuing awareness of the moral and ethical ramifications of assertive behavior. The following comments are offered for consideration of these matters, to stimulate the reader's own thinking. The issues are complex and we make no pretense of having arrived at definite answers even for ourselves.

Tolstoy has been credited with the observation that moral acts are distinguished from all other acts by the fact that they operate independently of any predictable advantage to ourselves or to others. This saying can be applied to our thinking about assertive acts. The crucial question is "Are there times in every life when one must sacrifice her or his own values in order to survive?" Analyze for example the following situation: You are taking a certain course of study which involves a period of three years of difficult work. In addition to the time and effort, you also are utilizing all of your savings plus going into debt in the process. Let us assume that you also are married and have two small children. Your studies are preparing you to enter a profession at a high level position with an excellent salary and fringe benefits. Near the end of your final year the vital culminating exam arrives on which you must show your knowledge. The first section of the exam involves three days of written questions; the second section is a three hour oral examination administered by a board of three of your teachers.

As you go through the testing procedure, you pass with a high score on the first section of the examination. During the second section, the oral exam, you appear to be answering very well up until one point toward the end. A question is asked by the most powerful and influential member of the board concerning his favorite area of study. The area is presently quite controversial, since new scientific knowledge has been discovered only recently. This individual is rigidly "set" in his belief that the new knowledge is meaningless and detrimental and dislikes anyone to challenge his views. In the past few years several candidates have flunked for holding opposite views. You have studied thoroughly this new data and believe very strongly that it is relevant, vital and will soon replace the older viewpoint. Question: Should you compromise your values and answer the way he wishes to hear, or should you severely jeopardize your future by standing up for your beliefs and risk flunking?

If one considers it legitimate and necessary to compromise one's values in transitory instances, should one compromise over an extended period of time? Occasional lapses are to be expected, in our opinion, but to sacrifice one's views to those of others over a long time span is not in one's own ultimate best interest, nor is it moral.

Other persons must also be taken into consideration. What about one's family, the spouse and children in the above case? If doing so presents a serious hazard to the welfare of others for whom I am responsible, do I still have a right to assert my beliefs?

Are there positive immoral acts as well as negative ones? For instance, I know certain information about a subject being discussed in English class that no one else knows or brings up. Am I "morally non-assertive" if I decide not to seem "know-it-allish" and therefore say nothing of my special knowledge? Does the situation change if the class is in history? Psychology? Driver training? First aid? Pharmacology? Heart surgery?

Perhaps the key issue is whether or not the assertion, which one feels morally obligated to make, in actuality will make any difference. It might be better for all to accept the fact that some things are better left as they are. Reinhold Niebuhr said it perhaps best of all: "God, give us serenity to accept what cannot be changed, courage to change what should be changed, and wisdom to distinguish the one from the other."

Beyond Assertiveness

As we bring this book to a conclusion, let us briefly summarize the more important points we have tried to express:

- Assertiveness, as other social behavior, is learned. You *can* change yourself if you wish to do so.
- Change is hard work. It usually comes slowly, and in small steps. Don't try to tackle too much at once. Succeed by taking *achievable* steps!
- There are no magic answers. While assertiveness doesn't always work (for us either!) it sure beats the alternatives - nearly all the time! Don't let failures at first stop you from trying again.
- Give yourself credit when you bring about changes in your life. Even the smallest accomplishments deserve a pat on the back!
- Don't hesitate to ask for help - including professional help when you need it. Everyone needs help at times. Remember,

you are working with an infinitely valuable resource - yourself.
Take good care!

You are unique, an individual, with your own size, shape, age,
ethnic and cultural background, sex, lifestyle, education, ideas,
values, occupation, relationships, behavior patterns. In this
book we have had to generalize a great deal. AT is not all things
to all people. *You* must decide what is relevant for you, and if
you choose to use AT as a tool to help you to become the person
you want to be, you must also decide how to apply its principles
to your own unique life situation.

Remember that assertiveness is *not* a tool for manipulation, or
intimidation, or getting your way. It is a means to stand up for
your own rights, to express your anger, to reach out to others,
to express your affection, to be more direct. Most importantly,
it is one means to become the person you want to be, to feel
good about yourself, and to demonstrate your respect for the
rights of others.

X

Assertive Behavior Situations

> *"Who does the observing of that self who performs on the stage? Is it not my own self? Then which is my real self, the actor or the observer? If you look closely you may discover another personage who deserves to be called self: he is the director of the play, the one who decides what to do and how to do it . . ."*
> —*J. Samuel Bois,* The Art of Awareness

The following examples depict typical situations in which assertive behavior is called for, but which often causes difficulty for non-assertive or aggressive persons. Each situation is presented without a response on the part of the principal "actor." Alternative responses are then described from which the actor may choose his behavior in the situation. Each alternative response may be characterized in the "non-assertive-aggressive-assertive" paradigm.

Each of the situations presented is designed for use as described in Chapter VI:

1. Select a situation appropriate to your needs.

2. Read the situation description, filling in such details as may be desired.

3. Follow Steps 4 to 7 utilizing the alternative responses suggested here for the situation, as well as others you may think of.

4. Enact the role-playing and feedback exercises described in Steps 8, 10, 11, and 12.

5. Continue with remaining steps of the Step-by-Step Process.

The examples are grouped according to several characteristic types of situations: close personal, consumer, employment, school and community, and social. In each case only a few situations are suggested although the number of categories and examples is as infinite as life. In addition to this series of representative illustrations, you may on your own initiative apply assertive behavior to examples from your own life.

CLOSE PERSONAL SITUATIONS

Slumber Party
Your twelve-year-old daughter is having a slumber party with five other girls. It is past 2 a.m. and the girls should have settled down to sleep by now, but are still quite noisy.
Alternative Responses:
(a) You toss and turn in bed wishing your spouse would get up and say something to the girls. You do a slow burn, but just lie there trying to block out the sounds.

(b) Jumping out of bed, you thoroughly scold and berate the girls, especially your daughter, for their unladylike conduct.

(c) Talking to girls in a tone which they will recognize as meaning business, you tell them that they have had enough fun for tonight. You point out that you need to arise early tomorrow, and that everyone needs to get to sleep.

Late for Dinner
Your husband was supposed to be home for dinner right after work. Instead, he returns hours later explaining he was out with the boys for a few drinks. He is somewhat tipsy.
Alternative Responses:
(a) You say nothing about how discourteous he has been to you, but simply start preparing something for him to eat.

(b) Screaming, yelling, or crying, you make the point very clear that you think he is a drunken fool, doesn't care about your feelings, is a poor example for the children, and ask what will the neighbors think. You tell him he can get his own dinner.

(c) You calmly and steadfastly let him know that he should have informed you beforehand that he was going out for a few drinks and would likely be late. You inform him that his cold dinner is in the kitchen.

Visiting Relative

Aunt Margaret, with whom you prefer not to spend much time, is on the telephone. She has just told you of her plans to spend three weeks visiting you, beginning next week.

Alternative Responses:

(a) You think "Oh, no!" but say "We'd love to have you come and stay as long as you like!"

(b) You tell her the children have just come down with bad colds, and the spare bed has a broken spring and you'll be going to Cousin Bill's weekend after next—none of which is true.

(c) You say "We'll be glad to have you come for the weekend, but we simply can't invite you for longer. A short visit is happier for everyone, and we'll want to see each other again sooner if we keep it brief."

"Past Midnight"

Your teenage son, Eric, has just returned from a school party. It is 3 o'clock in the morning, and you have been frantic, concerned primarily for his well being, since you had expected him home before midnight.

Alternative Responses:

(a) You turn over and go to sleep.

(b) You shout "Where the hell have you been? Do you have any idea what time it is? You've kept me up all night! You thoughtless, inconsiderate, selfish, no-good bum, I ought to make you sleep in the street!"

(c) You say "I have been very worried about you, son. You said you'd be home at midnight, and I have been frantic for hours. Are you alright? I wish you had called me!"

CONSUMER SITUATIONS

Haircut

At the barber shop, the barber has just finished cutting your hair and turns the chair toward the mirror so you can inspect. You feel that you would like the sides trimmed more.

Alternative Responses:

(a) You either nod your head in assent or say "That's ok" or say nothing.

(b) Abruptly you state that he should have done a more thorough job or say sarcastically "You sure didn't take much off the sides, did you?"

(c) You point out that you would like to have the sides trimmed more and ask if he would do so.

Short-changed

As you are leaving a store after purchasing some item, you discover that you have been short-changed by 70 cents.

Alternative Responses:

(a) Pausing for a moment, you try to decide if 70 cents is worth the effort. After a few moments, you decide it is not and go on your way.

(b) You hurry back in the store and loudly demand that you receive back your 70 cents, making a derogatory comment about "cashiers who can't add."

(c) Re-entering the store, you catch the attention of the clerk, saying that you believe you were short-changed by 70 cents. In the process of explaining you display the change you received back.

Waiting in Line

(a) You are standing near a cash register waiting to pay for your purchase and have it wrapped. Others, who come after you, are being waited on first. You are getting tired of waiting.

Alternative Responses:

(a) You either take the article back to where you picked it up or edge up closer trying to catch the eye of the clerk.

(b) Shouting that you sure get poor service in this store, you slam the intended purchase down on the counter and walk out of the store.

(c) In a voice loud enough to be heard, you tell the clerk you were ahead of people who had already been waited upon. Further state that you would like to be waited on now.

EMPLOYMENT SITUATIONS

Working Late

You and your spouse have an evening engagement which has been planned for several weeks. Today is the date and you plan to leave immediately after work. During the day, however, your supervisor indicates that he would like you to stay late this evening to work on a special assignment.

Alternative Responses:

(a) You say nothing about your important plans and simply agree to stay until the work is finished.

(b) In a nervous, abrupt voice you say "No, I will not work late tonight." Then you criticize the boss for not planning the work schedule better. You then turn back to the work you were doing.

(c) Talking to the supervisor in a firm, but pleasant voice, you tell of your important plans and say you will not be able to stay this evening to work on the special assignment.

Job Error

You have made a mistake on some aspect of your job. Your supervisor discovers it and is letting you know rather harshly that you should not have been so careless.

Alternative Responses:

(a) Overapologizing, you say you are sorry, you were stupid, how silly of you, you'll never let it happen again.

(b) You bristle up and say that he has no business whatsoever criticizing your work. You tell him to leave you alone and not bother you in the future because you are capable of handling your own work.

(c) You agree that you made the mistake, say you are sorry and will be more careful next time. You add that you feel he is being somewhat harsh and you see no need for that.

Tardy

One of your subordinates has been coming in late consistently for the last three or four days.

Alternative Responses:

(a) You grumble to yourself or to others about the situation, but say nothing to the person, hoping he will start coming in early.

(b) You tell the worker off, indicating that he has no right to take advantage of you and that he had better get to work on time or else you will see that he is fired.

(c) Approaching the worker, you point out that you have observed him coming in late recently and wonder if there is an explanation. If he does not have a legitimate excuse, you say firmly that he should start coming to work on time. If the excuse seems legitimate, you still say that he should have come to you and explained the situation rather than saying nothing at all, leaving you "up in the air."

SCHOOL AND COMMUNITY SITUATIONS

Quiet Prof
You are in a physics lecture with 300 students. The professor speaks softly and you know that many others are having the same trouble hearing him that you are experiencing.
Alternative Responses:
(a) You continue to strain to hear, eventually move closer to the front of the room, but say nothing about his too-soft voice.
(b) You yell out "Speak up!"
(c) You raise your hand, get the professor's attention, and ask if he would mind speaking louder.

Clarification
In an English class, the teacher is discussing the contributions of classical language to modern English. You are puzzled by several of the references, and believe he has misstated an important concept.
Alternative Responses:
(a) You say nothing, but continue to puzzle over the concept, looking up another source at the library later in the day.
(b) You interrupt, telling him he has made an error, pointing out the mistake and correcting him from your own knowledge of the subject. Your tone and choice of words make him look somewhat ill-at-ease.
(c) You ask the teacher to further explain the concept, expressing your confusion and noting the source of your conflicting information.

Morals
You are one of eleven students in a psychology group discussion on human sexuality. The concepts being supported by three or four of the more verbal students are contrary to your personal moral code.

Alternative Responses:

(a) You listen quietly, not disagreeing openly with the other members or describing your own views.

(b) You loudly denounce the views which have been expressed. Your defense of your own belief is strong, and you urge others to accept your point of view as the only correct one.

(c) You speak up in support of your own beliefs, identifying yourself with an apparently unpopular position, but not disparging the beliefs of others in the group.

"Know It All"

As a member of the community beautification committee, you are dismayed by the continued dominance of group discussion by Mr. Brown, an opinionated member who has "the answer" to every question. He has begun another tirade. As usual, no one has said anything about it after several minutes.

Alternative Responses:

(a) Your irritation increases, but you remain silent.

(2) You explode verbally, curse Mr. Brown for "not giving anyone else a chance", and declare his ideas out-of-date and worthless.

(3) You interrupt, saying "Excuse me Mr. Brown." When recognized, you express your personal irritation about Mr. Brown's monopoly on the group's time. Speaking to Mr. Brown as well as the other group members, you suggest a discussion procedure which will permit all members an opportunity to take part, and will minimize domination by a single outspoken individual.

SOCIAL SITUATIONS

Breaking the Ice

At a party where you don't know anyone except the host, you want to circulate and get to know others. You walk up to three people talking.

Alternative Responses:

(a) You stand close to them and smile but say nothing, waiting for them to notice you.

(b) You listen to the subject they are talkingabout, then break in and state you disagree with someone's viewpoint.

(c) You break in while they are talking and introduce yourself.

(d) You wait for a pause in the conversation then introduce yourself and ask if you may join in.

Making a Date

You are interested in a date with a person of the opposite sex whom you have met and talked with three or four times recently.

Alternative Responses:

(a) You sit around the telephone going over in your mind what you will say and how your friend will respond. Several times you lift the phone and are almost finished dialing, then hang up.

(b) You phone and as soon as your friend answers you respond by saying "Hi baby, we're going out together this weekend." Seemingly taken back, your friend asks who is calling.

(c) You call, and when your friend answers you ask how school (job, etc.) is going. The reply is "Fine, except I am worried about a test I will be taking soon." Following the lead, you talk for a few minutes about the test. Then you say that there is a show downtown this Friday evening and that you would like it if the two of you would go together.

Smoke Gets in Your Lungs

You are at a public meeting in a large room. A man enters the room and sits down next to you, puffing enthusiastically on a large cigar. The smoke is very offensive to you.

Alternative Responses:

(a) You suffer the offensive smoke in silence, deciding it is the right of the other person to smoke if he wishes.

(b) You become very angry, demand that he move or put out the cigar and loudly assail the evils and health hazards of the smoking habit.

(c) You firmly but politely ask him to refrain from smoking because it is offensive to you, or to sit in another seat if he prefers to continue smoking.

Part Two

For The Facilitator

XI

Facilitator Preparation

"How do therapists learn to be assertiveness trainers?" Since the first edition of *Your Perfect Right* thousands of human service professionals have asked that question. AT is now commonplace in graduate schools of counselor education, social work, psychology, nursing, theology and others. Indeed, you may be reading this book in conjunction with such a training program.

As a foundation for offering AT to others, it should be evident that we believe the therapist should be or become personally assertive in his/her *own* life. In addition, we mused, if the adage "A therapist must have therapy" applies to the assertive behavior facilitator, shouldn't potential assertiveness trainers have personal training themselves before being allowed to practice? (We could then set up exclusive and expensive workshops, certifying "qualified" assertive trainers . . .).

We do consider several steps to be important in becoming a *qualified* facilitator of assertive behavior in others. It is particularly important that professionals prepare themselves adequately to offer a high level of service, since an unfortunately large amount of work called "assertiveness training" is being done by persons who have no qualifications (other than the "assertiveness" to say "I am going to do assertiveness training")!

The statement of *Principles for Ethical Practice of Assertive Behavior Training* (Appendix B) identifies general and specific qualifications for AT interventions at three levels: assertive behavior *training*; assertive behavior *therapy*; and *training of trainers*. We support and advocate the minimum standards identified in that statement.

In brief, the "General Qualifications" considered to be a minimum requirement for professional facilitators in all settings and at all levels include:

A) Understanding of basic principles of learning and behavior;
B) Understanding of anxiety and its effects upon behavior;
C) Knowledge of limitations, contraindications, and potential dangers of AT;
D) Training as a facilitator under qualified supervision.

Additional "Specific Qualifications" detailed in the statement suggest the need for graduate level training in one of the human services professions (e.g., Psychology, education, social work, counseling, nursing, medicine, human development, theology, public health). The level of training proposed increases as one assumes increasing responsibility: least formal training is required for those who would do non-clinical *training*; more for those who would do AT as *therapy*; and most for those who would *train trainers*. The difference between training and therapy is not always clear, but the ethics statement offers guidelines to help the facilitator in deciding if his/her qualifications are adequate (see 3.2.A, 3.2.B, and 5.A-G).

(As this third edition of *Your Perfect Right* goes to press [March 1978], Dr. Pat Jakubowski has informed us of her very recent work in developing a set of "competencies" for AT facilitators. It is hoped that such behavioral criteria for qualification of facilitators will make "academic" credentials less important. Nevertheless, at this time, adequate formal training and the other qualifications identified in this chapter and in Appendix B are the most adequate criteria available. Updated information will be published in the *ASSERT* newsletter.)

In addition to the specific recommendations in the ethics statement, we suggest that potential facilitators acquire the following preparation:

Knowledge of Basic Learning Principles: Although this step ordinarily will have been accomplished in formal training as a facilitator, it would be helpful to study a text such as Bandura's (1969) *Principles of*

Behavior Modification, and Wolpe's *Practice of Behavior Therapy* (1973).

Familiarity with the Literature: The "annotated bibliography" and the remaining technical literature in the "references" section should be used as a guide to study. One should also keep abreast of pertinent material in current journals and books in the field. Perhaps the most comprehensive presentation of AT in print is Alberti's edited volume *Assertiveness: Innovations, Applications, Issues* (1977). Various training courses, workshops, institutes and graduate programs in assertiveness training are being offered currently and should be investigated. Especially helpful in announcing further training available to professionals are: *Journal of Behavior Therapy and Experimental Psychiatry*; the Association for Advancement of Behavior Therapy *Newsletter*; the American Psychological Association *Monitor*; the *Guidepost* of the American Personnel and Guidance Association; and *Assert: The Newsletter of Assertive Behavior and Personal Development* (available from Impact Publishers).

Practice with Components: Actually experiencing the full range of the assertive process in a variety of typical situations enables the facilitator more fully to understand what the client experiences. If a client is having difficulty expressing anger in a situation, you will be much more helpful if you yourself have experienced the situation covertly, modeled it, roleplayed, shaped and coached it. One approach is to work with a fellow staff member or a client volunteer. Get together and alternate the roles of client and facilitator, experiment with a variety of situations and techniques. Video tape equipment can be invaluable in your learning process. If available, some type of physiological measuring and feedback device may also provide useful data.

Personal Assertiveness: Anyone who sets out to increase assertiveness in others must first be *actively* assertive. The passive knowledge of assertive behavior gained by reading the first portion of *Your Perfect Right* is only a beginning. In our personal lives we are continually aware of situations in which these principles might be applied. For us this awareness has four benefits: 1) keeping the "air clear" in our own interpersonal functioning; 2) pursuing actual opportunities to practice in the "real world," 3) adding to our on-going examples to report to our individuals and groups,

4) minimizing our own cognitive dissonance which can result from "writing the book" on assertive training yet not acting assertively!

By experiencing ourselves the great potential of being in control of our own lives and realizing *how satisfying that feels*, we've become more convincing models and coaches of assertiveness. It is exciting for us to experience changes in our level of assertiveness over a period of years. We both believe we have improved a great deal in all phases of assertiveness as we have continued learning and practicing.

Commitment to Ethical Principles: Since AT has become so popular in recent years, we are concerned about high standards of AT practice, and appropriate qualifications and ethics of facilitators. Evaluate your own qualifications in the light of the statement of *Principles for Ethical Practice of Assertive Behavior Training*, and offer only those services for which you are truly qualified. We urge you to become familiar with the statement and, if you are or intend to be an AT facilitator, to support and function within its guidelines.

XII

Assessment of Non-Assertive, Aggressive and Assertive Behavior

Preliminary Considerations

The helping person who wishes to facilitate assertiveness must first ascertain as clearly as possible the exact nature of the other person's difficulty, *in order to decide if assertiveness training is appropriate or if it is necessary at all*. Perhaps the client needs support until a crisis blows over, in which case it would be premature to start assertiveness training. Moreover, the *generally non-assertive* individual may be so shy and withdrawn that even the suggestion of assertiveness training may cause somatic reactions such as flushing and stomach pains. The therapist must be especially careful not to overwhelm this type of client. In such cases, we may administer an anxiety measure, such as the *Willoughby Schedule* (Wolpe, 1958; Hestand, 1971) and/or the *Fear Survey Schedule* (Wolpe, 1969) and often find it necessary for these clients to experience systematic desensitization or other therapeutic measures to reduce fears of criticism and/or rejection. Even when assertiveness training is initiated, with such individuals it is best to start with a one-to-one situation rather than a group setting.

A *generally aggressive* individual may also be a poor candidate for AT until given other types of therapy. Although the actions may imply one

123

who is very brave and very capable, we often find that underneath he or she is easily hurt and has learned not to show it, but rather, to bluster or to manipulate. For this reason, facilitators may wish to hold these clients out of groups in which they would tend to dominate the non-assertive members, until therapy has helped them to deal less defensively and aggressively with their own anxiety.

Assessment Methods

The primary method we employ in assessing non-assertive or aggressive behavior patterns is simply listening to the individual describe relationships with others who are important in the client's life. One may carefully explore with the person interactions with (depending upon age and life style) parents, peers, co-workers, classmates, spouse, children, bosses, employees, teachers, salesmen, neighbors, relatives. In assessing, one may ask who is dominant in these specific relationships: Is the person easily taken advantage of in dealings with others? Are feelings and ideas openly expressed in most circumstances? Does he or she take advantage of and/or hurt others frequently?

In addition Wolpe (1969) and Lazarus (1971) suggest questions which are useful in the process of pinpointing responses which are maladaptive for an individual (e.g., Are you able to contradict a domineering person?). Responses are easily pursued to thoroughly explore the client's non-assertive, aggressive or assertive behavior. Keep in mind in your questioning to cover the area of very personal assertions as well as the more traditional areas. Once again, it should be remembered that behavior is person and situation specific, and must be examined in detail, rather than making generalized evaluations about the client's "personality."

Standardized Tests

Our emphasis is on locating current detailed examples of the client's behavior pattern. For this reason, if we use standardized tests in the diagnostic process, we first look at scores on individual scales, then attempt to discuss item-by-item with the client to find out exactly what was meant by the response. The process yields both insights of value in work with the client and practical experience in the training process.

Abundant standardized testing material is available. Most of the personality tests have scales which could be useful. Among those we have found valuable are the *Omnibus Personality Inventory,* the *Edwards Personal Preference Schedule, Eysenck Personality Inventory, Myers-Briggs Type Indicator,* and the *Marlow-Crowne Social Desirability Scale.*

Many scales have been developed to attempt to assess assertiveness directly. One of the most useful is the Gambrill-Richey "Assertion Inventory" (1975) in which the respondent is asked to report both the "degree of difficulty" in handling a series of situations, and the "response probability" that he or she will actually attempt to confront that scene.

Instruments which have been reported in the AT literature include the Action Situation Inventory (Friedman, 1971), the Adolescent Assertion Discrimination Test (Shoemaker, 1973 as cited in Bodner, 1975), the Adolescent Self-Expression Scale (McCarthy & Bellucci, 1974), the Adult Assertion Scale (Jakubowski & Wallace, 1975 as cited in Lange & Jakubowski, 1976), the Adult Self-Expression Scale (Gay, Hollandsworth & Galassi, 1975), the Assertion Inventory (Dalali, 1971), the Assertion Inventory (Fensterheim, 1971), The Assertion Inventory (Gambrill & Richey, 1975), the Assertiveness Inventory (Alberti & Emmons, 1974), the AQ test (Phelps & Austin, 1975), the College Self-Expression Scale (Galassi, DeLo, Galassi & Bastien, 1974), the Conflict Resolution Inventory (McFall & Lillesand, 1971) which was designed explicitly to measure refusal behavior, the Constriction Scale (Bates & Zimmerman, 1971), the Lawrence Assertive Inventory (Lawrence, 1970), the modified Rathus Assertiveness Schedule for the junior high level (Vaal & McCullagh, 1975), the Rathus Assertiveness Schedule (Rathus, 1973), the modified Rathus Assertiveness Schedule for Children (d'Amico, 1977), and the Wolpe-Lazarus Assertiveness Questionnaire (Wolpe and Lazarus, 1966).

We have often been asked about validation studies, scoring procedures, and norms for our *Assertiveness Inventory* (see Chapter IV). The *Inventory* is *not* a validated instrument and has no formalized "scoring" or normative data. It is useful as a clinical tool, primarily when the facilitator reviews each item individually with the trainee.

Note: we consider any assessment of assertiveness to be adequate only insofar as it takes into account the three dimensions we have discussed throughout this book: *attitudes, skills,* and *anxiety.*

In Vivo Behavioral Measures

It is desirable whenever possible to incorporate live behavioral tests to determine the degree of one's difficulty with assertiveness. Assessment may be based on post-situation self report, expert judgements of performance, and physiological measures of anxiety. Audio and video tape recording devices are useful in sampling client behavior in these situations. Examples of applications of such approaches are given in McFall and Marston (1970), Friedman (1971), and Eisler, Miller, and Hersen (1974). Another valuable contribution to behavioral measures is the "unobtrusive" approach of Cummins (1978).

Bodner (1975) has provided an excellent review of assessment in AT, including paper-and-pencil, observational, and behavioral measures. Galassi and Galassi (1977) have prepared an extensive discussion of AT assessment, with guidelines for developing an individualized scale.

XIII

Therapeutic Facilitation

We would like to begin this discussion by stressing that all clients, not only those who are considered to be generally non-assertive or generally aggressive, may need a more thorough treatment program than assertiveness training alone can provide. Emmons (1977, 1978) has recently written about a framework for a more complete therapeutic approach by placing AT into an "holistic-eclectic" format. Emphasizing the importance of going beyond a single method, and of dealing with "non-psychological" complaints. Emmons stresses that AT therapists should be concerned with treating (or referring to other specialists for treatment) the whole person: psychologically, physically, spiritually.

Assertiveness training is a very powerful way to help clients, but the facilitator should be prepared to assess the person's needs in all areas, in order to offer responsible treatment or referral. AT is *one* tool in an adequate therapeutic response to client needs. Thorough assessment of those needs, and a careful decision that AT is the most appropriate intervention, are mandatory elements in responsible application of assertiveness training.

Part 5 of the *Principles for Ethical Practice of Assertive Behavior Training* describes seven dimensions which should be evaluated in determining the appropriateness and level of an AT intervention: *client; problem/goals; facilitator; setting; time/duration; method; outcome.* (Refer to Appendix B for more detail).

Client Preparation

In Chapter IV we treated the basic elements of assertive motivation. We assume the professional reader is thoroughly familiar with that material, since the process of preparing for assertive living is essentially similar for facilitator or client. A key factor in the motivational process is familiarization with the difference between non-assertive, aggressive and assertive behavior. These distinctions should be well understood by the facilitator as well as the client.

Only when the facilitator feels the client is ready should the person be encouraged to initiate assertive behavior. Some will readily agree to try assertion on their own; these usually are the *situationally non-assertive* or *situationally aggressive.* With the *generally non-assertive* and *generally aggressive*, however, more caution is advised; work with a therapist is usually called for.

Even if the client desires to initiate assertion without prior practice, we have learned to coax him or her into a trial run anyway. Typically, persons who are asked if they need to roleplay a situation will decline. Going beyond this superficial confidence and coaxing the client to practice reveals the difficulties he/she may encounter. Similarly, a trainee who reports aggression may reveal in role-play that he/she was merely being angry, *not* aggressive. We all have a perfect right to be angry, but not to demean someone's character in the process; role-playing helps get across the distinction. The point here is that even though certain individuals *may not* need modeling, role-playing, etc., it is wise for the facilitator to check first by having the client demonstrate. The "Method of Contrasted Role Plays" (MacNeilage and Adams, 1977), described later in this chapter, is useful here as well.

One-to-One Facilitation

Understanding our step-by-step process of assertiveness training will be improved by studying the following practical example. Please review the "self-directed" steps described in Chapter VI before proceeding.

Step 1: Be certain you are adequately prepared as a facilitator.

Review Chapter XI and the statement of *Principles for Ethical Practice of Assertive Behavior Training.* Be sure you have the necessary qualifications before proceeding.

Step 2: Do a thorough preliminary assessment of the needs of the client.

Review Chapters IV and XII. Select an appropriate assessment procedure for the client, and implement it.

Step 3: Identify the situation that needs attention.

Example:

CLIENT: This one boy has called me twice to ask me out and he just won't take my hints. I don't want to hurt his feelings by telling him the truth; what should I do when he calls again?

Step 4: Set up the scene.

Work with the client to structure closely the potential situation, in order to present the covert scene accurately and to simulate the feelings one has in the real situation.

Example:

FACILITATOR: You've decided you don't like him?

CL: No, he's a nice person, but we just don't have the same interests. Besides, I'm not attracted to him physically. I can't tell him that though; it would crush him.

Step 5: Present the situation to the person for covert rehearsal.

Example:

FA: Are you sure? I'd like for you to go over the situation in your imagination now. Close your eyes and imagine yourself receiving tne next call. Let yourself respond in whatever way you feel.

CL: (Silent, imagines scene.)

Step 6: Model an assertive response for the particular situation.

Present audio and video models if available. You may wish to tape your modeling here also.

Example:

FA: Now I'll show you *one* way to approach him. Pretend I am you and you are him. Call me.

FA: Hello, this is Dorothy.

CL: Hi, this is Harold . . . (*small talk*) . . . Say, there is a great movie playing downtown on Friday, and I would love to have you go with me. I'll be so disappointed if you can't go.

FA: I really am busy on Friday, but I've been wanting to talk to you about us anyway, Harold. I feel I have been misleading you, and I want to straighten things out. I really am concerned about hurting you, but I don't see any future in our relationship.

CL: Why? What have I done wrong?

FA: That's just it; you've done nothing wrong. I feel that our interests aren't the same, and I'm not really attracted to you.

CL: Oh. (Pause).

FA: I hope you aren't too disappointed, but I had to be honest with you, so I wouldn't hurt you more later.

CL: Well, I appreciate that anyway. So, I guess I shouldn't call you anymore.

FA: That would be best.

CL: Goodby.

FA: Bye.

CL: What if he hangs up halfway through the conversation?

FA: If you are truly assertive, most likely that won't occur; but if it does, that is just the way it has to be.

Step 7: Answer the client's questions about how you handled the situation.

Point out the differences between assertive versus non-assertive and aggressive responses. Stress non-verbal factors if they are pertinent. Discuss philosophical concerns.

Example:

CL: Wouldn't it be better to tell white lies like "I have to wash my hair" so he'll get the hint?

FA: You've tried hints already and they haven't worked. Even if they eventually did work, you actually are hurting him and yourself more in the long run by not being honest with your feelings.

Step 8: Repeat Step 5.

Covert rehearsal based on the client's use of an effective model for handling the situation. Encourage client to imagine a positive outcome.

Step 9: Rehearse the scene once again.

This time the client role-plays him/herself. Audio or video tape if possible.

Step 10: Go over the performance.

Provide feedback and coaching where needed. Don't forget positive reinforcement.

Example:

FA: You did an excellent job! I liked the way you stuck to your point when he tried to persuade you to let him call again. Your voice was a little soft and somewhat shaky. Let's do it again and try to use a stronger voice.

Step 11: Repeat Steps 6 through 10 as often as needed.

Alternate between modeling and role-playing and provide coaching so as to shape the behavior to the *client's* satisfaction.

Step 12: The person is now ready to test the new response pattern in the actual situation.

Up to this point the preparation has taken place in a relatively secure environment. Nevertheless, careful training and repeated practice have developed a much more adequate reaction to the situation. The client should thus be reassured if necessary and encouraged to proceed *in vivo*. If he/she is unwilling to do so, further rehearsals may be needed.

Example:

FA: How do you feel about using your new approach with him when he calls again?

CL: I think I'm ready, and I know he's going to call.

FA: Well, I feel good about how you've handled it here, so I also think you're ready.

Step 13: The client should be encouraged to return as soon as practical following the in vivo trial, in order to review the effort.

The therapist should reward whatever degree of success the person experiences, and offer continued assistance.

Example:

FA: I want you to keep a record of how it goes, what he says, what you say, your feelings and so on. Then come in as soon as you can after it is over, so we can review how you did, O.K?

CL: O.K.

Further elaboration on Step 12 may be in order at this point:

The client's initial attempts at being assertive should be chosen for their high potential of success, so as to provide reinforcement. This point, of course, is important with all beginning asserters, but especially the *generally non-assertive* and *generally aggressive*. The more successfully one asserts the more likely one is to do so from then on. Additionally, the individual who reports to the facilitator an instance of successful assertion obtains added reinforcement. The facilitator must be very capable of providing verbal reinforcement for each of the trainee's successful assertive acts.

Initially then, the individual should begin with small assertions that are likely to be successful and rewarded, and from there proceed to more difficult assertions. Ideally each step should be explored with the facilitator until the client-trainee is capable of being fully in control of most situations. He or she should be warned against taking initiative to attempt a difficult assertion at first without special preparation. The facilitator also should particularly beware of instigating an assertion where the trainee is likely to fail miserably, thus inhibiting further attempts at assertiveness.

If the trainee does suffer a setback, which very well may happen, the facilitator must be ready to help analyze the situation and to help rebuild confidence. Especially in the early stages of assertion, trainees are prone to mistakes either of inadequate technique or of overzealousness to the point of aggression. Either miscue could cause negative returns, particularly if the other individual, the "receiver," becomes hostile and highly aggressive. Therefore, the facilitator must be prepared to serve as a buffer and to help re-establish motivation.

Most trainees will have more than one specific problem with being assertive. In the above case, for example, the woman may have difficulty returning items to a store or gaining her rights with roommates. The same basic process with variations may be used for each situation. The individuality of the client must always be accommodated. Facilitators are encouraged to provide a learning environment in which the trainee may grow in assertiveness, and carefully to avoid "shoving it down the throat."

Near the end of an assertiveness training process perhaps ranging from several weeks to several months duration, we point out important factors for the future. First, is the need for continued practice in real-life situations. We point out the desirability for the client to make conscious efforts to practice for a period of six months after leaving, and encourage re-reading this book as often as needed to provide continuing motivation and reinforcement for assertive ventures.

A final important factor in establishing a lasting, independent behavior pattern is to help the trainee understand the need for on-going self-reinforcement. It is necessary for the trainee, in order to maintain newly-developed assertive behavior, to achieve reinforcement within the immediate social environment. Without the benefit of regular reinforcement from the facilitator, the ex-client must gain rewards for assertiveness from other sources in his/her own unique life situation. Preparation for independent functioning must take place long before the end of the therapeutic intervention, of course.

Group Facilitation

When the first edition of *Your Perfect Right* was published, little work had been done on assertiveness training in groups. Since that time we have come to see the AT group as the "treatment of choice" for most persons who wish to develop their assertiveness. The process of assertive behavior development may be very effectively applied in a group setting. With many trainees this approach is more effective than one-to-one therapy because of the expanded potential for interaction with others during the training process.

Several specific advantages result from a small group. The non-assertive or aggressive person, as we have already demonstrated, typically encounters great anxiety in certain life situations when faced with confronting other people. Learning assertiveness in a group provides a "laboratory" of other people with whom to work. By discovering that they share similar problems, each is less "alone." A group is typically understanding and supportive—a social environment in which each person can be accepted, and thus be comfortable enough to experiment with new behavior.

With several individuals undertaking assertiveness training together, there is a broader base for social modeling. Each trainee sees several others learning to act assertively, and each is able to learn from the strengths and weaknesses of the others.

A group provides more diverse perspectives for feedback than can an individual facilitator. Hearing reactions from several different persons can speed the behavior-shaping process for each trainee.

Social situations involving a number of people are a frequent source of anxiety. Work in a group gives a realistic opportunity to face several people and overcome that difficulty in a relatively safe training environment.

The group is, of course, a powerful source of social reinforcement for each of its members. Knowing several others are "expecting" one's growth and active effort toward assertiveness, each member may be stimulated to greater achievement than when working alone. And, for its part, the group rewards new assertiveness with all the force of its social approval.

In the use of the small group setting for assertiveness training, it is important to recognize that some trainees are so anxious about their interpersonal contacts that they may be unable to face even a congenial group of others with similar problems. In such cases, of course, individual work is essential, at least until the trainee feels able to enter a group. Obviously group work is not called for in all cases, and the facilitator who works with both group and individual clients will consider the needs and capacities of each person in suggesting one or both approaches.

Preparation of the group for working effectively together will depend upon the institutional setting, the skill and attitudes of the facilitator, and the readiness of group members to respond openly and honestly to one another. Because a discussion of the process of personal interaction in groups is beyond the scope of this book, the interested reader is referred to the excellent treatises of Yalom (1970), and Houts and Serber (1972). It has been our experience with assertive behavior groups that an atmosphere of trust and concern by group members for one another will grow out of the training process, and that growth toward common objectives will provide the cohesiveness necessary to develop an effective working group. The facilitator, acting as model and guide, sets the tone, and by example encourages trust, support and positive regard for each member of the group.

The Make-up of Assertiveness Training Groups

Our typical assertiveness training group has from five to twelve members. Fewer than five restricts the potential for social modeling, limits the sources of feedback, and fails to provide the range of behavior styles needed for each trainee to experience a variety of others as each tries out new assertive behaviors. We prefer, when possible, to balance the number of men and women in our groups, since social relationships with the opposite sex are a frequent source of anxiety for our non-assertive and aggressive clients. A group with equal numbers of each sex has enhanced opportunity for helping its members to deal effectively with social situations involving the opposite sex. We recognize that much work has been done with same-sex groups, particularly for women. There is no doubt some value in such programs, but our preference is to create a more nearly representative microcosm of the "real world." For some clients, however, work in a same-sex group may be a desirable prerequisite to a mixed group.

Because we function in a university counseling center, our groups are usually scheduled to coincide with the academic term. Thus we typically meet one hour twice each week for eight or nine weeks—a total of sixteen to eighteen hours. We have experimented with alternatives to this approach. We have conducted a group for five or six weeks (10 or 12 one-hour sessions), then suspended meetings for approximately three weeks, reconvening again toward the end of the term for a follow-up meeting. This approach can be nearly as successful as our longer groups. The basic concepts of assertion can be covered and practiced within this short period of time. Motivation tends to remain high for both facilitator and members; absenteeism is almost non-existent. The break allows members time to identify any major obstacles which may need more attention. If necessary, further work with assertion on a one-to-one basis can be arranged. In selected cases additional therapeutic measures may also be needed. We have also worked on a two-hours-once-a-week schedule. The latter has the advantage of a longer and often more intensive session, but the long interval between sessions seems to be a significant loss to the behavior shaping process. Ideally, perhaps one-and-one-half hours twice each week would best achieve the goals of an assertive behavior group (we have no controlled experimental data to support this conclusion, however). Brief introductory groups as short as eight one-hour sessions have also been conducted with some success, particularly for those clients who are primarily in need of enhanced awareness of the potential of assertiveness.

Groups led by co-facilitators are, in our experience, more effective environments for client growth than those led by individual facilitators. Attrition is lower, enthusiasm higher, and both self report and facilitator observation of growth are greater. We have worked with each other, with other staff counselors, and with M.A.-level counselor-trainees. Co-facilitators are most effective when they are open and honest with each other and with group members, possess complimentary skills and facilitation styles, and are both openly enthusiastic about assertive training. In addition, although we have been consistently most effective in assertive groups when working together, we encourage a male-female co-facilitator team. Effective models of assertiveness of each sex are valuable resources for assertive behavior groups.

The Assertiveness Training Process in Groups

The first session of our training groups is devoted to a didactic presentation on assertive behavior, followed by the usual round of introduction of group members.

Opening with background material on what the group will be all about, we utilize the non-assertive-aggressive-assertive paradigm described in Chapter II. We call attention to the behavior-attitude cycle, and point out the importance of practice with support and reinforcement from the group. Members are cautioned that assertiveness training is not a panacea, and that they will not discover miraculous changes overnight. They are also told that occasional failure is to be expected, but will not stop long-term progress.

We give several typical examples to illustrate our contention that assertiveness is a better way than the other two alternatives. Next, we indicate how the group will be structured, outlining the exercises in which each will participate. We request that members keep an ongoing log of their progress emphasizing specific, detailed examples. In summing up, we give a basic pep talk about becoming thoroughly involved in changing, the need for risk-taking, and the progress others have made. Throughout, we encourage the participants to ask questions, even though getting a group of primarily non-assertive people to initiate questions is often difficult. At this time, each member is asked to write down specific behaviors within our non-assertive-aggressive-assertive framework which they wish to change.

Upon the completion of these preliminaries, we take time to go around the group and introduce ourselves. Even this initial exercise is handled as a demonstration of the facilitation process to be used in the group. The facilitator asks members to close their eyes and visualize themselves completing the task at hand, then models the self-introduction, emphasizing personal background and reasons for being involved in an assertive group. The covert step is then repeated, after which we go around with the self-introduction, including the co-therapist. Finally, we discuss what has taken place, giving impressions about how the exercise proceeded, and pointing out that this will be the style of operation for this group (covert, modeling, behavior rehearsal).

The format established in the first group meeting with the introductions exercise is followed throughout the life of the assertive training group: a situation is posed; the members are asked to fantasize their individual responses to it; a model (often but not always the facilitator) role-plays the scene; the group briefly discusses the modeling behavior; a new covert response is called for; individual members role-play and are given feedback. Thus the major three facilitative components of assertive training (covert rehearsal, modeling, and behavior rehearsal) are "built-in" to the group facilitation process for each separate situation covered.

Following this pattern, the first few weeks of group meetings are structured so that each member participates in several fundamental exercises (not necessarily in this order):

1. Breaking into a small group of strangers already engaged in conversation at a party.
2. Starting a conversation with a stranger in a classroom, on a bus, at a meeting. Maintaining a conversation.
3. Returning faulty or defective items to a store.
4. Assertiveness with significant others: parents, roommates, spouses, boy-girl friends.
5. Saying "no" to a request for a favor.

6. Assertive anger expression.

7. Asking for a date/refusing a date (telephone and face-to-face).

8. Compliments; caring; feelings; "soft assertions."

9. Public speaking.

10. Learning how to argue or stand up for oneself with a dominant or dogmatic opinionated person.

We operate with considerable flexibility, and may leave out some situations or add others, according to the apparent needs of a particular group.

After each member of the group has completed the basic exercises, we encourage them to bring to the group current life situations which are troubling them. Although no one is denied the opportunity to present a personal situation earlier in the group process, we find that most participants, as in more traditional forms of group therapy, are reluctant to expose much of themselves very early in the life of the group. Thus it is usually more valuable to structure the first meetings, and move toward member-initiated activities after the facilitation process is well established, and participants have come to trust one another more fully. At this point individual situations presented in the group frequently relate to intimate relationships: How can I tell my father to stop nagging me? How can I tell my boyfriend that I don't really love him? My roommate has terrible B.O! My boss keeps making passes at me. I yell at my wife and children every day when I get home from work. No one pays any attention to me.

Such situations strike very close to home, of course, and are more sensitive and difficult to handle than the "clerk-in-the-store" variety, since they involve on-going relationships with a great emotional investment. Sensitivity, patience, and careful attention to the principles of assertiveness—and to the consideration of consequences—are in order here, and the facilitator is cautioned against pat solutions to unique individual problems. Under these conditions other members of a perceptive and caring group are often the most valuable resource to the facilitator. In any event, rehearsing approaches to significant others is usually very worthwhile in the group, if only to gain a better understanding of one's own feelings about the person/situation. It is a rare group which does not offer support and caring in delicate situations.

Practice in the expression of caring for another is, of course, an important goal of an assertiveness training group (Chapter VII). We focus considerable attention upon the verbal expression of positive feelings toward oneself and others.

Similarly, at another point in the emotional spectrum, putting angry feelings into words is a useful group exercise. We have encouraged group members to practice anger (Chapter VIII).

As our assertive behavior group nears the end of its schedule, we assist each member to sensitize him/her self to sources of continuing reinforcement for assertion in his/her unique individual life environment. The group has been an important center of support for the developing assertiveness of each member. Now, however, each must take responsibility for identifying and expanding sources of support within his/her own "ecosystem."

The final meeting of our assertive behavior training group is usually devoted to a very positive uplifting emotional experience developed by psychologist Herbert Otto: the "Strength Bombardment." Each member of the group is given approximately one minute to speak about him/herself in only *positive* terms—no qualifiers, no criticisms, no "buts." Immediately thereafter, the rest of the group gives to this member an additional two minutes of *positive* feedback. The time may be varied to suit the group, but caution is urged: don't allow enough for embarrassing—and painful—silence. The "clock-watcher" can be flexible, but the important note is that this must be a positive experience for *each* member. The facilitator needs to be prepared to fill any gaps in the feedback portion for the most "unlovable" group member, and to encourage the too-modest reluctant starter. The facilitator is encouraged to be the first speaker in this exercise, as a model of self-assertion and to demonstrate appropriate positive statements to make about oneself.

On Improving Feedback in Groups

One of the important values of using a group format for AT is the diversity of viewpoints available for providing feedback to participants on the effectiveness of their assertions. Nevertheless, many group members find it difficult to give good feedback, and it is valuable to spend some time training a group in how the members can best help each other.

Toward that goal, it is suggested that a number of qualities of good interpersonal feedback be pointed out to the group. The following list should prove helpful, and the facilitator's experience will provide additional guidelines.

Helpful feedback:
- describes *specific* verbal and non-verbal behaviors in detail;
- avoids telling "how *I* would do it;"
- focuses on the *behavior*, not the *person*;
- gives *observations* and *descriptions*, not *opinions* and *judgements*;
- is for the benefit of the *receiver*, not the *giver*;
- gives *information*, not *instructions*, thus allowing the trainee to choose what he or she will do with the information.

One additional comment about feedback which may be of interest. A number of groups in Southern California have utilized poker chips as tokens, encouraging group members to toss a chip at the feet of a member to indicate—by chip color—whether a particular action was assertive, non-assertive, or aggressive. The immediacy of such feedback is valuable, and the chips themselves create a novel source of group interest (and fun!). However, such global feedback needs to be supplemented with specifics about behavior as soon afterward as possible, in order to be of maximum value in aiding the development of more effective behavior.

A Further Word on Assertive Groups
We have described here in considerable detail an approach to facilitating assertive groups which has worked well for us over a period of years. Our style has modified, of course, as we have found new and better means for achieving the goals of our group participants. Nevertheless, we are under no illusion that there is only one way to conduct effective assertive training groups. We know that many of our colleagues find other styles more appropriate in their own group work, some with more structure, some with less, some more rigorous in application of learning principles, others with a greater humanistic-existential flavor.

Although we have no quarrel with these and other approaches to the development of assertive behavior, we remain convinced that application of the principles detailed in this book will enable *clients* to achieve *their* behavioral goals. And that, for us, is the ultimate criterion.

Other Formats for Assertiveness Training

In the four years since publication of the second edition of *Your Perfect Right*, there has been a tremendous increase in the literature of assertive behavior training. At this writing over twenty books and hundreds of articles and papers have been published. We will highlight a number of the important contributions and contributors to AT which have appeared in books or other published sources.

It is worth noting here that as AT has grown, it has become more specialized, and so has its literature. Thus we find that contributions to the AT literature may be classified as dealing primarily with *research* (study of assertiveness or of the AT process and its effects), *practice* (direct service to clients or trainees), and *professional issues* (questions of ethics, qualification of trainers, "faddishness," etc.). Moreover, the literature of AT *practice* may be further classified according to the populations served. AT books have been written for women, children, and minorities, as well as the "general" population (Populations with which AT has been used are summarized in the next chapter).

This wide range of interests of AT practitioners, researchers, and theorists, has led to the development of a variety of approaches to meet special needs, and to suit the styles of the professionals involved. We consider this diversity to have been very healthy for AT, since the resulting process has been enriched by a relatively free exchange of ideas and discoveries, in contrast to the common experience in which a therapeutic modality has been limited by rigid adherence to "rules" established by its "founding guru."

We have benefited from the excellent work of many colleagues around the world who have helped to develop effective AT procedures. The following material is a very brief overview of some of the important recent contributions to AT. Space and time make a fully comprehensive review impractical. We encourage the interested professional to read each of the sources cited, in the process of developing and refining your own style. The contributions are presented under three general themes which help to organize the material. Some items are contributions to the *general conceptualization* of AT; others deal with *innovative procedures*; a group of *specific techniques* are worth noting.

General Conceptualization of Assertiveness Training

Four social myths which are responsible for much non-assertive behavior have been described by *Sherwin Cotler* and *Julio Guerra* (1976). The myths of *anxiety, obligation, modesty,* and the *good friend* help to explain much of the belief system which inhibits self-assertion as it is defined by the popular (pre-AT) culture. Trainee understanding of the false premises inherent in these myths does much to free them to attempt assertions.

AT as a part of the broader framework of behavior therapy has been a theme of *Herbert Fensterheim* (1975), and *Spencer Rathus* (1977). Their work has focused attention on the need to view the clinical client in a broad therapeutic framework, with emphasis on anxiety reduction as well as assertion skills training. Fensterheim has also identified a number of "clinical problem types" which are amenable to AT treatment.

Cognitive restructuring, the process of aiding clients to change their self-defeating thoughts and statements, has been developed and advocated particularly by *Iris Fodor* and *Janet Wolfe* (1975), and *Arthur Lange* and *Patricia Jakubowski* (1976). They have developed (independent but complementary) systems for helping clients to overcome faulty belief systems and to gain more positive and rational conceptions of their life situations. Much of their work has integrated the Rational Emotive Therapy of Albert Ellis with AT. Moreover, they have been outspoken advocates of *responsibility* as an element of assertiveness, and of high ethical standards for facilitators.

Innovative Procedures

Listening, often overlooked as a component of interpersonal competence, has been incorporated into the AT model espoused by *Lynn Bloom, Karen Coburn,* and *Joan Pearlman* (1975). They suggest that attention to the other person is critical to responsible assertiveness, and present a specific "listening training" procedure.

Scripts, and a procedure for developing your own assertive messages, is a central feature of the work of *Sharon Bower* (1976), who presents very detailed procedures for her approach to AT. She offers scripts for specific life events, and a general formula (Describe behavior; Express feelings; Specify desired change; Identify Consequences) for preparing scripts to meet any situation. Her procedures are very systematic and highly detailed.

Cultural differences have been taken into consideration by very few AT practitioners or writers. *Donald Cheek* (1976) offers a thorough analysis of cultural considerations in AT. His material examines the effect on behavior of the psycho-social history of a group (specifically Blacks in America), and presents a new AT methodology designed to accommodate the special needs of Black clients. Of particular note are his emphasis on *language barriers* between black and white, and his concern for adapting the assertive message to the *target person*.

Assessment instruments in AT are plentiful (See Chapter XII). Thoroughly researched instruments, however, are few. *Merna* and *John Galassi* (1977) have been active researchers and practitioners in AT, and have studied assessment devices extensively, including development of their own college and adult "Self Expression Scales." Moreover, their most recent work demonstrates a methodology for devising an individualized assessment scale tailored to the needs of each trainee. They have also been leaders in the move to establish ethical principles for AT practice. Among the most widely used AT measures are the "Rathus Assertiveness Schedule," by *Spencer Rathus* (1973), and the "Assertion Inventory" by *Eileen Gambrill* and *Cheryl Richey* (1975).

Sherwin Cotler and *Julio Guerra* (1976) have assembled one of the most comprehensive data collection packages in use in AT. Their concern for client needs includes anxiety measures, assertiveness scales, goal surveys and homework diaries. They have emphasized systematic monitoring of trainee anxiety through use in AT of the numerical "Subjective Unit of Disturbance" scale first presented by Joseph Wolpe. The "personal effectiveness" skills training program (which parallels AT), developed by *Robert Liberman* and his associates (1976), includes a group procedure which calls for planning, work, and evaluation sessions, so that time is clearly provided for each of those three group tasks.

Specific Techniques

We mentioned earlier in this chapter that we tend to avoid the use of "techniques" or "gimmicks" in our own AT work. Nevertheless, many specific techniques have been effectively utilized by other practitioners and are worthy of mention here. Although we have noted, in the brief summaries below, names of professionals whom we associate with the development of a particular procedure, the exact origin of many techniques is unknown or simultaneous, and we make no claim for the accuracy of our attributions.

Homework Assignments take AT from the training environment into the "life space" of the trainee. Responsible and appropriate assignments are those which would be natural to the client's life style, and would not demand that he or she behave in embarrassing, highly unusual or bizarre fashion. *John Shelton* (1976, 1977) has been a major developer of systematic homework in AT and other forms of therapy.

Contrasted Role Plays, an insight-oriented model for role playing in AT groups, is the work of *Linda MacNeilage* and *Kathleen Adams* (1977). The model incorporates a Gestalt notion of "reconciliation of opposites" by having the trainee enact three contrasting responses to a situation (unassertive, aggressive, assertive), thus experiencing the full range of emotional and behavioral alternatives.

Verbal Techniques have been widespread and take many forms. The DESC scripts of *Sharon Bower* (see "Innovative Procedures" above) are a very precise guide to assertive language. *Myles Cooley* and *James Hollandsworth* (1977) have devised a "components" strategy for teaching assertive verbal content. They identify seven verbal components of assertive statements, classified in three general areas: saying 'no' or taking a stand (position, reason, understanding); asking favors or asserting rights (problem, request, clarification); and expressing feelings (personal expression).

Among the "last resort" techniques used by some trainers are the "broken record," "fog," "selective ignoring," and "critical inquiry," (*Cotler and Guerra, 1976*). Each of these is an effort to overcome unfair manipulation or attack, and are considered appropriate only when the trainee has decided that the potential consequence of ending the relationship is worth risking. Briefly, "broken record" involves repetitive expression of one's position; "fog" is a passive-aggressive agreement with the other person ("whatever you say, dear"); "selective ignoring" is just that— withholding any response when one feels the other is being unreasonable, unfair, or aggressive; "critical inquiry" is an invitation to the critical person to *be* even more critical, and thus emphasize undesired behavior. Once learned, of course, these techniques may be *used* aggressively and not just in self-defense. Cotler and Guerra are careful to point out the dangers in these "last resort" approaches, and do not advocate their general use. (Nor do *we*, needless to say!)

XIV

Applications of Assertive Training

We have previously suggested that the procedures described here have application in a broad range of human activities. Although most individuals will themselves be better able to identify the usefulness of AT in their own situations, this chapter provides an organized approach to a variety of settings for the assertive behavior development process.

Most of the examples suggested here have been drawn from the experiences of the authors, friends, colleagues, and students, or from professional literature. Others will doubtless occur to the practitioner in his or her own setting. Thus, although an attempt has been made to arrange these examples according to a variety of school, professional and community settings, it is recommended that each reader review the entire list. Keep in mind that, although the settings may vary, we consider the general principles of AT—*including the ethical principles noted in Appendix B*—to apply.

School and College Applications

Teachers: The classroom teacher will frequently find students who are non-assertive or aggressive, particularly with respect to classroom behavior. Assertiveness training has been shown highly valuable for students who wish to become better able to raise questions in class, to make presentations and reports, to respond to teacher questions, to express opinions, or to participate in group discussions. Similarly, AT is pertinent to helping students who seem to "come on too strong" in asking questions, expressing opinions, and so on. An increasing volume of work with young children indicates tremendous potential for pre-school and early elementary age youngsters. A leader in this work is Dr. Pat Palmer of the Assertiveness Training Institute of Denver, Colorado, who has written two books on AT for children (1977).

Coaches: Every coach of athletic, music, drama or forensic groups has worked with students of considerable potential who were unwilling to try new behavior or to perform individually (e.g., carry the ball, solo) or, conversely, to be "part of the team." For the reluctant student who "wishes" to achieve his or her potential in these areas, assertive training in the area of desired development is suggested. (Indeed, the principles of behavior shaping have been successfully applied in these fields for years.) The aggressive individual can also be taught by the coach to temper an approach which seems to be out of line with what is generally accepted. There is great potential in any individual who has all of the necessary qualities, but who hinders results by being overly aggressive. If the coach can channel these abilities by fostering assertion, both the individual and the team will benefit.

Counselors: The mental health professional will readily recognize the potential of assertiveness training for clients who demonstrate poor social development, inadequate self-confidence, academic disinterest, inability to withstand peer, parental, or teacher pressure. The indecisive individual who wishes to improve capacity for decision-making, the non-dater who lacks rudimentary social skills, the student who fears going to see a teacher to ask legitimate questions about the subject matter, the student who eagerly expresses her- or himself but denies others their opportunity, the person who has made a well-considered decision to leave college but is unable to face parents—all of these and many more need to learn how they can more comfortably express themselves as they wish to, and AT can help.

College Student Development Staff: Individuals working in college residence halls, activities-union programs, student health centers, placement offices, special educational programs, financial aids offices, minority programs, campus religious programs, and deans' offices have broad contact with college students "where they're at." The perceptive residence hall advisor *knows* the student who cannot stand up to a roommate to ask relief from the stereo's unreasonable noise level. A would-be student leader who lacks the confidence to campaign for office will be recognized by staff members who work with organizations. Medical personnel recognize the rash on a shy student as symptomatic of anxiety over presenting a report in class tomorrow. The placement staff can readily spot in advance the student who will suffer in an upcoming job interview for not knowing how to act in that new and threatening situation. All of these student development staff members are very much aware also of the individual who seems to offend others by being too outspoken, brusque, or verbally or physically abusive. Because the assertive behavior shaping process is systematic and straightforward, these staff members can be of direct help *on the spot* to the student with such problems. There are obvious advantages to help offered by a *known* person, with little or no delay, without the need to seek out another office and establish a relationship with a new and unknown person.

Professional Applications

Therapists: Interpersonal anxiety is a common symptom in persons who have emotional difficulties. Assertiveness training can be a vital factor in reducing this anxiety. The basic principles we have proposed apply, regardless of the setting, be it in correctional work, private therapy practice, alcohol and drug abuse clinics, etc. Thus, persons who lack feelings of self-worth can be helped by facilitating their own development of "worthy person" behaviors (making their own choices, standing up for their rights successfully but non-aggressively). We find the changing of attitudes and feelings to be frequently a *result*—rather than *cause*—of changed behavior.

Dr. Arthur Hardy is a California physician who uses AT extensively with severely phobic patients and reports considerable success (1977).

Speech Therapists: Adult stutterers have responded well to AT by speech therapists in conjunction with other techniques of behavior therapy such as systematic desensitization, in addition to various speech therapy techniques. Stutterers usually have a long history of disfluency beginning in their elementary school years. Typically they have been "worried over" by parents and teachers, placed in special education classes for therapy, and teased by their peers. As time goes on they learn very well not to expose themselves to situations where attention will be focused on their speech. Essentially, these individuals learn to be very non-demanding of others to the exclusion of their own rights. Often they believe that they are not as good as others, and therefore have no right to be assertive. Because of their dread of interpersonal situations, they can benefit from AT to overcome or inhibit anxiety. Assertive acts such as use of the telephone, talking to sales clerks, asking questions, learning how to disagree, learning to say no, and so on, can be practiced successfully. Thus the long-established pattern of self-denial and lack of spontaneity can be altered significantly.

Social Welfare Workers: The welfare recipient is often a member of a minority group, living in sub-standard housing in the least "desirable" location in a community. In addition to the typically sub-human way in which members of minorities have often been treated in our society, the recipient has had to suffer the indignities of the welfare system. Assertiveness training holds great promise for this deprived individual. Helping to increase self-respect, teaching more adaptive ways of behaving in conjunction with gaining rights, helping to develop effective community leadership, assisting persons in methods of dealing with merchants, insuring fair treatment without self-denial or aggressive acts—are all possible applications of assertive training for the social worker. In addition, the frequent use of group work and the practice of family case work provide other opportunities for assertive behavior development in this field.

Employment Counselors: Efforts to place persons in productive and rewarding employment are greatly enhanced by the client's ability to demonstrate self-confidence and to communicate effectively with interviewers and employers. Often a simple rehearsal of interviewing behavior provides a client with the tools and confidence needed to gain an appropriate position. Another person may require more extensive help in building up good feelings about self, perhaps by developing assertive behaviors and recognizing that other people acknowledge his or her personhood. One who is *reinforced* for acting like a self-assured person begins to recognize her or his own strengths. Another individual may need awareness of coming across too aggressively and need to learn how to modify that approach.

Marriage Counselors: When a couple comes in for marriage counseling it is almost a foregone conclusion that they are not communicating successfully. Three situations are common: 1) the husband has been the dominant decision-maker throughout the marriage with the woman being the dutiful headnodder; 2) the reverse situation, in which the husband is quiet and indecisive, and the wife is dominant; and 3) neither partner is dominant throughout, but neither has really known the other's thoughts and feelings all these years. All three of these situations are responsive to the assertive training model. As noted earlier, learning assertiveness will change one's relationship with those closest. For this reason it is preferable to have both partners working on the relationship although they may be seen individually as well as conjointly during therapy. (Alberti and Emmons, 1977).

Such marital problems as sex, finances, and child-rearing may stem from one or both partners not being fully assertive. Breakdown in communication will at times occur in any marriage relationship, but if each spouse is truly assertive, the difficulty will not likely balloon into a major crisis.

We are convinced that the more honest and open each partner is about all aspects of the marital relationship the more successful that relationship will be. Similarly, families who encourage freedom of expression on the part of children provide more growth-enhancing environments for young persons *and* their parents. (Palmer, 1977).

Pastoral Counselors: One of our clients who had built up fears and doubts about being assertive could still remember from childhood a sign in a Sunday school room: "The formula for *JOY* is: *J*esus first, *O*thers second, *Y*ourself last." Unfortunately, to many youngsters (and oldsters), such messages mean quite pointedly "don't step out ahead of others," "let others take advantage of you," "turn the other cheek," "keep your feelings inside." There seems to be a religiously-based feeling among many people that they must never feel good about themselves. Because they must never hurt anyone's feelings, they will let others take advantage of them. It is a moot point whether or not it is indeed true that religious education in church or at home fosters ill feelings about one's right to feel good about one's self and to stand up for one's self. The goal is to help the individual to become self-confident. We feel that clients with religious-based barriers toward assertion need re-education about what it truly means to be assertive. There need be no incompatability between asserting one's perfect (i.e., God-given, natural, inherent) rights and having deep religious convictions.

A number of authors have addressed the area of assertiveness within a religious context. Ethan J. Allen, Jr. (1976) discusses the "nice-guy" syndrome. He states that those being trained to be priests have a reputation for being "too soft" because they are traditionally cheerful in the face of insult and unassertive when others disregard their rights. Allen feels that these characteristics lead others to regard the seminarian as a "Caspar Milquetoast."

Randy K. Sanders (1976) speaks of a theologically oriented approach to assertiveness training. He feels that devout Christians are likely to feel that their commitment to Christ requires such behavior as passively "turning the other cheek." Because of such conceptions, Sanders suggests that a religious AT facilitator may need to employ a method of teaching assertion which uses "scriptures exemplifying assertiveness."

Edward W. C. McAllister (1975), a member of the Psychology Department of Russell Sage College, advocates assertiveness training for Christian therapists as a useful tool to help their clients grow, relieve anxiety, and function better in interpersonal relationships. He feels that many Christians are in need of assertion training *because* they view being non-assertive as part of their Christianity.

In an unpublished manuscript, David Richardson, a Methodist minister, and Michael Emmons discuss key issues in the relationship between assertion training and religion. They note that the true meaning of "turn the other cheek," is not to run and hide from confrontation. Further, they view meekness, long-suffering, and loving in interpersonal relationships in an assertive context. In addition, Richardson and Emmons show that the behavior of Jesus may be interpreted as positive assertion.

Nurses and Allied Medical Personnel: Health care delivery systems have long been controlled in near-despotic fashion (albeit perhaps benevolent!) by physicians. Recently, however, nurses and other health care professionals have assumed more important roles in delivery of services to patients. As both cause and result, these health care staff are developing greater independence and personal/professional assertiveness. The new "Nurse Practitioner," for example, must often proceed independently under only limited physician supervision. Assertiveness training has become a vital part of nursing education programs throughout the country (Herman, 1977). And many health care professionals are advocating greater *patient* assertiveness as well! In a very important and therapeutic way, health care delivery is becoming a cooperative venture, involving physician, staff, and patient, and AT is a valuable tool in that process.

Rehabilitation Counselors: A particularly exciting area of AT application has evolved in work with handicapped and retarded persons. Although results are highly variable, and the work very difficult, a number of professionals have reported success in training for employment interviews, obtaining medical, educational and social services, dealing with relatives who treat the handicapped adult "like a child," gaining enough confidence to enroll in college, and developing skills in general social interaction. (Issue 13 of the *Assert* newsletter described several such programs in some detail.)

Non-Mental Health Applications

Management Development: Individuals who are concerned with staff development in industrial and/or governmental organizations may find that a systematic effort to train management and sales personnel in assertiveness will pay big dividends. Group training methods will be useful in large organizations, and assertive training can be effectively incorporated into other management development or staff training programs. Supervisorial personnel who understand, and can apply the assertive (non-aggressive) model to their interactions with subordinates are too few, and more effective management teams can be developed utilizing AT as a key to recognition of the rights and organizational parameters of each employee. For example, a supervisor who can firmly reprimand a subordinate's *error* without devastating that *person* is a valuable asset in any organization. Also, of course, the lower-level employee who can honestly and constructively criticize superiors or the operation—in an assertive fashion—without fear on the one hand, or aggressive attack on the other, can be a significant contributor to organizational productivity, and a happier person (Paulson, in press). (Issue 19 of the *Assert* newsletter featured AT in management.)

Teacher Education: Among the chief complaints we hear from teachers are difficulty in "handling the kids" (discipline), lack of communication with supervisors, and fear of parent conferences. If a teacher is non-assertive, the students will typically take advantage of the weakness. On the other hand, a tyrant, the overly aggressive teacher, will be feared but not respected, a counter-productive situation. Assertive communication with the principal is essential for teachers. Teachers must also learn that children and parents are people, their equals as human beings, and should be approached accordingly.

At a national convention of the American Personnel and Guidance Association, we conducted a workshop on assertive behavior facilitation. A teacher who took part in that program described the experience at her school district with an assertive training program. A faculty group set out to learn assertive techniques for helping their students. After a short time, they recognized many of their own non-assertive or aggressive responses to students, administrators, and parents, and began to focus upon their own need for assertiveness. The result was a highly-enthusiastic report about their growth in personal and professional assertiveness.

It is our opinion that student teachers should take part in assertiveness training as a routine segment of their preparation for classroom teaching.

Individual and Community Applications

Leadership Training for Community Organizations: Effective leadership at all levels is perhaps the greatest single area of difficulty facing volunteer community groups. School-parent associations, service clubs, auxiliaries, women's clubs, interest groups, churches, youth activities, social clubs, even community action agencies and political parties suffer from a lack of persons willing and able to assume key responsibilities. While it is obvious that lack of time for such involvement is an important reason for the dearth of willing individuals, it is also true that many persons simply consider themselves inadequately prepared to accept responsibility for a committee, or a club, or a community activity

(Lawson, et al, 1976). Leadership development in such groups—from securing volunteers for an arrangements committee to convincing candidates to accept the nominating committee's call to the presidency or chairmanship—can be enhanced by including a program of assertive behavior development for the "rank and file" membership as well as for those who have already attained identified leadership roles.

Youth Workers: Adult leaders in such organizations as YM and YWCA's, YM and YWHA's, Boy and Girl Scouts, 4-H, Future Farmers, community recreation programs, church and church school youth groups, and summer camps have considerable opportunity to observe the behavior of young people, notably in social settings where the youngsters are working and/or playing with their fellows. The apathetic, disinterested or asocial youth who is observed in such a group may well be non-assertive, may fear failure and subsequent rejection, refuse to try anything, or attempt to dominate peers by being brash and abrasive. The sensitive adult who notes such behavior may be able to help this young person by providing a non-threatening, secure environment (perhaps on a one-to-one basis at first) in which the youth can feel safe in trying some new activity. The process of shaping more confident behavior may be slow, but it can provide the youngster with opportunities to make choices among alternative ways of acting. This step toward independence is an important quality of all such youth-oriented programs.

Other Applications

Journalism: A university journalism instructor noticed the potential use of AT with photography students and asked us to make presentations and give demonstrations in his classes. We have found that assertive concepts can be important in the improvement of photographic skills. If the photographer is either overly shy and caution cautious or too overbearing and pushy, the results will be affected. By being assertive rather than aggressive one may be able to avoid the physical abuse and even law suits that press photographers experience.

Another application for journalists is in development of interviewing skills. For instance, how do you assertively approach the subject and obtain the story you need? How do you handle a domineering person who wants to take over the interview? What should you say if you deeply disagree with the person's views? Is there a way to put at ease a subject who is anxious or is trying too hard? Or to confront the person who feeds you information which you already know is false? All of these situations are natural opportunities for the assertive processes.

Human Liberation: Many women have learned not to feel good about themselves and their abilities for a variety of reasons. Women, like men, have a perfect right to feel good about their real selves and to be able assertively to stand up for themselves in life. Most of us are familiar with the aggressive female who has a "cause" which she pushes fanatically. Conversely, we are equally put off by her non-assertive counterpart, the frail female with little spunk and independence. The assertive person, female or male, is a beautiful person.

There now exist many broadly-based community programs of treatment for persons typically denied access to therapeutic services: the poor, minorities, working people. Women's consciousness efforts are growing in large and small communities throughout the world. (Phelps and Austin, 1975).

Application of assertive behavior principles is useful to any oppressed group; ethnic minorities, students, children, laborers, the poor, the aged, all have much to gain from assertion of their rights in accordance with the fundamental processes described in this book.

Others: AT with juvenile delinquents, consumers, the divorced, alcohol and substance abusers, senior citizens, families, and in weight control programs are among other applications of which we are aware. The *Assert* newsletter regularly carries reports of new AT programs.

The examples given in this chapter are by no means all-inclusive. The reader is encouraged to consult the literature, colleagues and friends, and to reflect on his/her own experience for other relevant applications of assertiveness training.

It should be noted, however, that although AT may have been utilized with a particular population—even successfully—there are no assurances that it will be of benefit to any individual or group. Facilitators are urged to thoroughly *assess* the needs of their clients—including those in "public" workshops—to determine the appropriateness of their interventions.

As a final comment, we urge professionals to integrate AT into a comprehensive approach to total client needs, and to operate within principles which advocate responsible self-expression which is non-hurtful to others.

SELECTED ANNOTATED BIBLIOGRAPHY*

Experimental Studies

Eisler, R.M., Hersen, M., and Miller, P.M. Effects of modeling on components of assertive behavior. *Journal of Behavior Therapy and Experimental Psychiatry*, 1973, *4*, 1-6.

Measured the effects of videotaped modeling on eight verbal and non-verbal aspects of assertive behavior. 30 male psychiatric patients with an average age of 44 years. Two additional groups were utilized: 1) practice-control and 2) test—retest. The modeling and practice groups participated in a behavioral assertiveness test (devised by the authors) six times during a three-day period. Video tapes of performances were rated by judges for duration of looking, loudness of speech, etc. Results showed the modeling group had significantly more change than the other two groups. Specifically, the modeling participants showed greater changes in five of the eight variables studied: 1) longest duration of reply, 2) greatest number of requests for new behavior, 3) greater affect, 4) louder speech, and 5) greatest overall assertiveness.

• Eisler, R.M., Hersen, M., Miller, P.M., and Blanchard, E.B. Situational determinants of assertive behaviors. *Journal of Consulting and Clinical Psychology*, 1975, *43*, 330-40.

The purposes of this study were to extend earlier findings regarding negative assertion to the area of positive assertion, to look at the effects of the social context of interpersonal behavior on assertion and to delineate behaviors differentiating high and low assertiveness with regard to three variables: male or female interaction partner, positive or negative responses, and familiar or unfamiliar interaction partner. Combining the three variables into 8 categories, 4 scenes were developed for roleplaying in each category, yielding 32 role play scenes. Assertiveness was measured by the Wolpe-Lazarus self report inventory and behavior ratings by two judges. Categories for behavior ratings were 5 verbal and 7 nonverbal behaviors in addition to an overall assertiveness score. Subjects were 60 male psychiatric patients. Results yielded significant interactions between the three variables substantiating the hypothesis that assertive behavior is functionally related to the social context of interpersonal interaction. Significant differences were found on 6 of the 7 nonverbal variables when positive and negative assertive situations were compared. Subjects exhibited greater assertion toward women than toward men in both positive and negative situations. In general, the results support a stimulus-specific theory of assertiveness as well as demonstrating the behavioral complexity of assertiveness.

Friedman, P.H. The effects of modeling and role-playing on assertive behavior. In R.D. Rubin, H. Fensterheim, A.A. Lazarus, & C.M. Franks (Eds.), *Advances in behavior therapy*, N.Y.: Academic Press, 1971 (a).

Author tested a number of hypotheses concerning the value of role-playing and modeling in assertive training. Students (from introductory psychology classes) who had low scores on self-report and behavioral tests of assertiveness were assigned to one of six treatments of 8-10 minutes duration; 1) modeling plus role-playing; 2) modeling; 3) directed role-playing; 4) improvised role-playing and 5) non-assertive script. Performances were taped and evaluated by judges. A two-week follow-up assessment and a four-week follow-up questionnaire were administered. Students in modeling plus role-playing showed significantly larger gains in a Sum Assertion score than all groups except that for improvised role-playing. Also M + R-P showed a greater percentage gain on the criterion behaviors than other groups except the modeling group. Overall success was dramatic considering that only 8-10 minutes of treatment were involved.

• Galassi, J.P. & Galassi, M.D. Relationship between assertiveness and aggressiveness. *Psychological Reports*, 1975, *36*, 352-354.

In recognition of the importance of differentiating assertive behavior from aggressive behavior, this study administered the College of Self Expression Scale (the authors' measure of assertiveness) and the Buss-Durkee Inventory (a measure of eight types of aggressiveness) to 100

---

*A number of items in this bibliography were prepared by Donna Moore, M.A., Director of the Women's Resources and Research Center, University of California, Davis, for publication in *Assertive Behavior Training: An Annotated Bibliography* (250 items), published by Impact Publishers, Inc. (1977).

female and 71 male college students. Male and female Ss were treated separately for analysis. The only significant positive relationship found was between the assertiveness scale and the verbal aggression scale for females. This led the authors to conclude that the College Self Expression Scale is not tapping aggressiveness as operationalized by the Buss-Durkee Inventory. There is nothing in this article of specific interest to trainers but it is one of the few studies which have looked at sex differences and also the only research to date looking at the relationship between aggression and assertion—a distinction which most trainers make.

Hedquist, F.J. and Weinhold, B.W. Behavioral group counseling with socially anxious and unassertive college students. *Journal of Counseling Psychology*, 1970, *17*, 237-241.

Two advanced doctoral students were trained to administer group therapy (co-leaders) to non-assertive, socially anxious, non-clinical population college students. Participants were chosen on the basis of two personality tests: 1) a modified form of the S-R Inventory of Anxiousness; 2) the AS scale of the Guilford-Zimmerman. A no-treatment control was compared with a Behavior-Rehearsal group (e.g., Lazarus) and a Social Learning group (e.g., Mainord). Each of the treatment groups had N = 10 and lasted 6 weeks. Treatment outcome was measured by the total number of self-reported verbal assertive responses for each group during treatment and at a two-week follow-up six weeks later. The treatment groups did not differ from each other in mean frequency of verbal assertive responses, but were both significantly higher than the control. The follow-up showed no significant differences among groups on the criterion. The authors concluded that the treatment effectiveness did not carry over into post-treatment real life.

• Hersen, M., Eisler, R.M., & Miller, P.M. An experimental analysis of generalization in assertiveness training. *Behavior Research and Therapy*, 1974, *12*, 295-310.

Beginning with a review of the many findings regarding effectiveness of various techniques in changing components of assertive behavior, the authors state that this study was to look at aspects of generalization for

different components of assertiveness. Hypotheses were: (1) effects of treatment on training scenes will be greater than on generalization scenes, (2) effects of treatment on independent measure of generalization will vary according to the instructions, and (3) generalization of AT to an independent situation will be weaker than transfer of training to generalization scenes. Ss were 50 male psychiatric patients who had scored low on the Wolpe-Lazarus Assertiveness Questionnaire and were assigned to one of the five following conditions: (1) Test-Retest, (2) Practice-Control, (3) Practice-Control with Instructions for Generalization, (4) Modeling and Instruction, and (5) Modeling and Instruction with Instructions for Generalization. Five standard interpersonal situations were used as training scenes with an additional five comprising the generalization series. All 10 scenes were administered individually to all Ss in a videotape studio. Instructions were given via a public address system by the experimenter who was in an adjacent room. Pre-post videotaped responses to the 10 scenes were rated on 8 behavioral components of assertiveness and high inter-rater reliability was obtained. Analysis of variance indicated no initial differences among groups on behavioral measures. Results indicated that the Modeling and Instructions groups effected the greatest changes on 7 of the 8 components for the training scenes but on only 5 of the 8 components for the generalization scenes. No differences were found between either of the two Practice-Control groups and the Test-Retest group. Transfer of training effects were obtained on the generalization scenes, but were minimal on an independent *in vivo* test of generalization and an instructional set designed to facilitate generalization to different situations was only partially effective. A discussion of previous findings regarding generalization leads the authors to conclude that generalization in AT cannot be left to chance and that specific training for each class of situations must be given.

Hersen, M., et al. Effects of practice, instruction, and modeling on components of assertive behavior. *Behaviour Research and Therapy*, 1973, *11*, 443-451.

Fifty hospitalized male psychiatric patients were divided into five treatment groups. Subjects were matched on age, years of education, low self-reported assertiveness, and diagnosis (alcoholic, neurotic or psychotic). The modeling aspect of treatment involved watching a videotaped male model. Pre- and post-responses to a Behavioral Assertiveness Test were videotaped and rated on seven components of behavior: 1) duration of looking, 2) duration of reply, 3) loudness of speech 4) compliance content, 5) requests for new behavior, 6) affect, and 7) overall assertiveness. Results showed that a modeling-plus-instructions group was more effective or as effective as instructions-alone or modeling-alone groups on components 1, 2, 5, 6, 7. No differences were reported between before and after measures of self-reported assertiveness.

• Hirsch, S.M. An experimental investigation of the effectiveness of assertion training with alcoholics. *Dissertation Abstracts International*, 36/06, 3044-B. Texas Technical University, Order No. 75-26843, 133 pgs.

In an attempt to delineate parameters of unassertiveness in alcoholics, 123 state hospitalized alcoholics were chosen as a standardization normalization group for the Rathus Assertiveness Scale. Comparing these patients with a group of college students, no significant differences were found in assertiveness of the two groups on the RAS. The second part of the study attempted to demonstrate that AT could be effective in working with alcoholic patients. 102 chronic alcoholics at two state hospitals were assigned to three groups: minimal assertive training (received regular state hospital program plus 2 hours of didactic presentation and group discussion on assertiveness); full scale AT (received regular state hospital program plus 10 hours of AT utilizing all the components of AT); and control group (received only the regular hospital treatment program). At the end of two weeks, all Ss were post-tested with the RAS, a taperecorded situational test of assertive behavior and an *in vivo* rating scale of assertiveness. The full scale AT group improved significantly on the RAS, the tape recorded situational test, and staff assessments of assertiveness.

Johnson, T., Tyler, V., Thompson, R. and Jones. Systematic desensitization and assertive training in the treatment of speech anxiety in middle-school students. *Psychology in the Schools*, 1971, 8 (3), 263-267.

Compared systematic desensitization with a type of assertive training (speech practice) for speech-anxious eighth graders. Groups met twice per week for a total of nine sessions. The group speech practice required members to give short talks before the group. These talks were audio-taped and immediately played back, after which the subject re-presented the talk. Some coaxing to speak plus information giving about speech and anxiety was utilized. Interestingly enough, no difference between the two groups was noted on a post-measure of speech anxiety which showed that both groups improved.

Lazarus, A.A. Behavior rehearsal vs. non-directive therapy vs. advice in effecting behavior change. *Behavior Research and Therapy*, 1966, 4, 209-212.

Gives examples of how one might use behavior rehearsal, presents a case history, then reports on a somewhat informal experiment comparing advice, reflection-interpretation and behavior rehearsal. He served as therapist in all cases. Results showed behavior rehearsal being much more effective.

Lomont, J.F., Gilner, F.H., Spector, N.J., & Skinner, K.K. Group assertive training and group insight therapies. *Psychological Reports*, 1969, 25, 463-470.

VA hospital inpatients divided into two groups. 1) assertive (N = 7) and 2) insight (N = 5), met for 1½ hours each day M-F for six weeks. Therapists were different for each group; both were established therapists. Assertion training consisted mainly of role-playing various situations. Patients were given scripts and took turns modeling behavior. The therapist served as a teacher-coach. Results showed that the assertion group had a significantly greater total reduction on the clinical scales of the MMPI and significant decreases on the D and Pt scales. The insight group had no test changes of significance.

McFall, R.M. & Lillesand, D.B. Behavior rehearsal with modeling and coaching in assertion training. *Journal of Abnormal Psychology*, 1971, 77, 313-323.

Subjects (introductory psychology) were placed in: 1) overt rehearsal with modeling and coaching (N = 11), 2) covert rehearsal with modeling and coaching (N = 11), and 3) placebo control (N = 11). Each member of each group was seen individually for two sessions, a week apart. Subjects were given 20 minutes of refusal training in the pre-treatment instructions. Models employed were one male and one female. The treatment was standardized and prerecorded except for two aspects: a) the overt group was to rehearse aloud; covert was to imagine, b) overt heard a recorded playback of their performance; covert reflected on their response. Results showed that the experimental subjects improved dramatically more than controls and that the covert rehearsal was at least as great if not greater in improvement than the overt rehearsal. The article also indicates how the *Conflict Resolution Inventory*, a self-report inventory of refusal behavior, was developed.

McFall, R.M. & Marston, A.R. An experimental investigation of behavior rehearsal in assertive training. *Journal of Abnormal Psychology*, 1970, 76, 295-303.

A semi-automated, standardized behavior rehearsal procedure on audio-tape was devised for use with non-assertive college students from undergraduate psychology classes. Pre- and post-treatment tests were administered, the primary device being a behavioral, role-playing test. Subjects were given tape-recorded situations to which they were to respond. They also rated each situation on two 5-point scales 1) degree of anxiety, 2) how well they felt they performed. E's checked response latencies on each performance. Tests administered were the Wolpe-Lazarus Assertive Scale (1966), Taylor Manifest Anxiety, and Wolpe-Lang Fear Survey Schedule. Pulse rate was recorded before and after each rehearsal.

Four groups were set up: 1) behavior rehearsal with feedback (N = 8), 2) behavior rehearsal without feedback (N = 9), 3) placebo insight therapy (N = 9), and 4) waiting list control (N = 10). Treatment was for four 1-hour meetings over a 2- or 3-week period of time. Treatment subjects were seen by two male advanced clinical graduate students although with the rehearsal groups all treatment was conducted by audio-tape, with or without feedback (re-listening to their performance) after an introduction about learning to overcome fears by practice. Group 3 was an assertive-insight group, no rehearsal, no role-play.

Follow-up 2 weeks later, in which subjects were exposed to a persuasive sales pitch telephone call, confirmed that the two behavior rehearsal groups fared better than the two controls in increasing assertive behavior. There was not a significant difference between feedback vs. no feedback.

McFall, R.M. & Twentyman, C.T. Four experiments on the relative contributions of rehearsal, modeling and coaching to assertion training. *Journal of Abnormal Psychology*, 1973.

Experiment 1—examined the effects of six treatment conditions: 1) rehearsal, modeling, coaching; 2) rehearsal and modeling; 3) rehearsal and coaching; 4) rehearsal only; 5) modeling and coaching; 6) control. Subjects were seen for two 45-minute sessions one week apart. The laboratory set-up was similar to the procedure used in McFall et al. above. The modeling was on audio tape and the coaching was live, administered by a non-therapist. Results showed that rehearsal and coaching treatment on assertive behavior both were effective and that these effects were independent and additive. Also, audio modeling added very little if anything to successful treatment.

Experiment 2—three treatments were investigated: a) covert rehearsal, modeling, coaching; b) covert rehearsal, coaching; c) covert rehearsal only. The set-up was essentially the same as above. Again modeling added little, if any, to the increase in assertiveness gained by rehearsal and coaching.

Experiment 3—compared the effect of the old audio models with a set of audio models who were more tactful, more hesitant, and less extreme in their responses. Also compared overt with covert rehearsal under several conditions. The results still supported that audio modeling, either old or new, didn't add to successful treatment effects. Results also made clearer the effects of overt and covert rehearsal, finding no differences between overt and covert when the playback component was eliminated. This indicates that the playback of response may be the variable causing earlier differences.

Experiment 4—compared audio modeling with audio-visual modeling. A professional TV video tape involved student actors, stage sets, three-camera dramatizations, etc. The sound track was utilized for the audio modeling subjects. Two treatments of 40-minute duration were given in refusal behavior. Results showed that the video tape of models did *not* improve the treatment results. Includes excellent extensive discussion of the results of the four experiments and limitations of the treatment approach.

* Percell, L.P., Berwick, P.T. & Beigel, A. The effects of assertive training on self-concept and anxiety. *Archives of General Psychiatry*, 1974, *31*, 502-504.

Two separate studies were conducted to test the relationships between assertiveness, self-esteem and anxiety. In the first study 50 male and 50 female outpatient psychiatric patients were given the Lawrence Interpersonal Behavior Test, the Self-Acceptance Scale of the California Psychological Inventory and the Taylor Manifest Anxiety Scale. Findings indicated a substantial positive relationship between assertiveness and self-acceptance for both males and females and a strong negative correlation between assertiveness and anxiety for women only. In the second study, 24 patients were assigned to either an AT group or a relationship control group for eight sessions. Ss in the AT group showed significant increases in assertiveness, self-acceptance and significant decreases in anxiety relative to controls. This is a particularly significant study for those who wish to explore the relationship between assertiveness and other factors (notably anxiety and self-esteem) which have often been assumed by trainers to be related. The weaknesses of the research (e.g., use of only psychiatric Ss, inability to get valid follow-up data) are well noted and discussed by the authors. Particularly interesting is the finding of negative relationships between assertiveness and anxiety for women only which is the opposite of what has been postulated by many authors due to cultural sex role expectations and should be explored further with larger, non-clinical populations.

Rathus, S. An experimental investigation of assertive training in a group setting. *Journal of Behavior Therapy and Experimental Psychiatry*, 1972, *3*, 81-86.

Assertive training was conducted with a non-clinical population of college women, who were treated in groups of six, once a week for seven weeks. The group was given discussion about assertion and encouraged to practice specific assertive tasks. Members rehearsed assertion in the group although no expert modeling took place. Results were compared with a Fear Discussion and a Control group. Outcomes were quite variable and inconclusive as to the value of assertion training compared to the Fear Discussion Group.

Rathus, Spencer A. Instigation of assertive behavior through video-tape mediated assertive models and directed practice. *Behavior Research and Therapy*, 1973, *11*, 57-65.

A group of 78 female college students was divided into groups: 1) assertive training—viewing of assertive video taped models, practicing assertive and aggressive types of behavior; 2) placebo treatment—viewing of video tapes concerning desensitization of fears, 3) no-treatment control. Results showed that assertive training members (N = 24) reported significantly more assertive behavior on the *Rathus Assertiveness Schedule* than the other groups.

* Rimm, D.C., Hill, G.A., Brown, N.N. & Stuart, J.E. Group-assertive training in treatment of expression of inappropriate anger. *Psychological Reports*, 1974, *34*, 791-798.

Ss were 13 college male volunteers who had difficulty controlling their tempers and wished help with the problem. Six control Ss participated in eight hours of discussion regarding anger; seven experimental Ss participated in eight hours of AT which focused on behavior rehearsal (role playing anger-inducing situations). Objective measures of assertion and comfort yielded significantly higher increases for experimental Ss than control Ss while subjective measures of discomfort and anger showed significantly higher decreases for experimental Ss than control Ss. No significant treatment effect for self-rated confidence or internal-external control was obtained. Results from a global assertiveness inventory were in the predicted direction but nonsignificant. Results support the value of AT in groups, and the value of AT for antisocial aggression. The study supports the idea that results of AT are situation-specific rather than generalized. This research is important because it is one of the few which uses AT to treat aggression in males, although the small number of all-male Ss and the nonpublished nature of their assertiveness measure are issues of concern.

Serber, M. & Nelson, P. The ineffectiveness of systematic desensitization and assertive training in hospitalized schizophrenics. *Journal of Behavior Therapy and Experimental Psychiatry*, 1971, 2, 107-109.

Assertive training was applied to 14 schizophrenics who manifested phobic deficits in interpersonal assertiveness. Up to 18 treatments were given in a six-week period. Two of the subjects were slightly improved in a 6-month follow-up. The two main problems with assertive training were 1) the subjects frequently were unable to project themselves as being assertive where they had previously been passive, 2) subjects were at the time not able to repeat the modeling and role-playing they observed.

Assertiveness in Children

Chittenden, G.E. An experimental study in measuring and modifying assertive behavior in young children. *Monographs of the Society for Research in Child Development*, 1942, VII (1, No. 31).

In an excellent background article on assertive behavior which was written in 1942, the author distinguishes between three kinds of behavior in children: domination, cooperation, non-assertion. She set up a training program for pre-school children designed to enhance assertion and decrease domination. A play technique utilized two dolls playing the roles of pre-school children encountering a problem. The child and adult worked out solutions in the play period. Results showed that trained children were less dominant than controls after treatment. Data did not, however, indicate a statistically significant increase in cooperative behavior. The techniques were effective in altering extreme behavior of children.

Gittelman, M. Behavior rehearsal as a technique in child treatment. *Journal of Child Psychology and Psychiatry*, 1965, 6, 251-255.

This treatment procedure involved first finding out the situations which have caused the child to be aggressive in the past. The child acts out situations with other group members. This approach is scored by other members with a system that gives more value to assertive rather than aggressive behavior. Gittelman describes one group of seven boys ages 12-14 which met once a week for two hours. One specific aggressive behavior was successfully modified in 12 group sessions.

• Mummery, D.V. Family backgrounds of assertive and non-assertive children. *Child Development*, 1954, 25, 63-80.

In an early review of the literature looking for information regarding what might lend to assertive/nonassertive children, and what makes for socially acceptable or socially unacceptable assertiveness, this author found that democratic homes which give guidance and control, nurturance, consideration for others and channel behavior into socially acceptable forms are most related to socially acceptable assertiveness. Children who are reared in a freedom-giving, exploration accepting, participatory, non-sheltering home appear to be most assertive. The author states that other factors which should be explored are parental attitudes regarding the acceptability of children's ascendant methods, parental modeling, quality of guidance a child receives regarding his peer relationships, and the child's first-hand experiences in participating in democratic attitudes and practices in daily home living. Overall, the conclusion seems to be that a sense of security and adequacy underlies both the capacity for assertiveness and the ability to determine methods of assertiveness which show concern for others. This review is important because it is one of the few which look at antecedent conditions for assertiveness rather than methods for reversing nonassertion. It would be important to do some current studies and reviews in this same manner.

O'Connor, R.D. Modification of social withdrawal through symbolic modeling. *Journal of Applied Behavior Analysis*, 1969, 2, 15-22.

O'Connor notes that typically severe withdrawal in social and interpersonal situations is evidence by two things: 1) deficits in social skills and 2) avoidance of interpersonal situations. The recommended treatment would allow one to learn new social competencies and to erase social fears.

He utilized a training film with severely socially withdrawn (isolates) nursery school children. The sound film showed peers engaged in progressively more active social interaction. The film also depicted reinforcement for social interaction such as peer approval (smiling, nodding, etc.), peer acceptance (invitations to join in, offering play materials, etc.).

The experimental group saw the sound color film which was 23 minutes in duration with 11 scenes graduated according to degree of threat. Two factors were considered: 1) the vigor of the social activity, and 2) the size of the group. Six children viewed the experimental film, seven children viewed the control film. Observation immediately after the film showed the experimental group to have significantly increased their social interaction whereas controls had not.

Follow-up observations were not conducted, but a second set of teacher's ratings were obtained at the end of the school year. The teachers were blind as to which children were experimentals and which controls. They were asked to choose their most extremely withdrawn children again. Only one of the experimentals was chosen again whereas four of the controls were again chosen.

Ross, D., Ross, S. and Evans. The modification of extreme social withdrawal by modeling with guided participation. *Journal of Behavior Therapy and Experimental Psychiatry*, 1971, 2 (4), 273-279.

The subject was a 6-year-old preschool boy who had been held back from entering public school because of his extreme social withdrawal. A 7-week (twenty-one 90-minute sessions) treatment program was administered by a female psychologist and a male undergraduate psychology student who served as the model. The first four sessions consisted of establishing in the boy generalized imitative behavior of the model. The remaining sessions focused on seven different approaches such as symbolic modeling presentations, giving information, role-playing, modeling, etc. Post-test and two-month follow-up data showed that the treatment was quite successful in increasing social interactions and decreasing avoidance behaviors in the child. An excellent discussion section is included in the article.

Case Studies

Edwards, N. Case conference: Assertive training in a case of

homosexual pedophilia. *Journal of Behavior Therapy and Experimental Psychiatry*, 1972, 3, 55-63.

The successful cure of homosexual pedophilia which had existed for 10 years. Primary treatment was assertive training especially focused on the client's relationship with his wife. Thought stopping was also utilized with his pedophilic fantasies. Results were obtained in 13 sessions over a period of four weeks. A 3-month follow-up showed the results were maintained.

• Eisler, R.M., Miller, P.M., Hersen, M. & Alford, H. Effects of assertive training on marital interaction. *Archives of General Psychiatry*, 1974, 30, 643-649.

Three passive-avoidant husbands were given short but intensive assertiveness training (four 45-minute sessions). AT was aimed at very specific difficulties each man was having in his marital relationship but was found to generalize to other areas of marital interaction. The three couples were video-taped in marital interactions pre- and post-training and the interactions rated by observers for behavioral deficits. Findings indicated that the husbands became more assertive, marital interactions improved in productivity and the wife's manner of relating to her husband changed as he became more assertive. Although the research gives support to the advantages of assertiveness training for family interaction, its outstanding weaknesses (e.g., no follow-up to test long-term effects, no self-reports of feelings about interactions, and small number of Ss) make it most valuable as an impetus for further research.

Macpherson, E. Selective operant conditioning and deconditioning of assertive modes of behavior. *Journal of Behavior Therapy and Experimental Psychiatry*, 1972, 3, 99-102.

Interesting case study of successful operant conditioning of assertive responses toward the patient's mother and deconditioning her aggressive responses toward her husband. Other symptoms also changed and progress was maintained at two-year follow-up.

Stevenson, I. & Wolpe, J. Recovery from sexual deviations through overcoming of nonsexual neurotic responses. *American Journal of Psychiatry*, 1960, *116*; 737-742.

Detailed case histories concerning the treatment of two homosexuals and one pedophile using assertive training. Each of the patients' deviant sexual behavior was replaced by heterosexual behavior after varying amounts of therapy. Each had had previous heterosexual experiences.

Wolpe, J. The instigation of assertive behavior: transcripts from two cases. *Journal of Behavior Therapy and Experimental Psychiatry*, 1970, *1* (2): 145-151.

A practical article which shows how the therapist utilized behavior rehearsal in assertive training in one case. The second case is the second interview with a client after assertive principles were presented during the first session.

Techniques

Bandura, A. Psychotherapy based upon modeling principles. In A.E. Bergin & S.L. Garfield (Eds.), *Handbook of psychotherapy and behavior change: an empirical analysis*. New York: Wiley & Sons, 1971.

Essential reading for anyone using modeling procedures. A comprehensive chapter covers a variety of topics such as: vicarious extinction, graduated modeling, multiple modeling, live vs. symbolic modeling, etc. He found that modeling with guided participation is the best method discovered so far for reducing fears of various kinds. A component analysis of this method is given.

Cautela, J.R. & Wisocki, P.A. The use of the reinforcement survey schedule in behavior modification. In Rubin, R.D., Fensterheim, H., Lazarus, A.A. & Franks, C.M. (Eds.), *Advances in behavior therapy*, New York: Academic Press, 1971.

A practical article dealing with the use of the Reinforcement Survey Schedule (identifying possible reinforcing stimuli) results. The authors show how a therapist might instruct the client in the use of covert reinforcement while imagining oneself performing some behavior which

ordinarily has a low response probability. Three examples are listed: 1) asking a girl for a date, 2) being assertive, 3) avoiding a favorite dessert.

Fensterheim, H. Behavior therapy: assertive training in groups. In C.J. Sayer & H.S. Kaplan (Eds.) *Progress in group and family therapy*. Brunner/Mazell: New York, 1972.

The author describes how he conducts a "typical" assertive group which meets once a week for 2¼ hours. First, clients go over their homework assignments, after which they may deal with special problems encountered. Then they deal with assertive experiences of the preceding week. Modeling and rehearsal techniques are used where needed and special exercises utilized, e.g., difficulty with expressing anger. Mini-groups in assertive training are used to achieve limited goals such as overcoming social isolation where, for this particular homogeneous group of three, he met for only four sessions.

Friedman, P.H. The effects of modeling, role-playing and participation on behavior change. In B. Maher (Ed.) *Progress in experimental personality research*. Vol. VI. New York: McGraw-Hill, 1971 (b).

Discusses modeling and role-playing from four viewpoints: a) information; b) rehearsal; c) motivational variables; d) cognitive variables. Also includes sections on combinations of modeling plus role-playing and modeling plus participation. Information is given on persistence of change, generalization and duration of results.

* Lange, A., Rimm, D.C., & Loxley, J.C. Cognitive-behavioral assertion training procedures. *The Counseling Psychologist*, 1975, *5* (4), 37-41.

The authors list what they consider to be the four outcome goals of AT, four stages which constitute the process of AT, and seven process goals for AT. Following these goals and stages, they give some in-depth information regarding the format of their AT programs which involve 8-12 persons (including a male-female co-trainer team) which meet for 2 hours per week over a 6-9 week period. Proceeding through a week-by-week description of an AT course, they include the goals for each session, exercises which are used in each week, and the rationale for each exercise they present. A section on homework includes the reasons for using homework as well as the need for reinforcement of work done outside the AT group. They close with a section on training issues which includes the philosophy that assertiveness is situation specific rather than global and that clients in AT courses should be given "permission" not to be assertive. Rather than teaching that assertiveness is a behavior to be used in all situations, it should be presented as simply another option to be added to the client's behavioral repertoire from which she/he can select the best alternative in each life situation.

Lazarus, A.A. Behavior therapy in groups. In Gazda, G.M. (Ed.) *Basic approaches to group psychotherapy and group counseling.* Springfield, Ill: Charles C. Thomas, 1968, 149-175.

In an "Assertive Training Group" section this author tells how he starts the group by an introductory speech followed by self-introductions which are audio-tape recorded and played back for feedback. During subsequent groups he employs behavioral rehearsal, shaping, positive and negative feedback, relaxation training and discussions about anxiety. He also uses desensitization for fears of rejection and criticism. He feels that the most significant learning and behavior changes occur in the first 15 to 20 sessions of an assertive group.

Palmer, R.D. Desensitization of the fear of expressing one's own inhibited aggression: Bioenergetic assertive techniques for behavior therapists. *Advances in behavior therapy.* New York Academic Press, 1972.

Describes how he uses Alexander Lowen's bioenergetic techniques with assertive training. Examples: 1) the client trying to take a towel from the therapist; 2) deliberately using obscenity; 3) temper tantrum exercises (lie on back, kick, hit, yell "no"). The therapist utilizes modeling and coaching techniques and doesn't allow the subjects to go overboard and get out of control. He stresses caution and the use of assertion rather than aggression in encounters. A good paper on non-verbal expression.

Piaget, G.W. & Lazarus, A.A. The use of rehearsal-desensitization. *Psychotherapy: Theory, Research and Practice,* 1969, 6 (4), 264-266.

Combines behavior rehearsal and systematic desensitization in a graduated approach to assertive training. Individualizes the assertive training process for people who may experience a great deal of fear with role-playing.

Sturm, I. Implications of role-playing methodology for clinical procedure. *Behavior Therapy.* 1971, 2, 88-96.

This intriguing article focuses mainly on a description of Stanislavski's "method" for teaching actors. The basic principles of the method are given and applied to improving both "psychodiagnostic testing," and the "psychodiagnostic aspects of role-playing." Includes discussion of improving the effectiveness of behavior therapy role-playing techniques.

Ullman, Leonard P. Making use of modeling in the therapeutic interview, in R.D. Rubin and C.M. Franks *Advances in behavior therapy.* New York: Academic Press, 1968.

This paper brings together material from modeling, operant, respondent, and rational-emotive techniques, and treats the use of prompting and fading in modeling procedures. One prompts the individual to do what the therapist has done then fades until the person repeats the task successfully without additional prompting. Suggests that the therapist should not start by exposing the final and perfect performance, but should shape towards the desired outcome, and then fade promptings. If the model gets too far ahead of the client's readiness, the step to reinforcement becomes too great. Also, he stresses that what truly maintains one's success is the consequence of the behavior; the therapist should be alert to question the client about real-life experiences utilizing the new learning and to react positively when the person has done well, pointing out to the person what was done differently to change old ways.

General

• Cotler, S.B. Assertion training: A road leading where? *Counseling Psychologist*, 1975, 5 (4), 20-29.

The author begins by stating that AT is a training for behavior change but then becomes a way of life and thinking which leads to increased self-esteem. He gives a very fine history of assertive training, indicating when new ideas and/or techniques entered the field, who was responsible for those changes, and the impact they had on AT, concluding that AT has grown from a treatment of patients with inhibitory personality traits to a broad range of applications with many populations. Ways to determine if AT is indicated include life history evaluations and assertiveness or personality assessment tools but he warns that these things must be treated quite cautiously and not done in a hurry without careful scrutiny. He states that all indications are that although AT began as individual therapy, it appears now that its most effective use is in groups. He then discusses some considerations in setting up group AT, e.g., number of sessions, what types of role playing situation to present, etc. Briefly mentions the use of both video and taping equipment. Following these general considerations is an in-depth discussion about group AT: group rules, specific techniques available, problems group members might present, stages of improvement that most people go through. Available evaluative tools were briefly discussed. The article closes by stating that AT has grown and expanded considerably since its inception in 1949 and will probably continue to do so both with regard to specific techniques and the populations being served, and that trainers must remember their responsibilities to both clients and those with whom clients interact.

• Flowers, J.V., & Booraem, C.D. Assertion training: The training of trainers. *Counseling Psychologist*, 1975, 5 (4), 29-36.

Stating that their purpose is to convince people to use AT with a variety of client populations in a systematic way, they list what they consider to be the 4 components of any effective change technique: 1) systematic small graded steps, 2) active client participation, 3) accurate feedback of results, and 4) reinforcement for change efforts and successes. Outlining one proposed method for doing AT, the

authors begin by having clients examine their attitudes and values regarding assertiveness. They believe group AT is most effective and must include rehearsal. The triad method of rehearsal (actor, receiver, coach) is discussed with a warning that training must take the form of successive approximation in order not to increase anxiety. Reinforcement is imperative and each session should begin with a report of successes. Reinforcement issues include: recognition of possible resistance from one's social world, an assessment of positive and negative consequences, and learning to administer self-reinforcement. Definitions, homework and goal clarification are covered. Nonverbal behaviors are covered in some length, including eye contact, posture, distance, latency, loudness and affect. They suggest that for training purposes, verbal behavior be separated into the areas of requests, refusals and expressions. This section is followed by an extensive treatment of techniques to be used when the verbal assertive techniques don't work: time out, broken record, repeat back, reversal, free information—all of these are more difficult than they sound and require that clients have practice. The article closes with several defensive techniques and negative assertions along with a caution against three techniques the authors don't use because of their manipulative nature (fogging, negative inquiry and process to content shifts). They stress AT as a healthy, nonmanipulative form of communication and pay great attention to the trainer's role/responsibility and ethical issues. Further, it is written with non-sexist language and examples.

• Galassi, J.P., Kostka, M.P. & Galassi, M.D. Assertive training: a one year follow-up. *Journal of Counseling Psychology*, 1975, 22, 451-452.

This study reports the results of a one-year follow-up on group AT with nonassertive college students. One year after training, experimental and control Ss were significantly different on two self-reports (The College Self-Expression Scale and the Subjective Unit of Disturbance Scale) and two of four behavior measures (assertive content and scene length). No differences were found on eye contact or response latency. The results indicated the long term effects of assertive training. (Authors' abstract) This is a particularly important study since it is one of the few which successfully measures long-term effects of AT. The authors suggest two possible reasons for their success: first, their original training was longer, more intensive and more complex than other researchers had used, and secondly, their follow-up procedure was conducted in the laboratory whereas other researchers had used *in vivo* follow-up (self-report diaries or phone calls). Although *in vivo* reports may be strong assessments of assertiveness, they are also strongly confounded by other variables which make them difficult to interpret.

* Gambrill, E.D. & Richey, C.A. An assertiveness inventory for use in assessment and research. *Behavior Therapy*, 1975, *6*, 550-561.

The Inventory, a 40-item self-report measure, permits respondents to indicate their degree of discomfort, probability of engaging in the behavior, and situations they would like to handle better. Normative data include college students and women taking part in AT groups. The inventory is reported to have value in both clinical settings and research. A particularly useful instrument for research on assertiveness, especially as a pre-post test to establish effectiveness of AT procedures between groups. Caution must be used regarding the population tested because the response instructions might make the test difficult to use with younger or less sophisticated populations.

Jakubowski-Spector, P. Facilitating the growth of women through assertive training. *The Counseling Psychologist* (Counseling Women), 1973, *4* (1), 75-86.

An excellent article which provides pertinent information for men and women facilitating or learning assertive behavior. Distinguishes between assertive and aggressive behavior for women. Good sections are included on awareness and motivation, developing a belief system, and anxieties about assertion. Several examples of client and therapist behavior are given.

* Lazarus, A.A. On assertive behavior: A brief note. *Behavior Therapy*, 1973, *4*, 697-699.

The author begins by stating that people who need assertive training are usually deficit in one or more of the following areas: the ability to say no, the ability to ask for favors or make requests, the ability to express positive and negative feelings, the ability to initiate, continue or

terminate general conversations. In order for AT to be successful, he believes it must be specific to the area in which the client is having difficulty because there is very little generalization across areas. The author then expresses his concern that most assertive training has focused on the negative aspects (e.g., saying no, expressing displeasure, etc.) which have too often been aggression under the guise of assertiveness. He suggests that AT should give more attention to the positive aspects of assertion (e.g., expressing affection, appreciation, etc.).

Prazak, J.A. Learning job-seeking interview skills. In Krumboltz, J.D. & Thoresen, C.E. (Eds.), *Behavioral Counseling, Cases and Techniques.* New York: Holt, Rinehart and Winston, 1969, 414-428.

Excellent article on all the particulars of job interviewing. Emphasizes five points: 1) ability to explain skills; 2) ability to answer problem questions (e.g., poor job history, little education, age, mental or physical illness, etc.); 3) appropriate appearance and mannerisms; 4) enthusiasm (e.g., Anything special I can learn? Can I work overtime?); 5) five points of interview (e.g., use of a "call-back" closing: "Would it be all right if I called you on Wednesday to find out about the job?"). Uses modeling, a film, role-playing, video tape.

* Rathus, S.A. A 30-item schedule for assessing assertive behavior. *Behavior Therapy*, 1973, *4*, 398-406.

A 30-item schedule for measuring assertiveness is shown to have moderate to high test-retest reliability and split-half reliability. Validity in terms of the impressions respondents make on other people and in terms of their indication of how they would behave in specific situations in which assertive, outgoing behavior can be used with profit is satisfactory. Item analysis shows good correlation with the total scale score and with external criteria. A shorter version of the scale is discussed. Also, it was found that assertiveness varies negatively with impressions of niceness. This is one of the few scales which has been experimentally tested for validity and reliability and should be considered if one is doing assertiveness research. Norms are available with males scoring higher than females. Additionally, the items are general enough to be useful for pre-post testing with non-college or college populations if assertiveness trainers wish to test the effectiveness of their groups.

- Wolfe, J.L., & Fodor, I.G. A cognitive-behavioral approach to modifying assertive behavior in women. *Counseling Psychologist*, 1975, 5 (4), 45-52.

Beginning with a typical discussion of the sex-role socialization which occurs for women, thus leading to non-assertion, the authors continue by giving the outline for an AT group which first attempts to dispute irrational attitudes and beliefs, and then gives members of the group practice in new forms of behavior. A very nice chart of traditional beliefs with ways of disputing irrational ideas is included. Lengthy scripts for role played situations are also included. Discussion of what to do with assertive failures, why homework is important, differences between AT and consciousness raising groups. A nice chart on typical assignments which is divided into target problem, behavioral assignment and cognitive assignment sections. This is a useful article for persons thinking about working with women in AT groups.

169

REFERENCES

Alberti, R.E. Assertive behavior training: definitions, overview, contributions. In R.E. Alberti (Ed.), *Assertiveness: Innovations, Applications, Issues.* San Luis Obispo, California: Impact Publishers, Inc., 1977.

Alberti, R.E. Issues in assertive behavior training. In R.E. Alberti (Ed.), *Assertiveness: Innovations, Applications, Issues.* San Luis Obispo, California: Impact Publishers, Inc., 1977.

Alberti, R.E. Was that *assertive* or *aggressive? ASSERT: The Newsletter of Assertive Behavior*, 1976, *1* (7), 2.

Alberti, R.E. and Emmons, M.L. Assertion training in marital counseling. *Journal of Marriage and Family Counseling,* January 1976, 49-54. Also in R.E. Alberti (Ed.), *Assertiveness: Innovations, Applications, Issues.* San Luis Obispo, California: Impact Publishers, Inc., 1977.

Alberti, R.E. and Emmons, M.L. *Stand Up, Speak Out, Talk Back!* New York: Pocket Books, Inc., 1975.

Alberti, R.E. and Emmons, M.L. *Your Perfect Right: A Guide to Assertive Behavior.* San Luis Obispo, California: Impact Publishers, Inc., 1970 (1st edition), 1974 (2nd edition).

Allen, E.J., Jr. Repression-sensitization and the effect of assertion on anxiety. Senior Research Paper. St. Meinrad College, St. Meinrad, Indiana, May, 1976.

Arkowitz, H., Lichtenstein, E. & McGovern, K. A behavioral approach to social inhibition. Paper read at American Psychological Association, 1971.

Arkowitz, H., Lichtenstein, E. & McGovern, K. The behavioral assessment of social competence in males. Paper read at Western Psychological Association, 1971.

Atkinson, D. Effect of selected behavior modification techniques on student-initiated action. *Journal of Counseling Psychology*, 1971, *18* (5), 395-400.

Bach, G. and Deutsch, R. *Pairing.* New York, Avon Books, 1970.

Bach, G. and Wyden, P. *The Intimate Enemy: How to Fight Fair in Love and Marriage.* New York, William Morrow and Company, Inc., 1968.

Baer, J. *How to Be an Assertive (Not Aggressive) Woman in Life, in Love, and on the Job.* New York: Signet (New American Library), 1976.

Balson, P. The use of behavior therapy techniques in crisis-intervention: A case report. *Journal of Behavior Therapy and Experimental Psychiatry*, 1971, *2* (4), 297-300.

Bandura, A. *Aggression: A Social Learning Analysis.* Englewood Cliffs: Prentice-Hall, 1973.

Bandura, A. Analysis of modeling processes. In A. Bandura (Ed.), *Psychological Modeling: Conflicting Theories.* Chicago: Aldine-Atherton, 1971.

Bandura, A. Behavioral modification through modeling procedures. In L. Krasner and L. P. Ullman (Eds.), *Research in Behavior Modification.* New York: Holt, Rinehart, Winston, 1965, 310-340.

Bandura, A. Influence of models' reinforcement contingencies on the acquisition of imitative responses. *Journal of Personality and Social Psychology*, 1965, *1*, 589-595.

Bandura, A. *Principles of Behavior Modification.* New York: Holt, Rinehart, Winston, 1969.

Bandura, A. Psychotherapy based upon modeling principles. In A.E. Bergin & S.L. Garfield (Eds.), *Handbook of psychotherapy and behavior change: an empirical analysis.* New York: Wiley & Sons, 1971.

Bandura, A. Blanchard, E.B., and Ritter, B. Relative efficacy of desensitization and modeling approaches for inducing behavioral, affective, and attitudinal changes. *Journal of Personality and Social Psychology*, 1969, *13*, 173-199.

Bandura, A., Ross, D., and Ross, S. Vicarious reinforcement and imitative learning. *Journal of Abnormal Social Psychology*, 1963, 67, 601-607.

Bandura, A. and Walters, R.H. *Adolescent Aggression.* New York: Ronald Press, 1959.

Bandura, A. and Wlaters, R.H. *Social Learning and Personality Development.* New York: Holt, Rinehart, and Winston, 1963.

Bates, H.D. and Zimmerman, S.F. Toward the development of a screening scale for assertive training. *Psychological Reports*, 1971, 28, 99-107.

Bean, K.L. Desensitization, behavior rehearsal, then reality: a preliminary report on a new procedure. *Behavior Therapy*, 1970, 1, 542.

Berkowitz, L. The concept of aggressive drive: some additional considerations. In L. Berkowitz (Ed.), *Advances in Experimental Social Psychology*, Vol. 2. New York: Academic Press, 1965.

Berkowitz, L. *Roots of Aggression: A Re-examination of the Frustration-Aggression Hypothesis.* New York: Atherton Press, 1969.

Bloom, L.Z., Coburn, K., and Pearlman, J. *The New Assertive Woman.* New York: Delacorte Press, 1975.

Bodner, G.E. The role of assessment in assertion training. *The Counseling Psychologist*, 1975, 5 (4), 90-96.

Booraem, C.D. and Flowers, J.V. Reduction of anxiety and personal space as a function of assertion training with severely disturbed neuropsychiatric inpatients. *Psychological Reports*, 1972, 30, 923-929.

Boulette, T.R. Determining needs and appropriate counseling approaches for Mexican American women: a comparison of therapeutic listening and behavioral rehearsal. Unpublished dissertation, University of California, Santa Barbara, June, 1972.

Bourdon, R.D. Imitation: Implications for counseling and therapy. *Review of Educational Research*, 1970, 40, 429-457.

Bower, S.A. and Bower, G.H. *Asserting Yourself.* Reading, Massachusetts: Addison-Wesley, 1976.

Bumpus, F. Toward assertive therapy: A discussion of various behavioral techniques. Paper read at Western Psychological Association, Portland, Oregon, 1972.

Buss, A.H. *The Psychology of Aggression.* New York: Wiley, 1961.

Buss, A. & Durkee. An inventory for assessing different kinds of hostility. *Journal of Consulting Psychology*, 1957, 21, 343-348.

Cameron, D.E. The conversion of passivity into normal self-assertion. *American Journal of Psychiatry*, 1951, 108, 98.

Cautela, J.R. Behavior therapy and self-control: techniques and implications. In C.M. Franks (Ed.), *Behavior Therapy: Appraisal and Status.* New York: McGraw-Hill, 1969.

Cautela, J.R. Covert processes and behavior modification. *Journal of Nervous and Mental Disease*, 1973, 157, 27-36.

Cautela, J.R. Covert reinforcement. *Behavior Therapy*, 1970, 1, 33-50.

Cautela, J.R. Covert sensitization. *Psychological Reports*, 1967, 20, 459.

Cautela, J.R. & Wisocki, P.A. The use of the reinforcement survey schedule in behavior modification. In Rubin, R.D., Fensterheim, H., Lazarus, A.A. & Franks, C.M. (Eds.), *Advances in behavior therapy*, N.Y.: Academic Press, 1971.

Cheek, D.K. Assertive behavior and black lifestyles. In R.E. Alberti (Ed.), *Assertiveness: Innovations, Applications, Issues.* San Luis Obispo, California: Impact Publishers, Inc., 1977.

Cheek, D.K. *Assertive Black . . . Puzzled White.* San Luis Obispo, California: Impact Publishers, Inc., 1976.

Chittenden, G.E. An experimental study in measuring and modifying assertive behavior in young children. *Monographs of the Society for Research in Child Development*, 1942, 7 (1, Serial #31).

Cooley, M. A model for assertive statements. *ASSERT: The Newsletter of Assertive Behavior*, 1976, *1* (6), 2.

Cooley, M.L. and Hollandsworth, J.G., Jr. A strategy for teaching verbal content of assertive responses. In R.E. Alberti (Ed.), *Assertiveness: Innovations, Applications, Issues*. San Luis Obispo, California: Impact Publishers, Inc., 1977.

Corsini, R.J. *Roleplaying in psychotherapy: A manual*, Chicago: Aldine, 1966.

Corsini, R.J., et al. *Roleplaying in business and industry*, New York: Free Press, 1961.

Cotler, S.B. and Cotler, S.M. Four myths of nonassertiveness in the work environment. In R.E. Alberti (Ed.), *Assertiveness: Innovations, Applications, Issues*. San Luis Obispo, California: Impact Publishers, Inc., 1977.

Cotler, S.B. and Guerra, J.J. *Assertion Training: A Humanistic-Behavioral Guide to Self-Dignity*. Champaign: Research Press, 1976.

Cummins, D.E. On the use of unobtrusive measures of assertion. *Assert: The Newsletter of Assertive Behavior and Personal Development*, February, 1978, p. 1.

Cummins, D.E. On the use of unobtrusive measures of assertion. *Assert: The Newsletter of Assertive Behavior*, 18, February 1978.

Dalali, I.D. The effect of active-assertion and feeling clarification training on factor analyzed measures of assertion. Doctoral dissertation, University of California, Los Angeles, 1971. *Dissertation Abstracts International*. 1971, *32*, 1B-1291B, University Microfilms No. 71-21, 322.

D'Amico, W. Case studies in assertive training with adolescents. In R.E. Alberti (Ed.), *Assertiveness: Innovations, Applications, Issues*. San Luis Obispo, California: Impact Publishers, Inc., 1977.

D'Amico, W. *Revised Rathus Assertiveness Scale for Children, Grades 3-8*. Marblehead, Mass.: Educational Counseling and Consulting Services, 1976.

Danish, S.J. & Kagan, N. Emotional simulation in counseling and psychotherapy. *Psychotherapy: Theory, Research and Practice*, 1969, 6, 261-263.

D'Zurilla, T.J. Reducing heterosexual anxiety. In J.D. Krumboltz and C.E. Thoresen (Eds.), *Behavioral Counseling: Cases and Techniques*. New York: Holt, Rinehart, and Winston, 1969.

Edwards, N.B. Case conference: assertive training in a case of homosexual pedophilia. *Journal of Behavior Therapy and Experimental Psychiatry*, 1972, *3*, 55-63.

Efran, J.S. & Korn, P.R. Measurement of social caution: Self-appraisal, role-playing, and discussion behavior. *Journal of Consulting and Clinical Psychology*, 1969, *33*, 78-83.

Eisler, R.M., Miller, P.M., and Hersen, M. Components of assertive behavior. *Journal of Clinical Psychology*, 1973, *29*, 295-299.

Eisler, R.M., Hersen, M., and Agras, W.S. Videotape: a method for the controlled observation of nonverbal interpersonal behavior. *Behavior Therapy*, 1973, *4*, 420-425.

Eisler, R.M., Hersen, M., and Miller, P.M. Effects of modeling components of assertive behavior. *Journal of Behavior Therapy and Experimental Psychiatry*, 1973, 4, 1-6.

Eisler, R.M., Miller, P.M., Hersen, M., and Alford, H. Effects of assertive training on marital interaction. *Archives of General Psychiatry*, 1974, *30*, 643-649.

Ekman, P. Differential communication of affect by head and body cues. *Journal of Personality and Social Psychology*, 1965, *2*, 726-735.

Ekman, P., Friessen, W.V., and Taussig, T. VID-R and scan: tools and methods in the analysis of facial expression and body movements. In G. Gerbner, O. Holsti, K. Knippendorff, W. Paisley, and P. Stone (Eds.), *Content Analysis*. New York: Wiley, 1969.

Emmons, M.L. Assertion training within an holistic-eclectic framework. In R.E. Alberti (Ed.), *Assertiveness: Innovations, Applications, Issues*. San Luis Obispo, California: Impact Publishers, Inc., 1977.

Emmons, M.L. *The Inner Source: A Guide to Meditative Therapy*. San Luis Obispo, California: Impact Publishers, Inc., 1978.

Epstein, D. Aggression toward outgroups as a function of authoritarianism and imitation of aggression models. *Journal of Personality and Social Psychology*, 1966, *3*, 574-579.

Evans, D. Specific aggression, arousal and reciprocal inhibition therapy. *Western Psychologist*, 1970, *1* (4), 125-130.

Fensterheim, H. Personal communication. January, 1977.

Fensterheim, H. Assertive methods and marital problems. In R. Rubin, H. Fensterheim, J. Henderson, and L. Ullmann (Eds.), *Advances in Behavior Therapy*. New York: Academic Press, 1972.

Fensterheim, H. "Behavior therapy: assertive training in groups" in C.J. Sayer & H.S. Kaplan (Eds.), *Progress in Group and Family Therapy*. New York: Brunner/Mazel, 1972.

Fensterheim, H. *Help Without Psychoanalysis*. New York: Stein and Day, 1971.

Fensterheim, H. and Baer, J. *Don't Say Yes When You Want To Say No*. New York: Dell, 1975.

Feshbach, S. Dynamics of morality of violence and aggression: some psychological considerations. *American Psychologist*, 1971, *26*, 281-291.

Flanders, J.P. A review of research on imitative behavior, *Psychological Bulletin*, 1968, *69*, 316-337.

Flowers, J., Booraem, C., Brown, T., and Harris, D. An investigation of a technique for facilitating patient to patient therapeutic interaction in group therapy. *Journal of Community Psychology*, 1974, *2* (1), 39-42.

Flowers, J. and Guerra, J. The use of client-coaching in assertion training with a large group. *Journal of Community Health*, 1974.

Fodor, I.G. and Wolfe, J.L. Assertiveness training for mothers and daughters. In R.E. Alberti (Ed.), *Assertiveness: Innovations, Applications, Issues*. San Luis Obispo, California: Impact Publishers, Inc., 1977.

Franzini, L.R. Review of *The Assertive Woman*. *Behavior Therapy*, 1976, 7, 418-419.

Freedman, J.L. & Fraser, S.C. Compliance without pressure: The foot-in-the-door technique. *Journal of Personality and Social Psychology*, 1966, *4*, 195-202.

Freud, S. *Civilization and Its Discontents*. London: The Hogarth Press, Ltd., 1962.

Friedman, P.H. The effects of modeling and role playing on assertive behavior. In R. Rubin, A. Lazarus, H. Fensterheim, and C. Franks (Eds.), *Advances in Behavior Therapy*. New York: Academic Press, 1971.

Friedman, P.H. The effects of modeling, role playing, and participation on behavior change. In B.A. Maher (Ed.), *Progress in Experimental Personality Research*, Vol. 6. New York: Academic Press, 1972.

Fromm, E. *The Art of Loving*. New York: Harper and Row, 1956.

Galassi, J.P. *Assertive Training in Groups Using Video Feedback*. Final progress report in National Institute of Mental Health Small Research Grant MH22392-01, 1973.

Galassi, J.P., DeLo, J.S., Galassi, M.D., and Bastien, S. The College self-expression scale: a measure of assertiveness. *Behavior Therapy*, 1974, *5*, 165-171.

Galassi, J.P. and Galassi, M.D. Assessment procedures for assertive behavior. In R.E. Alberti (Ed.), *Assertiveness: Innovations, Applications, Issues*. San Luis Obispo, California: Impact Publishers, Inc., 1977.

Galassi, J.P. and Galassi, M.D. Relationship between assertiveness and aggressiveness. *Psychological Reports*, 1975, *36*, 352-354.

Galassi, J.P. and Galassi, M.D. Validity of a measure of assertiveness. *Journal of Counseling Psychology*, 1974, *21*, 248-250.

Galassi, J.P., Galassi, M.D., and Litz, C.M. Assertive training in groups using video feedback. *Journal of Counseling Psychology*, 1974, *21*, 390-394.

Galassi, J.P., Hollandsworth, J.G., Jr., Radecki, J.C., Gay, M.L., Howe, M.R., and Evans, C.L. Behavioral performance in the validation of an assertiveness scale. *Behavior Therapy*, 1976, *7*, 447-452.

Galassi, M.D. and Galassi, J.P. A critical review of assertive behavior: definition and assessment. *Psychotherapy: Theory, Research and Practice*, 1976, in press.

Galassi, M.D. and Galassi, J.P. *Assert Yourself! How to Be Your Own Person*. New York: Human Sciences Press, 1977.

Gambrill, E.D. and Richey, C.A. An assertion inventory for use in assessment and research. *Behavior Therapy*, 1975, *6*, 550-561.

Gambrill, E.D. and Richey, C.A. *It's Up to You: The Development of Assertive Social Skills*. Millbrae, California: Les Femmes, 1976.

Garnett, L. Assertion training with juvenile delinquents. In R.E. Alberti (Ed.), *Assertiveness: Innovations, Applications, Issues*. San Luis Obispo, California: Impact Publishers, Inc., 1977.

Gay, M.L., Hollandsworth, J.G. Jr., and Galassi, J.P. An assertiveness inventory for adults. *Journal of Counseling Psychology*, 1975, *22*, 340-344.

Geisinger, D.L. Controlling sexual and interpersonal anxieties. In J. Krumboltz and C. Thoresen (Eds.), *Behavioral Counseling: Cases and Techniques*. New York: Holt, Rinehart, and Winston, 1969.

Gillis, J.S. & Jesser, R. Effects of brief psychotherapy on belief in internal control: An exploratory study. *Psychotherapy: Theory, Research and Practice*, 1970, *7*, 135-137.

Gittelman, M. Behavior rehearsal as a technique in child treatment. *Journal of Child Psychology and Psychiatry*, 1965, *6*, 251.

Goldfried, M.R. & D'Zurilla, T.J. A behavior-analytic model for assessing competence. In C.D. Spielberger (Ed.), *Current topics in clinical and community psychology*, Vol. I, New York: Academic Press, 1969.

Goldiamond, I. Self-control procedures in personal behavior problems. *Psychological Reports*, 1965, *17*, 851-868.

Goldstein, A.J., Serber, M., & Piaget, G. Induced anger as a reciprocal inhibitor of fear. *Journal of Behavior Therapy & Experimental Psychiatry*. 1970, 67-70.

Goldstein, A.P. The use of modeling to increase independent behavior. *Behavior Research and Therapy*, 1973, *11*, 31-42.

Gordon, T. *Parent Effectiveness Training*. New York: Wyden, 1970.

Green, A.H. & Marlatt, G.A. Effects of instruction and modeling upon affective and descriptive verbalization. *Journal of Abnormal Psychology*. 1972, *80*, 189-196.

Grodner, B.S. Assertiveness and anxiety: a cross-cultural and socio-economic perspective. In R.E. Alberti (Ed.), *Assertiveness: Innovations, Applications, Issues*. San Luis Obispo, California: Impact Publishers, Inc., 1977.

Guerra, J.J. and Taylor, P.A. The four assertive myths: a fable. In R.E. Alberti (Ed.), *Assertiveness: Innovations, Applications, Issues.* San Luis Obispo, California: Impact Publishers, Inc., 1977.

Hardy, A.B. Assertive training in the treatment of phobias. In R.E. Alberti (Ed.), *Assertiveness: Innovations, Applications, Issues.* San Luis Obispo, California: Impact Publishers, Inc., 1977.

Hedquist, F.J. and Weinhold, B.K. Behavioral group counseling with socially anxious and unassertive college students. *Journal of Counseling Psychology*, 1970, *17*, 237-242.

Heller, K. Effects of modeling procedures in helping relationships. *Journal of Consulting and Clinical Psychology*, 1969, *33*, 522-526.

Henderson, J.M. The effects of assertiveness training on self-actualization in women. Unpublished doctoral dissertation, University of Northern Colorado, 1976.

Herman, S.J. Assertiveness: one answer to job dissatisfaction for nurses. In R.E. Alberti (Ed.), *Assertiveness: Innovations, Applications, Issues.* San Luis Obispo, California: Impact Publishers, Inc., 1977.

Hersen, M., Eisler, R.M., and Miller, P.M. An experimental analysis of generalization in assertive training. *Behavior Research and Therapy*, 1974, *12*, 295-310.

Hersen, M., Eisler, R.M., and Miller, P.M. Development of assertive responses: clinical, measurement and research considerations. *Behavior Research and Therapy*, 1973, *2*, 505-521.

Hersen, M., et al. Effects of practice, instructions, and modeling on components of assertive behavior. *Behaviour Research and Therapy*, 1973, *11*, 443-451.

Hestand, R., et al. The Willoughby Schedule: a replication. *Journal of Behavior Therapy and Experimental Psychiatry*, 1971, *2*, 111-112.

Hewes, D.D. On effective assertive behavior: a brief note. *Behavior Therapy*, 1975, 6, 269-271.

Hicks, W. Imitation and retention of film-mediated aggressive peer and adult models. *Journal of Personality and Social Psychology*. 1965, *2*, 97-100.

Hill, J.H., et al. Vicarious extinction of avoidance behavior through films: an initial test. *Psychological Reports*, 1968, *22*, 192.

Hirsch, S. An experimental investigation of the effectiveness of assertion training with alcoholics. Research Report, Texas Department of Mental Health and Mental Retardation, Austin, Texas, 1975. Contract No. (74-75)-1973, Texas Commission on Alcoholism.

Hirsch, S.M. Assertiveness training with alcoholics. In R.E. Alberti (Ed.), *Assertiveness: Innovations, Applications, Issues.* San Luis Obispo, California: Impact Publishers, Inc., 1977.

Hokanson, J.E. Psychophysiological evaluation of the catharsis hypothesis. In E.I. Megargee and J.E. Hokanson (Eds.), *The Dynamics of Aggression.* New York: Harper and Row, 1970.

Hollandsworth, J.G. Differentiating assertion and aggression: some behavioral guidelines. *Behavior Therapy*, in press.

Hollandsworth, J.G. Jr., Galassi, J.P., and Gay, M.L. The adult self-expression scale: validation using the multitrait-multimethod procedure. *Journal of Clinical Psychology*, 1976, in press.

Homme, L.E. Perspectives in psychology: XXIV. Control of coverants, the operants of the mind. *Psychological Record*, 1965, *15*, 501-511.

Houts, P. and Serber, M. *After The Turn-On, What?* Champaign, Illinois: Research Press, 1972.

Hwang, P.O. Assertion training for Asian-Americans. In R.E. Alberti (Ed.), *Assertiveness: Innovations, Applications, Issues.* San Luis Obispo, California: Impact Publishers, Inc., 1977.

Ivey, A.E., Normington, C.J., Miller, D., and Morrill, W.H. Microcounseling and attending behavior, *Journal of Counseling Psychology*, 1968, *15* (5), 1-12.

Jacobson, E. *Progressive Relaxation*, Chicago: University of Chicago Press, 1938.

Jakubowski, P.A. Assertive behavior and clinical problems of women. In R.E. Alberti (Ed.), *Assertiveness: Innovations, Applications, Issues.* San Luis Obispo, California: Impact Publishers, Inc., 1977.

Jakubowski, P.A. and Lacks, P.B. Assessment procedures in assertion training. *The Counseling Psychologist*, 1975, *5* (4), 84-90.

Jakubowski-Spector, P. An introduction to assertive training procedures for women. Paper presented to American Personnel and Guidance Association, Washington, D.C., 1973.

Jakubowski-Spector, P. Facilitating the growth of women through assertive training. *The Counseling Psychologist*, 1973, *4* (1), 75-86.

Johnson, S.M. & White, G. Self-observation as an agent of behavioral change. *Behavior Therapy*, 1971, *2*, 488-497.

Johnson, T., Tyler, V., Thompson, R., and Jones, E. Systematic desensitization and assertive training in the treatment of speech anxiety in middle-school students. *Psychology in the Schools*, 1971, *8*, 263-267.

Kanfer, F.H. & Duerfeldt, P.H. Learner competence, model competence and number of observation trials in vicarious learning. *Journal of Educational Psychology*, 1969, *58*, 153-157.

Kanfer, R.H. & Goldfoot, D.A. Self-control and tolerance of noxious stimulation. *Psychological Reports*, 1966, *18*, 79-85.

Katz, R. Case conference: Rapid development of activity in a case of chronic passivity. *Journal of Behavior Therapy and Experimental Psychiatry*, 1971, *2*, 187.

Kaufmann, H. Definitions and methodology in the study of aggression. *Psychological Bulletin*, 1965, *64*, 351-361.

Kaufmann, L.M. and Wagner, B.R. Barb: a systematic treatment technology for temper control disorders. *Behavior Therapy*, 1972, *3*, 84.

Kazdin, A.E. Effects of covert modeling and reinforcement on assertive behavior. *Proceedings of the 81st Annual Convention of the American Psychological Association*, 1973, *8*, 537-538.

Krop, H., Calhoon, B., & Verrier, R. Modification of the "self-concept" of emotionally disturbed children by covert reinforcement. *Behavior Therapy*, 1971, *2*, 201-204.

Krumboltz, J.D. and Thoresen, C.E. *Behavioral Counseling: Cases and Techniques*. New York: Holt, Rinehart, and Winston, 1969.

Laird, J.D. The effect of facial expression on emotional experience. Paper presented at Eastern Psychological Association, 1967.

Landau, P. and Paulson, T. COPE: a wilderness workshop in AT. In R.E. Alberti (Ed.), *Assertiveness: Innovations, Applications, Issues.* San Luis Obispo, California: Impact Publishers, Inc., 1977.

Landau, P. and Paulson, T. Group assertion training for Spanish speaking Mexican-American mothers. In R.E. Alberti (Ed.), *Assertiveness: Innovations, Applications, Issues.* San Luis Obispo, California: Impact Publishers, Inc., 1977.

Lange, A.J. and Jakubowski, P. *Responsible Assertive Behavior: Cognitive/Behavioral Procedures for Trainers*. Champaign: Research Press, 1976.

Lawrence, P.S. The assessment and modification of assertive behavior. Doctoral dissertation, Arizona State University, 1970. *Dissertation Abstracts International*, 31,
1B-1601B (University Microfilms No. 70-11, 888).

Laws, D.R. and Serber, M. Measurement and evaluation of assertive training. Paper
presented at the meeting of the Association for Advancement of Behavior Therapy,
Washington, D.C., September, 1971.

Laws, D.R. and Serber, M. Measurement and evaluation of assertive training with
sexual offenders. In R.E. Hosford and S. Moss (Eds.), *The Crumbling Walls;
Treatment and Counseling of the Youthful Offender*, 1972.

Lawson, J.D., Griffin, L.G., and Donant, F.D. *Leadership is Everybody's Business.*   San
Luis Obispo, California: Impact Publishers, Inc., 1976.

Lazarus, A.A. Behavior rehearsal vs. non-directive therapy vs. advice in effecting
behavior change. *Behavior Research and Therapy*, 1966, *4*, 209-212.

Lazarus, A.A. *Behavior Therapy and Beyond.* New York: McGraw-Hill, 1971.

Lazarus, A.A. Behavior therapy in groups. In G.M. Gazda (Ed.), *Basic Approaches to
Group Psychotherapy and Group Counseling.* Springfield, Illinois: Charles C.
Thomas, 1968.

Lazarus, A.A. Behavior therapy, incomplete treatment, and symptom substitution.
The Journal of Nervous and Mental Disease, 1965, *140*, 180.

Lazarus, A.A. Broad-spectrum behavior therapy and the treatment of agoraphobia.
Behavior Research and Therapy, 1966, *4*, 95.

Lazarus, A.A. (Ed.), *Clinical behavior therapy.* New York: Brunner/Mazel, 1972.

Lazarus, A.A. and Fay, A. *I Can If I Want To.* New York: William Morrow and
Company, Inc., 1975.

Lazarus, A.A. and Serber, M. Is systematic desensitization being misapplied?
Psychological Reports, 1968, *23*, 215.

Lefcourt, H.M. Internal versus external control of reinforcement: A review.
Psychological Bulletin, 1960, *65*, 206-220.

Lehman-Olson, D. Assertiveness training: theoretical and clinical implications. In D.
Olson (Ed.), *Treating Relationships*. Lake Mills, Iowa: Graphics Publishing Co.,
1976.

Leibowitz, G. Comparison of self-report and behavioral techniques of assessing aggression.
Journal of Consulting and Clinical Psychology, 1968, *32*, 21-25.

Lewinsohn, P.M., Weinstein, M.S. & Shaw, D.A. Depression: A clinical-research
approach. In R.D. Rubin & C.M. Franks (Eds.), *Advances in behavior therapy.* New
York: Academic Press, 1969.

Liberman, R. A behavioral approach to group dynamics. *Behavior Therapy*, 1970, *1*,
141-175.

Liberman, R. Behavioral approaches to family and couple therapy. *American Journal of
Orthopsychiatry.* 1970, *40*, 106-118.

Liberman, R.P., King, L.W., DeRisi, W.J., and McCann, M. *Personal Effectiveness.*
Champaign, Illinois: Research Press, 1976.

Lomont, J.F., Gilner, F.H., Spector, N.J., & Skinner, K.K. Group assertive training and
group insight therapies. *Psychological Reports*, 1969, *25*, 463-470.

Loo, R.M.Y. The effects of projected consequences and overt behavior rehearsal on
assertive behavior. Unpublished doctoral thesis. University of Illinois, Urbana, 1971.

Lorenz, K. *On Aggression.* New York: Harcourt, Brace and World, 1966.

Ludwig, L.D. & Lazarus, A.A. A cognitive and behavioral approach to the treatment of
social inhibition. *Psychotherapy: Theory, Research and Practice*, 1972, *9*, 204-206.

Maass, M. Situational role playing: a technique for learning to be more loving. *Marriage and Family Counselors Quarterly*, 1972, 7, 34-39.

MacDonald, M.L. A behavioral assessment methodology applied to the measurement of assertion. Doctoral dissertation, University of Illinois, Urbana, 1974.

MacNeilage, L.A. and Adams, K.A. The method of contrasted role-plays: An insight-oriented model for role playing in assertiveness training groups. Paper presented at the American Psychological Association, 1977.

Macpherson, E. Selective operant conditioning and deconditioning of assertive modes of behavior. *Journal of Behavior Therapy and Experimental Psychiatry*, 1972, 3, 99-102.

Mahoney, M.J. *Cognition and Behavior Modification*. Cambridge: Ballinger, 1974.

Manderino, M.A. Effects of a group assertive training procedure on undergraduate women. Unpublished doctoral dissertation, Arizona State University, 1973.

Manis, M. Social interaction and the self-concept. *Journal of Abnormal and Social Psychology*, 1955, 51, 262-370.

Martinson, W.D. & Zerface, J.P. Comparison of individual counseling and a social program with nondaters. *Journal of Counseling Psychology*, 1970, 17, 36-40.

Masters, J.C. & Branch, M.N. Comparison of the relative effectiveness of instruction, modeling, and reinforcement procedures for inducing behavior change. *Journal of Experimental Psychology*, 1969, 80, 364-368.

Maultsby, M.C. Systematic, written homework in psychotherapy. *Psychotherapy: Theory, Research and Practice*, 1971, 8, 195-198.

McAllister, E.W. Assertive training and the Christian therapist. *Journal of Psychology and Theology*, Winter, 1975, p. 19-24.

McFall, R.M. Analogue methods in behavioral assessment: Issues and prospects. In J. Cone and R. Hawkins (eds.), *Behavioral Assessment: New Directions in Clinical Psychology*. New York: Brunner/Mazel, in press.

McFall, R.M. Assertion training. In B.B. Wolman (Ed.), *International Encyclopedia of Neurology, Psychiatry, Psychoanalysis, and Psychology*. In press, 1977.

McFall, R.M. and Lillesand, D.B. Behavior rehearsal with modeling and coaching in assertive training. *Journal of Abnormal Psychology*, 1971, 77(3), 313-323.

McFall, R.M. and Marston, A.R. An experimental investigation of behavior rehearsal in assertiveness training. *Journal of Abnormal Psychology*, 1970, 76, 295-303.

McFall, R.M. and Twentyman, C.T. Four experiments on the relative contributions of rehearsal, modeling, and coaching to assertion training. *Journal of Abnormal Psychology*, 1973, 81, 199-218.

McMillan, M. Assertiveness as an aid to weight control. In R.E. Alberti (Ed.), *Assertiveness: Innovations, Applications, Issues*. San Luis Obispo, California: Impact Publishers, Inc., 1977.

McMillan, M.M. Relative efficacy of assertive training and self-control procedures in a weight control program. Unpublished doctoral dissertation, Arizona State University, 1975.

McNamara, J.R. The broad based application of social learning theory to treat aggression in a preschool child. *Journal of Clinical Psychology*, 1970, 81, 199.

McPhail, G.W. Developing adolescent assertiveness. In R.E. Alberti (Ed.), *Assertiveness: Innovations, Applications, Issues*. San Luis Obispo, California: Impact Publishers, Inc., 1977.

Megargee, E.I. and Mendelsohn, G.A. A cross-validation of twelve MMPI indices of hostility and control. *Journal of Abnormal and Social Psychology*, 1962, 65, 431-438.

Mehrabian, A. Inference of attitudes from the posture, orientation and distance of a communicator. *Journal of Consulting & Clinical Psychology*, 1968, *32*, 296-308.

Mehrabian, A. and Ferris, S.R. Inference of attitudes from non-verbal communication in two channels. *Journal of Consulting Psychology*, 1967, *31*, 248-252.

Mehrabian, A. Relationship of attitude to seated posture orientation and distance. *Journal of Personality and Social Psychology*, 1968, *10*, 26-30.

Meichenbaum, D. *Cognitive Behavior Modification*. Morristown: General Learning Press, 1974.

Meichenbaum, D. and Cameron, R. Stress-inoculation training: a skills approach to anxiety management. Unpublished manuscript, University of Waterloo, 1973.

Meichenbaum, D. and Turk, D. Stress-inoculation training. In P.O. Davidson (Ed.), *The Behavioral Management of Anxiety, Depression, and Pain*. New York: Brunner/ Mazel, 1976.

Melnick, J. A comparison of replication techniques in the modification of minimal dating behavior. *Journal of Abnormal Psychology*, 1973, *81*, 51-59.

Meyer, R. The art of refusal. *British Journal of Criminology*. 1971, *11* (3), 265-274.

Miller, P.M., Hersen, M., Eisler, R.M., and Hilsman, G. Effects of social stress on operant drinking of alcoholics and social drinkers. *Behavior Research and Therapy*, 1974, *12*, 67-72.

Mischel, W. *Personality and Assessment*. New York: Wiley, 1968. '

Moore, D. *Assertive Behavior Training: An Annotated Bibliography*. San Luis Obispo, California: Impact Publishers, Inc., 1977.

Moreno, J.L. *Psychodrama: Vol. I*, New York: Beacon House, 1971.

Morrow, W.R. *Behavior Therapy Bibliography: 1950-1969*. Columbia: University of Missouri Press, 1971.

Mowrer, O.H. The behavior therapies with special reference to modeling and imitation, *American Journal of Psychotherapy*, 1966, *20*, 439-461.

Nachman, G. Squeak up! *Newsweek*, April 5, 1977, p. 13. Also in R.E. Alberti (Ed.), *Assertiveness: Innovations, Applications, Issues*. San Luis Obispo, California: Impact Publishers, Inc., 1977.

Neuman, D. Using assertive training. In J. Krumboltz and C. Thoreson (Eds.), *Behavioral Counseling: Cases and Techniques*. New York: Holt, Rinehart, and Winston, 1969.

Novotny, H. Social competence training. A paper presented at the meeting of the Western Psychological Association, Sacramento, California, May, 1975.

O'Connor, R.D. Modification of social withdrawal through symbolic modeling. *Journal of Applied Behavior Analysis*, 1969, *2*, 15-22.

O'Connor, R.D. The relative efficacy of modeling, shaping and combined procedures for the modification of social withdrawal. Unpublished manuscript, University of Illinois, 1970.

Osborn, S.M. and Harris, G.G. *Assertive Training for Women*. Springfield, Illinois: Charles C. Thomas, 1975.

Otto, H. *More Joy in Your Marriage*. New York: Hawthorn Books, Inc., 1969.

Palmer, P. *Liking Myself*. San Luis Obispo, California: Impact Publishers, Inc., 1977.

Palmer, P. *The Mouse, the Monster, and Me: Assertiveness for Young People*. San Luis Obispo, California: Impact Publishers, Inc., 1977.

Palmer, R.D. Desensitization of the fear of expressing one's own inhibited aggression: Bioenergetic assertive techniques for behavior therapists. *Advances in behavior therapy*. New York: Academic Press.

Patterson, G.R. *Families: applications of social learning to family life*. Champaign, Ill.: Research Press, 1971.

Patterson, G.R. & Reid, J.B. Reciprocity and coercion: Two factors of social systems. In C. Neuringer and J.L. Michael (Eds.), *Behavior modification in clinical psychology*. New York: Appleton-Century-Crofts, 1970.

Patterson, R. Time-out and assertive training for a dependent child. *Behavior Therapy*, 1972, *3*, 466-468.

Paulson, T. *Assertive Management*. New York: Harper and Row, (in press, 1978)

Paulson, T.L. and Landau, P. Divorce recovery: assertion training for the divorced. In R.E. Alberti (Ed.), *Assertiveness: Innovations, Applications, Issues*. San Luis Obispo, California: Impact Publishers, Inc., 1977.

Paulson, T. The differential use of self-administered and group administered token reinforcement in group assertion training for college students. Unpublished doctoral dissertation. Fuller Graduate School of Psychology, 1974.

Pendleton, L., Shelton, J., and Wilson, S. Social interaction training using systematic homework. *The Personnel and Guidance Journal*, *54* (9), 484-487.

Percell, L.P. Assertive behavior training and the enhancement of self-esteem. In R.E. Alberti (Ed.), *Assertiveness: Innovations, Applications, Issues*. San Luis Obispo, California: Impact Publishers, Inc., 1977.

Percell, L.P., Berwick, P.T., and Beigel, A. The effects of assertive training on self-concept and anxiety. *Archives of General Psychiatry*, 1974, 502-504.

Perls, F.S. *Gestalt Therapy Verbatim*. Lafayette, California: Real People Press, 1969.

Perls, F., Hefferline, R.F., and Goodman, P. *Gestalt Therapy*. New York: Dell, 1951.

Phelps, S. and Austin, N. The assertive woman: developing an assertive attitude. In R.E. Alberti (Ed.), *Assertiveness: Innovations, Applications, Issues*. San Luis Obispo, California: Impact Publishers, Inc., 1977.

Phelps, S. and Austin, N. *The Assertive Woman*. San Luis Obispo, California: Impact Publishers, Inc., 1975.

Phillips, L., & Zigler, E. Social competence: The action-thought parameter and vicariousness in normal and pathological behaviors. *Journal of Abnormal & Social Psychology*, 1961, *63*, 137-146.

Piaget, G.W. and Lazarus, A.A. The use of rehearsal-desensitization. *Psychotherapy: Theory, Research and Practice*, 1969, 6, 264.

Pierce, R.M., Schauble, P.G. & Farkas. Teaching internalization behavior to clients. *Psychotherapy: Theory, Research and Practice*, 1970, 7, 217-220.

Potter, S. *Gamemanship*. New York: Holt, 1948.

Potter, S. *One Upmanship*. New York: Holt, Rinehart, and Winston, 1970.

Potter, S. *Upmanship*. New York: Holt, Rinehart, and Winston, 1970.

Prazak, J.A. Learning job-seeking interview skills. In Krumboltz, J.D. & Thoresen, C.E. (Eds.), *Behavioral counseling: cases and techniques*. New York: Holt, Rinehart and Winston, 1969, 414-428.

Rathus, S.A. A 30-item schedule for assessing assertive behavior. *Behavior Therapy*, 1973, *4*, 398-406.

Rathus, S.A. An experimental investigation of assertive training in a group setting. *Journal of Behavior Therapy and Experimental Psychiatry*, 1972, *3*, 81-86.

Rathus, S.A., and Nevid, J.S. *BT: Behavior Therapy*. New York: Doubleday, 1977.

Rathus, S. Instigation of assertive behavior through videotape-mediated assertive models and directed practice, *Behaviour Research and Therapy*, 1973, *11*, 57-65.

Rathus, S.A. Principles and practices of assertive training: an eclectic overview. *Counseling Psychologist*, 1975, *5* (4), 9-20.

Rathus, S.A. and Ruppert, C.A. Assertion training in the secondary school and the college. *Adolescence*, 1973, 8:257-263.

Rehm, L.P. & Marston, A.R. Reduction of social anxiety through modification or self-reinforcement. *Journal of Consulting and Clinical Psychology*, 1968, *32*, 565-574.

Rich, A.R. and Schroeder, H.E. Research issues in assertiveness training. *Psychological Bulletin*, 1976, *83*, 6, 1081-1096.

Rimm, D.C. Assertive training and the expression of anger. In R.E. Alberti (Ed.), *Assertiveness: Innovations, Applications, Issues*. San Luis Obispo, California: Impact Publishers, Inc., 1977.

Rimm, D.C. Thought stopping and covert assertion in the treatment of phobias. *Journal of Consulting and Clinical Psychology*, 1973, *41* (3), 466-467.

Rimm, D.C., Hill, G.A. Brown, N.N., and Stuart, J.E. Group assertive training in the treatment of inappropriate anger expression. *Psychological Reports*, 1974, *34*, 791-798.

Rimm, D.C., Keyson, M., and Hunziker, J. Group assertive training in the treatment of antisocial aggression. Unpublished manuscript, Arizona State University, 1971.

Rimm, D.C. and Masters, J.C. *Behavior Therapy: Techniques and Empirical Findings*. New York: Academic Press, 1974.

Rimm, D.C., Snyder, J.J., Depue, R.A., Haanstad, M.J., and Armstrong, D.P. Assertive training versus rehearsal, and the importance of making an assertive response. *Behavior Research and Therapy*, 1976.

Ringer, R. *Winning Through Intimidation*. New York: Funk & Wagnalls, 1976.

Rogers, C.R. *On Becoming a Person*. Boston: Houghton-Mifflin, 1961.

Rosenblum, L. Telephone therapy. *Psychotherapy: Theory, Research and Practice*, 1969, *6*, 241-242.

Ross, D., Ross, S. and Evans. The modification of extreme social withdrawal by modeling with guided participation. *Journal of Behavior Therapy and Experimental Psychiatry*, 1971, *2* (4), 273-279.

Rotter, J.B. Generalized expectancies for internal versus external control of reinforcement. *Psychological Monographs*, 1966, *80*, 1-28.

Salter, A. *Conditioned Reflex Therapy*. New York: Farrar, Straus, and Giroux, 1949 (Capricorn Books edition, 1961).

Salter, A. On assertion. In R.E. Alberti (Ed.), *Assertiveness: Innovations, Applications, Issues*. San Luis Obispo, California: Impact Publishers, Inc., 1977.

Sanders, R. The effectiveness of a theologically oriented approach to assertive training for refusal behaviors. Masters Thesis. S.F. Austin State University, 1976. Masters abstracts, 1976, 14, 252. (University Microfilm No. 13-08786).

Sarason, I. Verbal learning, modeling, and juvenile delinquency. *American Psychologist*, 1968, *23*, 254-266.

Sarason, I.G., and Ganzer, V.J. Modeling and group discussion in the rehabilitation of juvenile delinquents. *Journal of Counseling Psychology*, 1973, *20*, 442.

Sarason, I.G. & Ganzer, V.J. Social influence techniques in clinical and community psychology. In C.D. Spielberger :Ed.), *Current Topics in Clinical and Community Psychology*. New York: Academic Press, 1969, 1-66.

Scoresby, J.E. Imitative learning and reinforcement of decisions in counseling. *Dissertation Abstracts International*, 1969, *30*, 2344.

Seitz, F.C. Behavior modification techniques for treating depression. *Psychotherapy: Theory, Research and Practice*, 1971, *8*, 181-184.

Seligman, M.E. Fall into helplessness. *Psychology Today*, 1973, June, 43.

Seligman, M.E. For helplessness: can we immunize the weak? *Psychology Today*, 1969, June, 42.

Seligman, M.E. and Maier, S.F. Failure to escape traumatic shock. *Journal of Experimental Psychology*, 1976, 74, 1.

Seligman, M.E., Maier, S.F., and Greer, J.H. Alleviation of learned helplessness in the dog. *Journal of Abnormal Psychology*, 1968, 73, 256.

Serber, M. Book review of *Your Perfect Right. Behavior Therapy*, 1971, 2, 253-254.

Serber, M. Teaching the non-verbal components of assertive training. *Journal of Behavior Therapy and Experimental Psychiatry*, 1972, 3, 1-5. Also in R.E. Alberti (Ed.), *Assertiveness: Innovations, Applications, Issues*. San Luis Obispo, California: Impact Publishers, Inc., 1977.

Serber, M. & Nelson, P. The ineffectiveness of systematic desensitization and assertive training in hospitalized schizophrenics. *Journal of Behavior Therapy and Experimental Psychiatry*, 1971, 2, 253-254.

Sheehy, G. *Passages: Predictable Crises of Adult Life*. New York: E.P. Dutton and Company, 1976.

Shelton, J.L. Homework in AT: promoting the transfer of assertive skills to the natural environment. In R.E. Alberti (Ed.), *Assertiveness: Innovations, Applications, Issues*. San Luis Obispo, California: Impact Publishers, Inc., 1977.

Shelton, J. and Ackerman, M. *Homework in Counseling and Psychotherapy: Examples of Systematic Assignments for Therapeutic Use by Mental Health Professionals*. Springfield, Illinois: Charles C. Thomas, 1974.

Shoemaker, M.E. Developing assertiveness: training or therapy? In R.E. Alberti (Ed.), *Assertiveness: Innovations, Applications, Issues*. San Luis Obispo, California: Impact Publishers, Inc., 1977.

Shoemaker, M.E. Group assertiveness training for institutionalized delinquents. Unpublished doctoral dissertation, Fuller Graduate School of Psychology, 1974.

Shoemaker, M.E. and Paulson, T.L. Group assertion training for mothers: a family intervention strategy. In E.J. Mash, L.C. Handy, and L.A. Hamerlynck (Eds.), *Behavior Modification Approaches to Parenting*. New York: Brunner/Mazel, Inc., 1976.

Shoemaker, M.E. and Satterfield, D.O. Assertion training: an identity crisis that's coming on strong. In R.E. Alberti (Ed.), *Assertiveness: Innovations, Applications, Issues*. San Luis Obispo, California: Impact Publishers, Inc., 1977.

Simon, S.B. *Values Clarification*. New York: Hart Publishing Co., 1972.

Singer, E. *Key concepts in psychotherapy*. New York: Random House, 1965.

Smaby, M.H. and Tamminen, A.W. Counselors can be assertive. *Personnel and Guidance Journal*, 1976, 54, 420-424.

Smith, M. *When I Say No, I Feel Guilty*. New York: Dial Press, 1975.

Spiegler, M.D., et al. Experimental development of a modeling treatment to extinguish persistent avoidance behavior. In Rubin, R.D. & Frank, C.M. (Eds.), *Advances in behavior therapy, 1968*. New York: Academic Press, 1969, 45-51.

Spivack, G. and Shure, M. *Social Adjustment of Young Children*. San Francisco: Josey-Bass, 1974.

Stanislavsky, C. *An Actor Prepares*. New York: Theater Arts, 1936.

Stevenson, I. and Wolpe, J. Recovery from sexual deviation through overcoming non-sexual neurotic responses. *American Journal of Psychology*, 1960, 116, 737.

Stuart, R.B. Analysis and illustration of the process of assertive conditioning. University of Michigan. Unpublished manuscript.

Sturm, I. Implications of role-playing methodology for clinical procedure. *Behavior Therapy*, 1971, 2, 88-96.

Sturm, I.E. The behavioristic aspect of psychodrama. *Group Psychotherapy*, 1965, *18*, 50-64.

Taubman, B. *How To Become An Assertive Woman*. New York: Pocket Books (Simon and Schuster), 1976.

Taylor, J.A. A personality scale of manifest anxiety. *Journal of Abnormal and Social Psychology*, 1953, *48*, 285-290.

Thoft, J.S. Developing assertiveness in children. In R.E. Alberti (Ed.), *Assertiveness: Innovations, Applications, Issues*. San Luis Obispo, California: Impact Publishers, Inc., 1977.

Thoresen, C.E., et al. " 'I can't say no': Social modeling for unassertive clients," Stanford University. Unpublished manuscript, 1972.

Thoresen, C.E. and Stuhr, D.E. Social modeling and counseling: theory, research and practice. Paper presented at the American Educational Research Association Convention, Chicago, April, 1972.

Thornton, J.W. and Jacobs, P.D. Learned helplessness in human subjects. *Journal of Experimental Psychology*, 1971, *87*, 367.

Ullman, L.P. Making use of modeling in the therapeutic interview. In Rubin, R.D. & Frank, C.M. (Eds.), *Advances in behavior therapy*. New York: Academic Press, 1968.

Vaal, J.J. and McCullagh, J. The Rathus assertiveness schedule: reliability at the junior high school level. *Behavior Therapy*, 1975, *6*, 566-567.

Varenhorst, B.B. Helping a client speak up in class. In J.E. Krumboltz and C.E. Thoresen (Edgs.), *Behavioral Counseling: Cases and Techniques*. New York: Holt, Rinehart, and Winston, 1969.

Videbeck, L. Self-conception and the reaction of others. *Sociometry*, 1960, *23*, 351-359.

Wallace, C.J., Teigen, J.R., Liberman, R.P., and Baker, V. Destructive behavior treated by contingency contracts and assertive training: a case study. *Journal of Behavior Therapy and Experimental Psychiatry*, 1973, *4*, 273.

Walters, R.H. and Brown, M. Studies of reinforcement of aggression: III. Transfer of responses to an interpersonal situation. *Child Development*, 1963, *24*, 563-571.

Waters, W.F. and McDonald, D.G. Autonomic response to auditory, visual, and imagined stimuli in a systematic desensitization context. *Behavior Research and Therapy*, 1973, *11*, 577-585.

Watzlawick, P., Beavin, J. & Jackson, D. *Pragmatics of human communication*. New York: W.W. Norton, 1967.

Weinman, B., et al. Inducing assertive behavior in chronic schizophrenics. *Journal of Consulting and Clinical Psychology*, 1972, *37*(2), 246-252.

Wells, W.P. Relaxation-rehearsal: A variant of systematic desensitization. *Psychotherapy: Theory, Research and Practice*, 1970, 7, 224-225.

Whalen, C. Effects of a model and instructions on group verbal behaviors. *Journal of Consulting and Clinical Psychology*, 1969, *33*, 509-521.

Wheeler, K. Assertiveness and the job hunt. In R.E. Alberti (Ed.), *Assertiveness: Innovations, Applications, issues*. San Luis Obispo, California: Impact Publishers, Inc., 1977.

White, R.W. The concept of healthy personality: what do we really mean? *The Counseling Psychologist*, 1973, *4*, 3.

Winship, B.J. and Kelley, J.D. A verbal response model of assertiveness. *Journal of Counseling Psychology*, 1976, *23*, 215-220.

Wolfe, J. and Fodor, I. A cognitive/behavioral approach to modifying assertive behavior in women. *The Counseling Psychologist*, 1975, *5* (4), 45-52.

Wolfe, J. and Fodor, I. Modifying assertive behavior in women: a comparison of three approaches. *Behavior Therapy*, 1976.

Wolpe, J. Neurotic depression: experimental analog, clinical syndromes and treatment. *American Journal of Psychotherapy*, 1971, *25*, 362.

Wolpe, J. *Psychotherapy by Reciprocal Inhibition*. Stanford: Stanford University Press, 1958.

Wolpe, J. Reciprocal inhibition as the main basis of psychotherapeutic effects. *Archives of Neurology and Psychiatry*, 1954, *72*, 205-226.

Wolpe, J. *The Practice of Behavior Therapy*. New York: Pergamon Press, 1969, 1973.

Wolpe, J. Supervision transcript V: mainly about assertive training. *Journal of Behavior Therapy and Experimental Psychiatry*, 1973, *4*, 141-148.

Wolpe, J. Transcript of initial interview in a case of depression. *Journal of Beahvior Therapy and Experimental Psychiatry*, 1970, *1* (1), 71.

Wolpe, J. The instigation of assertive behavior: transcripts from two cases. *Journal of Behavior Therapy and Experimental Psychiatry*, 1970, *1* (2): 145-151.

Wolpe, J. The systematic desensitization of neuroses. *Journal of Nervous and Mental Diseases*, 1961, *132*, 189-203.

Wolpe, J. *The Case of Mrs. Schmidt*. Nashville, Tenn: Counselor Recordings, 1964.

Wolpe, J. & Lange, P. A fear survey schedule for use in behavior therapy. *Behavior Research and Therapy*, 1964, *2*, 27-30.

Wolpe, J. & Lang, P. *The fear survey schedule*. San Diego, Calif.: Knapp, 1969.

Wolpe, J. and Lazarus, A.A. *Behavior Therapy Techniques*. New York: Pergamon Press, 1966, (Now out of print).

Yalom, I.D. *The Theory and Practice of Group Psychotherapy*. New York: Basic Books, 1970, 1975 (Second Edition).

APPENDIX A

THE UNIVERSAL DECLARATION
OF HUMAN RIGHTS

WHEREAS recognition of the inherent dignity and of the equal and inalienable rights of all members of the human family is the foundation of freedom, justice and peace in the world,

WHEREAS disregard and contempt for human rights have resulted in barbarous acts which have outraged the conscience of mankind, and the advent of a world in which human beings shall enjoy freedom of speech and belief and freedom from fear and want has been proclaimed as the highest aspiration of the common people,

WHEREAS, it is essential, if man is not to be compelled to have recourse, as a last resort, to rebellion against tyranny and oppression, that human rights should be protected by the rule of law,

WHEREAS it is essential to promote the development of friendly relations between nations,

WHEREAS the peoples of the United Nations have in their Charter reaffirmed their faith in fundamental human rights, in the dignity and worth of the human person and in the equal rights of men and women and have determined to promote social progress and better standards of life in larger freedom,

WHEREAS Member States have pledged themselves to achieve, in cooperation with the United Nations, the promotion of universal respect for and observance of human rights and fundamental freedoms,

WHEREAS a common understanding of these rights and freedoms is of the greatest importance for the full realization of this pledge,

NOW, THEREFORE, THE GENERAL ASSEMBLY PROCLAIMS this Universal Declaration of Human Rights as a common standard of achievement for all peoples and all nations, to the end that every individual and every organ of society, keeping this Declaration constantly in mind, shall strive by teaching and education to promote respect for these rights and freedoms and by progressive measures, national and international, to secure their universal and effective recognition and observance, both among the peoples of Member States themselves and among the peoples of territories under their jurisdiction.

Article 1. All human beings are born free and equal in dignity and rights. They are endowed with reason and conscience and should act towards one another in a spirit of brotherhood.

Article 2. Everyone is entitled to all the rights and freedoms set forth in this Declaration, without distinction of any kind, such as race, colour, sex, language, religion, political or other opinion, national or social origin, property, birth or other status.

Furthermore, no distinction shall be made on the basis of the political, jurisdictional or international status of the country or territory to which a person belongs, whether it be independent, trust, non-self-governing or under any other limitation of sovereignty.

Article 3.   Everyone has the right to life, liberty and security of person.

Article 4.   No one shall be held in slavery or servitude; slavery and the slave trade shall be prohibited in all their forms.

Article 5.   No one shall be subjected to torture or to cruel, inhuman or degrading treatment or punishment.

Article 6.   Everyone has the right to recognition everywhere as a person before the law.

Article 7.   All are equal before the law and are entitled without any discrimination to equal protection of the law. All are entitled to equal protection against any discrimination in violation of this Declaration and against any incitement to such discrimination.

Article 8.   Everyone has the right to an effective remedy by the competent national tribunals for acts violating the fundamental rights granted him by the constitution or by law.

Article 9.   No one shall be subjected to arbitrary arrest, detention of exile.

Article 10.   Everyone is entitled in full equality to a fair and public hearing by an independent and impartial tribunal, in the determination of his rights and obligations and of any criminal charge against him.

Article 11.   (1) Everyone charged with a penal offence has the right to be presumed innocent until proved guilty according to law in a public trial at which he has had all the guarantees necessary for his defence.

(2) No one shall be held guilty of any penal offence on account of any act or omission which did not constitute a penal offence, under national or international law, at the time when it was committed. Nor shall a heavier penalty be imposed than the one that was applicable at the time the penal offence was committed.

Article 12.   No one shall be subjected to arbitrary interference with his privacy, family, home or correspondence, nor to attacks upon his honour and reputation. Everyone has the right to the protection of the law against such interference or attacks.

Article 13.   (1) Everyone nas the right to freedom of movement and residence within the borders of each state.

(2) Everyone has the right to leave any country, including his own, and to return to his country.

Article 14.   (1) Everyone has the right to seek and to eenjoy in other countries asylum from persecution.

(2) This right may not be invoked in the case of prosecutions genuinely arising from non-political crimes or from acts contrary to the purposes and principles of the United Nations.

Article 15.   (1) Everyone has the right to a nationality.

(2) No one shall be arbitrarily deprived of his nationality nor denied the right to change his nationality.

Article 16.   (1) Men and women of full age, without any limitation due to race, nationality or religion, have the right to marry and to found a family. They are entitled to equal rights as to marriage, during marriage and at its dissolution.

(2) Marriage shall be entered into only with the free and full consent of the intending spouses.

(3) The family is the natural and fundamental group unit of society and is entitled to protection by society and the State.

Article 17. (1) Everyone has the right to own property alone as well as in association with others.

(2) No one shall be arbitrarily deprived of his property.

Article 18. Everyone has the right to freedom of thought, conscience and religion; this right includes freedom to change his religion or belief, and freedom, either alone or in community with others and in public or private, to manifest his religion or belief in teaching, practice, worship and observance.

Article 19. Everyone has the right to freedom of opinion and expression; this right includes freedom to hold opinions without interference and to seek, receive and impart information and ideas through any media and regardless of frontiers.

Article 20. (1) Everyone has the right to freedom of peaceful assembly and association.

(2) No one may be compelled to belong to an association.

Article 21. (1) Everyone has the right to take part in the government of his country, directly or through freely chosen representatives.

(2) Everyone has the right of equal access to public service in his country.

(3) The will of the people shall be the basis of the authority of government; this will shall be expressed in periodic and genuine elections which shall be by universal and equal suffrage and shall be held by secret vote or by equivalent free voting procedures.

Article 22. Everyone, as a member of society, has the right to social security and is entitled to realization, through national effort and international cooperation and in accordance with the organization and resources of each State, of the economic, social and cultural rights indispensable for his dignity and the free development of his personality.

Article 23. (1) Everyone has the right to work, to free choice of employment, to just and favourable conditions of work and to protection against unemployment.

(2) Everyone, without any discrimination, has the right to equal pay for equal work.

(3) Everyone who works has the right to just and favourable remuneration ensuring for himself and his family an existence worthy of human dignity, and supplemented, if necessary, by other means of social protection.

(4) Everyone has the right to form and to join trade unions for the protection of his interests.

Article 24. Everyone has the right to rest and leisure, including reasonable limitation of working hours and periodic holidays with pay.

Article 25. (1) Everyone has the right to a standard of living adequate for the health and well-being of himself and of his family, including food, clothing, housing and medical care and necessary social services, and the right to security in the event of unemployment, sickness, disability, widowhood, old age or other lack of livelihood in circumstances beyond his control.

(2) Motherhood and childhood are entitled to special care and assistance. All children, whether born in or out of wedlock, shall enjoy the same social protection.

Article 26. (1) Everyone has the right to education. Education shall be free, at least in the elementary and fundamental stages. Elementary education shall be compulsory. Technical and professional education shall be made generally available and higher education shall be equally accessible to all on the basis of merit.

(2) Education shall be directed to the full development of the human personality and to the strengthening of respect for human rights and fundamental freedoms. It shall promote understanding, tolerance and friendship among all nations, racial or

religious groups, and shall further the activities of the United Nations for the maintenance of peace.

(3) Parents have a prior right to choose the kind of education that shall be given to their children.

Article 27. (1) Everyone has the right freely to participate in the cultural life of the community, to enjoy the arts and to share in scientific advancement and its benefits.

(2) Everyone has the right to the protection of the moral and material interests resulting from any scientific, literary or artistic production of which he is the author.

Article 28. Everyone is entitled to a social and international order in which the rights and freedoms set forth in this Declaration can be fully realized.

Article 29. (1) Everyone has duties to the community in which alone the free and full development of his personality is possible.

(2) In the exercise of his rights and freedoms, everyone shall be subject only to such limitations as are determined by law solely for the purpose of securing due recognition and respect for the rights and freedoms of others and of meeting the just requirements of morality, public order and the general welfare in a democratic society.

(3) These rights and freedoms may in no case be exercised contrary to the purposes and principles of the United Nations.

Article 30. Nothing in this Declaration may be interpreted as implying for any State, group or person any right to engage in any activity or to perform any act aimed at the destruction of any of the rights and freedoms set forth herein.

APPENDIX B

As AT gained in popularity during the mid-1970's, an increasing concern developed among responsible practitioners for the misuse of the process: unqualified trainers, illegitimate purposes, contraindicated clients. At the December 1975 meeting of the Association for Advancement of Behavior Therapy in San Francisco, a group of nationally recognized AT professionals met to initiate work on a statement of ethical principles. The following statement is the result of their work.

Further discussion of this proposal occurred at the First International Conference on Assertive Behavior Training in Washington, D.C., in August, 1976, and at the Association for Advancement of Behavior Therapy in New York City, December, 1976. Although no amendments to the original statement have been formalized, considerable concern has been expressed about the academic credentials suggested herein for qualifying facilitators. It is likely that a competency based criterion for qualification will emerge.

Moreover, AABT itself is preparing a statement of ethics for the practice of behavior therapy generally, which may have direct application to AT, although AT is not considered solely a "behavior therapy" by a considerable number of its practitioners.

Meanwhile, however, this statement remains the only public declaration by a group of professionals which is directed toward greater ethical responsibility in the practice of AT. Practitioners are urged to consider its implications for their own work.

PRINCIPLES FOR ETHICAL PRACTICE
OF ASSERTIVE BEHAVIOR TRAINING

With the increasing popularity of assertive behavior training, a quality of "faddishness" has become evident, and there are frequent reports of ethically irresponsible practices (and practitioners). We hear of trainers who, for example, do not adequately differentiate assertion and aggression. Others have failed to advocate proper ethical responsibility and caution to clients—e.g., failed to alert them to and/or prepare them for the possibility of retaliation or other highly negative reactions from others.

The following statement of "Principles for Ethical Practice of Assertive Behavior Training" is the work of the professional psychologists and educators listed below, who are actively engaged in the practice of facilitating assertive behavior (also referred to as "assertive therapy," "social skills training," "personal effectiveness training," and "AT"). We don't intend by this statement to discourage untrained individuals from becoming more assertive on their own, and we don't advocate that one must have extensive credentials in order to be of help to friends and relatives. Rather, these principles are offered to help foster responsible and ethical teaching and practice by human services professionals. Others who wish to enhance their own assertiveness or that of associates are encouraged to do so, with awareness of their own limitations, and of the importance of seeking help from a qualified therapist/trainer when necessary.

We hereby declare support for and adherence to the statement of principles, and invite responsible professionals in our own and other fields who use these techniques to join us in advocating and practicing these principles.

Robert E. Alberti, Ph.D.
Counseling Psychologist & Professor
California Polytechnic State University
San Luis Obispo, CA

Michael L. Emmons, Ph.D.
Counseling Psychologist and Professor
California Polytechnic State University
San Luis Obispo, CA

Iris G. Fodor, Ph.D.
Associate Professor, Educational Psychology
New York University, Washington Square
New York, NY

John Galassi, Ph.D.
School of Education
University of North Carolina
Chapel Hill, NC

Merna D. Galassi, Ed.D.
Meredith College
Raleigh, NC

Lynne Garnett, Ph.D.
Counseling Psychologist
University of California
Los Angeles, CA

Patricia Jakubowski, Ed.D.
Associate Professor, Behavioral Studies
University of Missouri
St. Louis, MO

Janet L. Wolfe, Ph.D.
Director of Clinical Services
Institute for Advanced Study in Rational
  Psychotherapy
New York, NY

1. Definition of Assertive Behavior

For purposes of these principles and the ethical framework expressed herein, we define assertive behavior as that complex of behaviors, emitted by a person in an interpersonal context, which express that person's feelings, attitudes, wishes, opinions or rights directly, firmly, and honestly, while respecting the feelings, attitudes, wishes, opinions and rights of the other person(s). Such behavior may include the expression of such emotions as anger, fear, caring, hope, joy, despair, indignation, embarrassment, but in any event is expressed in a manner which does not violate the rights of others. Assertive behavior is differentiated from aggressive behavior which, while expressive of one person's feelings, attitudes, wishes, opinions or rights, does not respect those characteristics in others.

While this definition is intended to be comprehensive, it is recognized that any adequate definition of assertive behavior must consider several dimensions:

A. *Intent:* behavior classified as assertive is not intended by its author to be hurtful of others.

B. *Behavior:* behavior classified as assertive would be evaluated by an "objective observer" as itself honest, direct, expressive and non-destructive of others.

C. *Effects:* behavior classified as assertive has the effect upon the receiver of a direct and non-destructive message, by which a "reasonable person" would not be hurt.

D. *Socio-cultural Context:* behavior classified as assertive is appropriate to the environment and culture in which it is exhibited, and may not be considered "assertive" in a different socio-cultural environment.

2. Client Self-Determination

These principles recognize and affirm the inherent dignity and the equal and inalienable rights of all members of the human family, as proclaimed in the "Universal Declaration of Human Rights" endorsed by the General Assembly of the United Nations.

Pursuant to the precepts of the Declaration, each client (trainee, patient) who seeks assertive behavior training shall be treated as a person of value, with all of the freedoms and rights expressed in the Declaration. No procedure shall be utilized in the name of assertive behavior training which would violate those freedoms or rights.

Informed client self-determination shall guide all such interventions:

A. the client shall be fully informed in advance of all procedures to be utilized;
B. the client shall have the freedom to choose to participate or not at any point in the intervention;
C. the client who is institutionalized shall be similarly treated with respect and without coercion, insofar as is possible within the institutional environment.
D. the client shall be provided with explicit definitions of assertiveness and assertive training.
E. the client shall be fully informed as to the education, training, experience or other qualifications of the assertive trainer(s).
F. the client shall be informed as to the goals and potential outcomes of assertive training, including potentially high levels of anxiety, and possible negative reactions from others.
G. the client shall be fully informed as to the responsibility of the assertion trainer(s) and the client(s).
H. the client shall be informed as to the ethics and employment of confidentiality guidelines as they pertain to various assertive training settings (e.g. clinical vs. non-clinical).

3. Qualifications of Facilitators

Assertive behavior training is essentially a therapeutic procedure, although frequently practiced in a variety of settings by professionals not otherwise engaged in rendering a "psychological" service. Persons in any professional role who engage in helping others to change their behavior, attitudes, and interpersonal relationships must understand human behavior at a level commensurate with the level of their interventions.

3.1 General Qualifications

We support the following minimum, general qualifications for facilitators at all levels of intervention (including "trainers in training"—preservice or inservice—who are preparing for professional service in a recognized human services field, and who may be conducting assertive behavior training under supervision as part of a research project or practicum):

A. Fundamental understanding of the principles of learning and behavior (equivalent to completion of a rigorous undergraduate level course in learning theory);
B. Fundamental understanding of anxiety and its effects upon behavior (equivalent to completion of a rigorous undergraduate level course in abnormal psychology);
C. Knowledge of the limitations, contraindications and potential dangers of assertive behavior training; familiarity with theory and research in the area.
D. Satisfactory evidence of competent performance as a facilitator, as observed by a qualified trainer, is strongly recommended for all professionals, particularly for those who do not possess a doctorate or an equivalent level of training. Such evidence would most ideally be supported by:
   1) participation in at least ten (10) hours of assertive behavior training as a client (trainee, patient); and
   2) participation in at least ten (10) hours of assertive behavior training as a facilitator under supervision.

3.2 Specific Qualifications

The following additional qualifications are considered to be the minimum expected for facilitators at the indicated levels of intervention:

A. *Assertive behavior training*, including non-clinical workshops, groups, and individual client training aimed at teaching assertive skills to those persons who require only encouragement and specific skill training, and in whom no serious emotional deficiency or pathology is evident.

1) For trainers in programs conducted under the sponsorship of a recognized human services agency, school, governmental or corporate entity, church, or community organization:
   a) An advanced degree in a recognized field of human services (e.g. psychology, counseling, social work, medicine, public health, nursing, education, human development, theology/divinity), including at least one term of field experience in a human services agency supervised by a qualified trainer; *or*
   b) certification as a minister, public school teacher, social worker, physician, counselor, nurse, or clinical, counseling, educational, or school psychologist, or similar human services professional, as recognized by the state wherein employed or by the recognized state or national professional society in the indicated discipline; *or*
   c) one year of paid counseling experience in a recognized human services agency, supervised by a qualified trainer; *or*
   d) qualification under items 3.2B or 3.2C below.

2) For trainers in programs including interventions at the level defined in this item (3.2A), but without agency/organization sponsorship:
   a) An advanced degree in a recognized field of human services (e.g. psychology, counseling, social work, medicine, public health, nursing, education, human development, theology/divinity) including at least one term of field experience in a human services agency supervised by a qualified trainer; *and*
   b) certification as a minister, social worker, physician, counselor, nurse, or clinical, counseling, educational, or school psychologist, or similar human services professional, as recognized by the state wherein employed or by the recognized state or national professional society in the indicated discipline; *or*
   c) qualification under items 3.2B or 3.2C below.

B. *Assertive behavior therapy*, including clinical interventions designed to assist persons who are severely inhibited by anxiety, or who are significantly deficient in social skills, or who are controlled by aggression, or who evidence pathology, or for whom other therapeutic procedures are indicated:
   1) For therapists in programs conducted under the sponsorship of a recognized human services agency, school, governmental or corporate entity, church, or community organization:
      a) An advanced degree in a recognized field of human services (e.g. psychology, counseling, social work, medicine, public health, nursing, education, human development, theology/divinity) including at least one term of field experience in a human services agency supervised by a qualified trainer; *or*
      b) certification as a minister, social worker, physician, counselor, nurse, or clinical, counseling, educational, or school psychologist, as recognized by the state wherein employed or by the recognized state or national professional society in the indicated discipline; *or*
      c) qualification under item 3.2C below.
   2) For therapists employing interventions at the level defined in this item (3.2B), but without agency/organization sponsorship:
      a) An advanced degree in a recognized field of human services (e.g. psychology,

counseling, social work, medicine, public health, nursing, education, human development, theology/divinity) including at least one term of field experience in a human services agency supervised by a qualified trainer; *and*

b) certification as minister, social worker, physician, counselor, nurse, or clinical, counseling, educational, or school psychologist, as recognized by the state wherein employed or by the recognized state or national professional society in the indicated discipline; *and*

c) at least one year of paid professional experience in a recognized human services agency, supervised by a qualified trainer; *or*

d) qualification under item 3.2C below.

C. *Training of trainers*, including preparation of other professionals to offer assertive behavior training/therapy to clients, in school, agency, organization, or individual settings.

1) A doctoral degree in a recognized field of human services (e.g. psychology, counseling, social work, medicine, public health, nursing, education, human development, theology/divinity) including at least one term of field experience in a human services agency supervised by a qualified trainer; *and*

2) certification as a minister, social worker, physician, counselor, nurse, or clinical, counseling, educational, or school psychologist, as recognized by the state wherein employed, or by the recognized state or national professional society in the indicated discipline; *and*

3) at least one year of paid professional experience in a recognized human services agency, supervised by a qualified trainer; *and*

4) advanced study in assertive behavior training/therapy, including at least two of the following:

a) At least thirty (30) hours of facilitation with clients;

b) participation in at least two different workshops at professional meetings or professional training institutes:

c) contribution to the professional literature in the field.

3.3 We recognize that counselors and psychologists are not certified by each state. In states wherein no such certification is provided, unless contrary to local statute, we acknowledge the legitimacy of professionals who: A) are otherwise qualified under the provisions of items 3.1 and 3.2; and B) would be eligible for certification as a counselor or psychologist in another state.

3.4 We do not consider that participation in one or two workshops on assertive behavior, even though conducted by a professional with an advanced degree, is adequate qualification to offer assertive behavior training to others, *unless the additional qualifications* of items 3.1 and 3.2 are also met.

3.5 These qualifications are presented as *standards* for professional facilitators of assertive behavior. No "certification" or "qualifying" agency is hereby proposed. Rather, it is incumbent upon each professional to evaluate himself/herself as a trainer/therapist according to these standards, and to make explicit to clients the adequacy of his/her qualifications as a facilitator.

4. Ethical Behavior of Facilitators

Since the encouragement and facilitation of assertive behavior is essentially a *therapeutic* procedure, the ethical standards most applicable to the practice of assertive behavior training are those of psychologists. We recognize that many persons who practice some form of assertive behavior training are not otherwise engaged in rendering a "psychological" service (i.e. teachers, personnel/training directors). To all we support the statement of "Ethical Standards for Psychologists" as adopted by the American Psychological Association as the standard of ethical behavior by which assertive behavior training shall be conducted.

We recognize that the methodology employed in assertive behavior training may include a wide range of procedures, some of which are of unproven value. It is the responsibility of the facilitators to inform clients of any experimental procedures. Under no circumstances should the facilitator "guarantee" a specific outcome from an intervention.

5. Appropriateness of Assertive Behavior Training Interventions

Assertive behavior training, as any intervention oriented toward helping people change, may be applied under a wide range of conditions, yet its appropriateness must be evaluated in each individual case. The responsible selection of assertive behavior training for a particular intervention must include attention to at least the following dimensions:

A. *Client:* The personal characteristics of the client in question (age, sex, ethnicity, institutionalization, capacity for informed choice, physical and psychological functionality).
B. *Problem/Goals:* The purpose for which professional help has been sought or recommended (job skills, severe inhibition, anxiety reduction, overcome aggression).
C. *Facilitator:* The personal and professional qualifications of the facilitator in question (age, sex, ethnicity, skills, understanding, ethics—see also Principles 3 and 4 above).
D. *Setting:* The characteristics of the setting in which the intervention is conducted (home, school, business, agency, clinic, hospital, prison). Is the client free to choose? Is the facilitator's effectiveness systematically evaluated?
E. *Time/Duration:* The duration of the intervention. Does the time involved represent a brief word of encouragement, a formal training workshop, an intensive and long-term therapeutic effort?
F. *Method:* The nature of the intervention. Is it "packaged" procedure or tailored to client needs? Is training based on sound principles of learning and behavior? Is there clear differentiation of aggressiveness, assertiveness and other concepts? Are definitions, techniques, procedures and purposes clarified? Is care taken to encourage small, successful steps and to minimize punishing consequences? Are any suggested "homework assignments" presented with adequate supervision, responsibility, and sensitivity to the effect upon significant others of the client's behavior change efforts? Are clients informed that assertiveness "doesn't always work?"
G. *Outcome:* Are there follow-up procedures, either by self-report or other post-test procedures?

6. Social Responsibility

Assertive behavior training shall be conducted within the law. Trainers and clients are encouraged to work assertively to change those laws which they consider need to be changed, and to modify the social system in ways they believe appropriate—in particular to extend the boundaries of human rights. Toward these ends, trainers are encouraged to facilitate responsible change skills via assertive behavior training. All those who practice, teach, or do research on assertive behavior are urged to advocate caution and ethical responsibility in application of the technique, in accordance with these Principles.